Contents

The Future of Business

Inter@ctive Edition

Lawrence J. Gitman

San Diego State University

Carl McDaniel

University of Texas, Arlington

Prepared by

Jonas Falik

Queensborough Community College

Brenda Hersh

Queensborough Community College

SOUTH-WESTERN

TM

THOMSON LEARNING

Australia · Canada · Mexico · Singapore · Spain · United Kingdom · United States

Study Guide for *The Future of Business, Interactive Edition* by Jonas Falik and Brenda Hersh

Team Leader/Publisher: Dave Shaut
Sr. Acquisitions Editor: Scott Person
Developmental Editor: Mary Draper, Draper Development
Marketing Manager: Marc Callahan
Production Editor: Kelly Keeler
Manufacturing Coordinator: Sandee Milewski
Printer: Globus Printing

Printed in the United States of America
1 2 3 4 5 04 03 02 01

For more information contact South-Western Publishing, 5101 Madison Road, Cincinnati, Ohio, 45227 or find us on the Internet at http://www.swcollege.com

For permission to use material from this text or product,contact us by
• telephone: **1-800-730-2214**
• fax: **1-800-730-2215**
• web: **http://www.thomsonrights.com**

ISBN: 0-324-11353-6

To the Student

This student study guide has been designed for use with *The Future of Business*, Inter@ctive Edition, by Gitman and McDaniel to help you master the concepts presented within the textbook. The first step in ensuring your success in this course is to read the textbook chapters and become familiar with the principles and terminology being presented. Second, take notes while you read and study the key terms defined in the margins and included in the glossary at the end of the text. Third, identify the areas where you need additional help by using the integrated learning system—a study system used in the textbook and in this student study guide. At the beginning of each chapter in the textbook, learning goals identify the most important topics in the chapter. These learning goals provide a framework for studying the chapters and are used in this study guide to help you focus on areas where you need further study.

This student study guide contains a number of sections that are designed to reinforce key concepts and to prepare you for quizzes and exams. The student study guide includes the following:

1. Chapter Outline
2. Multiple Choice Questions
3. True/False Questions
4. Enhance Your Vocabulary
5. Review Your Key Terms
6. Critical Thinking Activities

The Multiple Choice and True/False questions are organized by learning goals so you can maximize your study time by targeting specific areas that you wish to review. The Enhance Your Vocabulary and Review Your Key Terms sections have been created so that you can improve your comprehension of the textbook, expand your business vocabulary, and become familiar with the language that is an instrumental part of success in the business world.

Once you have answered the questions, check your accuracy in the back of the study guide and refer to the textbook for additional review if necessary.

You are also invited to visit the Gitman/McDaniel Web site at **http://gitman.swcollege.com** for additional online quizzes, Internet exercises, and downloadable resources that will help you to achieve greater success in the course.

Chapter 1

Your Future in Business Begins Now

OUTLINE

I. The Nature of Business
    A. For-profit and Not-for-profit Organization
    B. Factors of Production-The Building Blocks of Business

II. Social Trends
    A. Component Lifestyles
    B. The Changing Role of Families and Women

III. Demographic Trends
    A. Generation Y-Born to Shop
    B. Generation X-Savvy and Cynical
    C. Baby Boomers-America's Mass Market
    D. Older Consumers-Not Just Grandparents
    E. Americans on the Move
    F. Growing Ethnic Markets

IV. Evolving Global Economic Systems
    A. The Growth of Capitalism
    B. The Command Economy
    C. Socialism
    D. Mixed Economic Systems

V. Technological Trends

VI. Trends in Global Competition
    A. Technology and Communication
    B. Improvements in Productivity
    C. Global Standards

VII. The Talent War Among Employers

MULTIPLE CHOICE

Directions: Place the letter of the response that best completes the questions that follow in the blank space at the left.

>lg 1

How do businesses and not-for-profit organizations help create our standard of living?

  _d_   1. An organization that strives to make a profit by providing goods and services that its customers desire is called a:
        a. free enterprise   c. not-for-profit
        b. open enterprise   d. business

C **2.** Tangible items manufactured for sale by business firms are known as:
   a. national outputs   **c.** goods
   b. services   **d.** needs

a **3.** The standard of living of any country is measured by the ability of people to purchase:
   a. goods and services
   b. goods only
   c. services only
   d. items that improve their quality of life

b **4.** Profit is:
   a. the potential to lose time and money when accomplishing organizational goals
   b. the money left over after all expenses are paid
   c. expenses for such items as rent, salaries, and services
   d. salaries earned after allowing for normal business risks

C **5.** Not-for-profit organizations:
   a. now account for 50% of all economic activity in the United States
   b. do not, as a rule, have to follow sound business practices in order to succeed
   c. exist to achieve some goal other than the usual business goal of profit
   d. often compete directly with each other in order to provide goods and services

C **6.** The resources that are used to create goods and services are known as factors of production. They include:
   a. labor
   b. natural resources
   c. entrepreneurship
   d. all of these are considered factors of production

C **7.** Capital in the form of money is not considered a factor of production because it:
   a. is difficult to count
   b. is considered a basic input
   c. does not directly produce anything
   d. is necessary in the production of services only

>lg 2

How are social trends, such as more women entering the workforce, affecting business?

d **8.** Social change is the most difficult environmental factor to integrate into a business's plans for the future. This is true because managers find social change hard to:
   a. forecast   **c.** integrate
   b. influence   **d.** all of these answers are correct

a **9.** An individual's lifestyle is:
   a. the way one chooses to live his/her life
   b. impossible to define
   c. determined mostly by traditional stereotypes
   d. a simple set of interests and choices

C **10.** Component lifestyles have evolved because consumers:
   a. have limited choices of goods as a result of increased hours of work
   b. can choose from a growing number of goods and services
   c. now rely on single income and single decision maker families
   d. are overwhelmed by the increased number of goods and services available to them

>lg 3

How are demographic trends creating new opportunities for business?

_d_ 11. Demography includes the study of people's:
 a. age   c. ethnicity
 b. race   d. all of these answers are correct

_b_ 12. Generation Y consists of individuals who are:
 a. above 16 years of age
 b. below 16 years of age
 c. between the ages of 20 and 31
 d. above 31 years of age

_c_ 13. Generation Y members are said to be born to:
 a. drop out   c. shop
 b. be savvy   d. be cynical

_d_ 14. Generation X members are said to be born to:
 a. drop out
 b. families where only one parent was employed
 c. shop
 d. be savvy and cynical

_c_ 15. Parents of baby boomers raised their children to:
 a. drop out
 b. be cooperative
 c. think for themselves
 d. rely on such skills as teamwork

>lg 4

What are the primary features of the world's economic systems?

_d_ 16. Capitalism is an economic system that is based upon:
 a. unregulated freedom of business operation
 b. a small number of businesses selling to mass markets
 c. a small number of large buyers who control prices
 d. competition in the marketplace and private ownership of resources

_b_ 17. The economic rights of the capitalist economic system include the right of:
 a. government to own large industries
 b. businesses to make a profit
 c. government to control all competition
 d. government to set all prices

_d_ 18. The following represents an economic right under a capitalist system:
 a. ownership of property by individuals
 b. the right to earn a profit when selling good and services
 c. freedom of choice
 d. all of these answers are correct

_b_ 19. Under a command economy:
 a. individuals demand goods and services from the government
 b. a planned economy is controlled and directed by the government
 c. production volume is determined by the marketplace
 d. the supply of raw materials is determined by the marketplace

_a_ 20. Socialism is an economic system where:
 a. basic industries are owned or strongly controlled by the government
 b. social organizations, such as the American Automobile Association, control key industries

        c. pure competition is essential in determining which individuals control social organizations

        d. services, such as medical care, are virtually nonexistent

C   **21.** Mixed economies:

        a. are found primarily in developing countries

        b. combine only central control with limited socialism

        c. combine the use of more than one economic system

        d. are not found in highly developed economic systems

>lg 5   How can technological effectiveness help a firm reach its goals?

d   **22.** The application of technology can stimulate growth:

        a. only in a centrally controlled economy

        b. only in a socialist economic system

        c. only in mixed economies

        d. in any economic system

C   **23.** Productivity is:

        a. the quantity of raw materials that it takes to make a product

        b. a reflection of the number of individuals who are unemployed in a country

        c. the amount of goods and services one worker can produce

        d. an unimportant component of an economic system

>lg 6   What are the trends in global competition?

a   **24.** Exports include:

        a. all goods and services sold outside a firm's domestic market

        b. all goods and services sold outside the local area in which a firm is located

        c. the value of products sold that contributes to gross domestic product

        d. the total value of foreign products sold in the domestic market

b   **25.** Gross domestic product is defined as:

        a. the total market value of goods and services produced within a nation's borders minus the value of imports

        b. the total market value of all final goods and services produced within a nation's borders in a year

        c. the total market value of goods and services produced within a nation's borders minus the value of social security payments

        d. the total market value of goods and services produced less items that are considered "gross"—that is, not suitable for the marketplace

C   **26.** Customer value:

        a. does not have any association with continuous product improvement

        b. has only limited association with innovation

        c. is a measure of the benefits that a customer receives in relation to the sacrifices necessary to obtain those benefits

        d. is the ratio of brand name to durability which adds to product life

d   **27.** Continuous improvement:

        a. was popular in the 1930's during the Depression

        b. is too expensive for application in modern manufacturing

        c. cannot be adequately applied in the era of downsizing

        d. is a popular approach to constantly seek better ways of maintaining and improving quality

TRUE/FALSE

Directions: Place a T or an F in the space provided to the left of each question to indicate whether it is True or False.

>lg 1 **How do businesses and not-for-profit organizations help create our standard of living?**

F   1. Services are considered tangible offerings of businesses that can be held, touched, or stored.

T   2. The measurement of the output of goods and services that people in a country can buy with the money that they have is known as the nation's standard of living.

F   3. Several countries, such as Switzerland and Germany, have higher wages as well as a higher standard of living than that of the United States.

F   4. Quality of life issues such as life expectancy, educational standards, health, sanitation, and leisure time are not related to such business activities as providing jobs and goods and services to society.

T   5. Risk is the potential to lose time and money or otherwise not be able to accomplish an organization's goals.

F   6. Revenue is the money a firm spends on expenses for such items as rent, salaries, supplies, and transportation.

F   7. Revenue is the money left over after all of a company's expenses are paid.

F   8. A not-for-profit organization exists to achieve the usual business goal of profit as well as to provide other beneficial goals.

T   9. In addition to natural resources, labor, capital, and entrepreneurship, *knowledge* is being increasingly recognized as the fifth factor of production.

>lg 2 **How are social trends, such as more women entering the workforce, affecting business?**

F   10. Social factors include our attitudes, values, and lifestyles. They influence the products people buy, the prices paid for them, and how, where, and when people expect to purchase products.

T   11. A component lifestyle is a lifestyle made up of a complex set of interests and choices.

F   12. A person's profession, such as being an attorney or physician, defines his or her lifestyle because this is the most significant component of this person's life.

T   13. Component lifestyles have evolved because consumers have more goods and services to choose from. The increase in purchasing power that has enabled these goods to be purchased has resulted largely from the growth of dual income families.

>lg 3 **How are demographic trends creating new opportunities for business?**

F   14. Demography has little to do with the determination of markets because the study of a people's vital statistics is an uncontrollable factor in the business environment.

F   15. Individuals who belong to Generation Y are considered to be cautious consumers of modern technological products-especially in the area of personal computers and educational software.

I   **16.** Generation X members are the product of dual-career parents who encouraged them to succeed in the job market through competitive drive more than cooperative spirit, and individual skills more than teamwork.

I   **17.** The parents of baby boomers consistently ranked "to think for yourself" as the number one trait that they sought to nurture in their children.

F   **18.** The change taking place within the United States in relation to the representation of major ethnic groups is away from greater multiculturalism.

>lg 4   **What are the primary features of the world's economic systems?**

F   **19.** Capitalism is characterized by government ownership of virtually all resources and economic decision making.

F   **20.** A command economy is characterized by competition in the marketplace and private ownership of natural resources, labor, capital, entrepreneurship, and knowledge.

I   **21.** Socialism is an economic system in which the basic industries are owned by the government or by the private sector under strong government control.

F   **22.** In a socialist state, private industry controls critical, large scale industries such as transportation, communications, and utilities.

F   **23.** The United States is not an example of a mixed economic system because the government is involved in the economy through taxing, spending, and welfare activities.

>lg 5   **How can technological effectiveness help a firm reach its goals?**

I   **24.** Technology is the application of science and engineering skill and knowledge to solve production and organizational problems.

F   **25.** Productivity is the sum total of output in goods and services that one firm can produce in one year.

F   **26.** The application of technology is not a significant component of a nation's ability to build wealth because technological advances are future oriented and not concerned with current economic growth.

>lg 6   **What are the trends in global competition?**

I   **27.** Gross domestic product is the total market value of goods and services produced within a nation's borders in a year.

I   **28.** If current trends continue, world exports will continue to become a larger share of world gross domestic product.

F   **29.** Downsizing of American businesses resulted in a reduction of production efficiencies and competitiveness in world markets.

I   **30.** Customer value, the ratio of benefits to the sacrifices necessary to obtain those benefits, is provided in the form of well-known brand names, durability, design, ease of use, and customer service.

F   **31.** Continuous improvement requires that companywide teams trouble-shoot problems as they arise, rather than systematically attempt to avert them.

ENHANCE YOUR VOCABULARY

Affluence	A plentiful supply of material goods; wealth
Ailment	A physical or mental disorder, especially a mild illness
Burrowing	Digging or tunneling
Cornerstone	A fundamental basis; a stone at the corner of building
Deploying	To put into use or action
Diversification	To vary
Evolving	To develop or achieve gradually
Grassroots	People at a local level rather than at the center of political activity
Initiative	The ability to begin a plan or task
Integrate	To make into a whole by bringing all parts together
Latchkey child	Usually a school-age child who comes home from school (opening the door with their own keys) and who regularly spends part of day unsupervised at home
Mainstream	The prevailing current of thought, influence, or activity
Savvy	Well informed and perceptive; shrewd
Site	The place or setting of something
Visionary	Characterized by vision or foresight

Directions: Select the definition in Column B that best defines the word in Column A.

	Column A		Column B
d	1. Affluence	a.	The place or setting
g	2. Ailment	b.	To vary
b	3. Diversification	c.	Shrewd
j	4. Evolving	d.	Wealth
h	5. Grassroots	e.	Characterized by foresight
i	6. Integrate	f.	The prevailing thought
f	7. Mainstream	g.	A mild illness
c	8. Savvy	h.	People at a local level
a	9. Site	i.	To make into a whole
e	10. Visionary	j.	To develop gradually

REVIEW YOUR KEY TERMS

Directions: Select the definition in Column B that best defines the word in Column A.

	Column A		Column B
c	1. Business	a.	Goods and services sold outside a firm's domestic market.
e	2. Goods	b.	The total market value of all final goods and services produced within a nation's borders in a year.
m	3. Services	c.	An organization that strives for a profit by providing goods and services desired by its customers.
Q	4. Standard of living	d.	The combined talents and skills of the workforce.
W	5. Quality of life	e.	Tangible items manufactured by businesses.

_G_ **6.** Risk

_S_ **7.** Revenue

_GG_ **8.** Costs

_HH_ **9.** Profit

_ee_ **10.** Not-for-profit organization

_F_ **11.** Factors of production

_P_ **12.** Capital

_T_ **13.** Entrepreneurs

_D_ **14.** Knowledge

_i_ **15.** Component lifestyle

_K_ **16.** Demography

_J_ **17.** Generation Y

_N_ **18.** Generation X

_BB_ **19.** Baby boomers

_aa_ **20.** Multiculturalism

_Y_ **21.** Capitalism

_DD_ **22.** Command economy

____ **23.** Socialism

_U_ **24.** Mixed economies

_CC_ **25.** Technology

f. The resources used to create goods and services.

g. The potential to lose time and money or otherwise not be able to accomplish an organization's goals.

h. The ratio of benefits to the sacrifices necessary to obtain those benefits.

i. A lifestyle made up of a complex set of interests and choices.

j. Americans born after 1982.

k. The study of people's vital statistics, such as their age, race and ethnicity, and location.

l. A set of five technical standards of quality management that were created in the 1980s by the International Organization for Standardization to provide a uniform way of determining whether manufacturing plants and service organizations have sound quality procedures.

m. Intangible offerings of businesses that can't be held, touched, or stored.

n. Americans born between 1968 and 1979.

o. A commitment to constantly seek better ways of doing things so as to maintain and increase quality.

p. The inputs, such as tools, machinery, equipment, and buildings, used to produce goods and services and get them to the consumer.

q. A country's output of goods and services that people can buy with the money they have.

r. An economic system in which the basic industries are owned either by the government, itself, or by the private sector under strong government control.

s. The money a company earns from providing services or selling goods to customers.

t. People who combine the inputs of natural resources, labor, and capital to produce goods or services with the intention of making a profit or accomplishing a not-for-profit goal.

u. Economies that combine several economic systems; for example, an economy where the government owns certain industries but others are owned by the private sector.

v. Goods and services that offer customer value and satisfaction.

w. The general level of human happiness based on such things as life expectancy, educational standards, health, sanitation and leisure time.

x. A set of technical standards designed by the International Organization for Standardization to help ensure clean production processes to protect the environment.

y. An economic system based on competition in the marketplace and private ownership of the factors of production.

FF____ **26.** Productivity

z. An award bestowed on U.S. companies whose goods and services offer world-class quality.

B____ **27.** Gross domestic product

aa. The condition when all major ethnic groups in an area, such as a city, county, or census tract, are equally represented.

V____ **28.** Quality

bb. Americans born between 1946 and 1964.

H____ **29.** Customer value

cc. The application of science and engineering skills and knowledge to solve production and organizational problems.

D____ **30.** Continuous improvement

dd. An economic system characterized by government ownership of virtually all resources along with economic decision making by central government planning; also known as communism.

Z____ **31.** Malcolm Baldrige National Quality Award

ee. An organization that exists to achieve some goal other than the usual business goal of profit.

I____ **32.** ISO 9000

ff. The amount of goods and services one worker can produce.

X____ **33.** ISO 14000

gg. Expenses incurred in creating and selling goods and services; for example, expenses for rent, salaries, supplies, and transportation.

α____ **34.** Exports

hh. The money left over after all expenses are paid.

CRITICAL THINKING ACTIVITIES

1. P.O.V. (Point of View)

Directions: In this exercise you will be asked to provide your personal opinion regarding some of the topics discussed in the chapter. At the completion of this exercise, your instructor may wish to poll the entire class regarding their responses.

a. The quality of life in a country reflects the general level of human happiness. It is based on such things as: life expectancy, educational standards, health, leisure time, etc. The improvement of the general quality of life is solely the responsibility of the government.

Agree _____   Disagree _✓_

Explain:

Building a high quality of life is a combined effort of businesses, government, and not for-profit organizations.

b. Everywhere we look there are not-for-profit organizations providing some service or other. This would include such nationally known institutions as: Public Television, the Heart Association, the Muscular Dystrophy Association, and Students for the American Way. Not-for-profit organizations continue to grow and now account for more that twenty–eight percent of economic activity in the United States. These organizations are exempt from paying Federal Income Taxes. The taxpaying citizens of the United States are being forced to subsidize these organizations as a result of their tax-exempt status. The tax exemption is unfair.

Agree _____   Disagree ✓

Explain:

Successful not-for-profit organizations follow sound business principles. These groups have goals they hope to accomplish, but the goals are not focused on profits.

2. Using the Internet

Directions: The U.S. central bank is known as the Federal Reserve System. It carries out monetary policy in order to maintain high levels of employment and stable prices. Your success in business will be determined, in part, by your ability to understand how the Federal Reserve System works. Click on **http://www.federalreserve.gov** then click on general information.

a. How many members are on the Board of Governors? *7 of the federal Reserve System*

consists of 12 members

b. Name the Federal Reserve District banks. *The Federal reserve the central bank of the U.S.*

c. What is the Federal Reserve Open Markets Committee?

d. What are the monetary policy tools of the Federal Reserve? *Open market operations, the discount rate, and reserve requirements.*

3. Writing Skills

Directions: You are an author for a large publisher. Write a one-page memorandum to your editor, Frank Gomez, about a potential book concerning baby boomers. Use a total of at least ten words from Enhance Your Vocabulary and Review Your Key Words. (Presented earlier in this chapter).

Chapter 2

Understanding Evolving Economic Systems and Competition

OUTLINE

MULTIPLE CHOICE

Directions: Place the letter of the response that best completes the questions that follow in the blank space to the left.

>lg 1   **What is economics and how are the three sectors of the economy linked?**

_____   **1.** A nation's combination of policies, laws, and choices made by its government to establish the systems that determine the production and allocation of goods and services is known as a(n):

     a. macro system   **c.** economic system

     b. micro system   **d.** political system

_____   **2.** Economics involves the study of how a society utilizes:

     a. scarce resources   **c.** political choices

     b. legal services   **d.** distribution systems

_____   **3.** Macroeconomics is the study of the economy as a:

     a. series of households or business firms

     b. whole utilizing aggregate data

     c. cluster of decision-making enterprises

     d. series of economic expectations

_____   **4.** Microeconomics is the study of the economy:

     a. focusing on individual parts of the economy

     b. excluding households and firms

     c. as a cluster of decision-making enterprises

     d. through consumer expectations

_____   **5.** The circular flow concept is:

     a. designed to primarily show how goods flow within the economy

     b. another way to demonstrate how microeconomics works

     c. focused primarily on the government sector of the economy

     d. a way to see how the sectors of the economy interact

>lg 2   **How do economic growth, full employment and price stability indicate a nation's economic health?**

_____   **6.** The business cycle reflects:

     a. only downward changes in the level of economic activity

     b. only upward changes in the level of economic activity

     c. both upward and downward changes in the level of economic activity

     d. the government's ability to control economic activity

_____   **7.** Full employment as defined by the government occurs when:

     a. all able bodied people are employed

     b. 94 to 96 percent of those available for work have jobs

     c. 100 percent employment takes place

     d. all temporary unemployment ends

_____   **8.** The unemployment rate measures the percentage of the total labor force:

     a. that is not working

     b. employed for more that 3 years

     c. not seeking work

     d. not working but actively seeking work

_____ 9. Voluntary short-term unemployment that is not related to the business cycle is:
   a. seasonal unemployment   **c.** frictional unemployment
   b. structural unemployment   **d.** cyclical unemployment

_____ 10. Involuntary short-term unemployment unrelated to the business cycle is:
   a. structural unemployment   **c.** frictional unemployment
   b. seasonal unemployment   **d.** cyclical unemployment

>lg 3

What is inflation, how is it measured, and what causes it?

_____ 11. The situation in which the average of all prices of goods and services is rising is known as:
   a. deflation   **c.** disinflation
   b. reinflation   **d.** inflation

_____ 12. The type of inflation wherein the supply of goods is not sufficient to keep up with the quantity of goods consumers wish to purchase is known as:
   a. cost-push inflation   **c.** demand-push inflation
   b. creeping inflation   **d.** demand-pull inflation

_____ 13. The type of inflation whereby increased production expenses lead to price increases is known as:
   a. cost-push inflation   **c.** demand-push inflation
   b. creeping inflation   **d.** demand-pull inflation

>lg 4

How does the government use monetary policy to achieve its macroeconomic goals?

_____ 14. Monetary policy refers to the government's programs for controlling:
   a. employment and unemployment
   b. productivity and output
   c. money in circulation and interest rates
   d. taxation and government spending

_____ 15. The primary role of the Federal Reserve System is to:
   a. collect taxes and make disbursements for the government
   b. control how much money is in circulation
   c. deal with foreign central banks
   d. serve as a watchdog over the Treasury Department

_____ 16. Fiscal policy refers to the government's:
   a. program of taxation and spending
   b. program to increase the money supply
   c. control of interest rates
   d. control of the money supply

_____ 17. Crowding out refers to the government policy of:
   a. taking more money from the private sector and increasing federal spending
   b. taking less money from the private sector and decreasing federal spending
   c. printing more money for use in the private sector
   d. printing more money for use in the public sector

_____ 18. To reduce a federal budget deficit it would make the most sense for the federal government to:
   a. increase spending and decrease taxes
   b. increase spending and increase taxes
   c. decrease spending and increase taxes
   d. decrease spending and decrease taxes

>lg 5   **What are the basic microeconomic concepts of demand and supply and how do they establish prices?**

_____ 19. Microeconomics is the study of the economy as a:
a. series of households, businesses, and industries
b. whole
c. cluster of decision-making enterprises
d. series of economic expectations

_____ 20. The nature of the demand for goods and services in an economic system will result in:
a. increases in the quantity demanded as prices rise and vice versa
b. increases in prices which lead increased demand and vice versa
c. decreases in demand which lead to higher prices and vice versa
d. decreases in the quantity demanded as prices rise and vice versa

_____ 21. The nature of the supply of goods and services in an economic system will result in:
a. increases in prices which decrease the quantity supplied and vice versa
b. increases in the quantity supplied as prices rise and vice versa
c. decreases in the quantity supplied as prices rise and vice versa
d. decreases in the quantity supplied without regard to changes in prices

_____ 22. The equilibrium point on a supply and demand curve is the point where:
a. supply exceeds demand
b. demand exceeds supply
c. there is balance between supply and demand
d. government steps in to buy all remaining supply

>lg 6   **What are the four types of market structure?**

_____ 23. The main characteristics of pure competition include:
a. a large number of firms in the market
b. firms selling similar or identical products
c. no single firm controlling the price at which their product is sold
d. all of these answers are correct

_____ 24. Pure monopoly is characterized by:
a. ease of entry by new firms into the market
b. a single firm that accounts for all sales in an industry
c. three or fewer firms accounting for all sales in an industry
d. all of these answers are correct

_____ 25. Monopolistic competition is characterized by:
a. many firms in the market
b. products that are close substitutes but still somewhat different
c. relative ease of entry into the market
d. all of the above are correct

_____ 26. Oligopoly is characterized by:
a. a single firm that accounts for all sales in an industry
b. ease of entry into the market
c. a few firms that produce most of the output
d. minimal capital requirements that limits the number of firms in the market

>lg 7   **Which trends are reshaping micro and macro economic environments?**

_____ 27. Customer value:
  a. is the customer's perception of the ratio of benefits to the sacrifice necessary to obtain those benefits
  b. is the business firm's perception of the ratio of benefits to the sacrifice necessary to obtain those benefits
  c. does not involve any tangible or intangible sacrifice on the part of customers
  d. is concerned with the quality of products being offered for sale

_____ 28. A strategic alliance:
  a. can only result in increasing the number of firms that a large corporation uses as suppliers
  b. allows the larger corporation to dominate and control other partners
  c. will usually lead to increased costs
  d. is a cooperative agreement between business firms

TRUE/FALSE

Directions: Place a T or an F in the space provided to the left of each question to indicate whether it is True or False.

>lg 1   **What is economics and how are the three sectors of the economy linked?**

_____ 1. Economics is the study of how a society uses only its most plentiful resources to produce goods and services.

_____ 2. Macroeconomics utilizes aggregate data to study the economic system as a whole.

_____ 3. Microeconomics, like macroeconomics, emphasizes the use of aggregate data to make economic decisions.

_____ 4. Interactions within the economy can be demonstrated using the circular flow concept, which examines the flow of inputs and outputs between economic sectors.

>lg 2   **How do economic growth, full employment, and price stability indicate a nation's economic health?**

_____ 5. Economic growth is always beneficial because the gains in production that it brings more than offset any economic strains that it might cause.

_____ 6. GDP is the total market value of all goods and services produced within a nation's borders each year.

_____ 7. Business cycles vary in length and represent upward and downward changes in economic activity.

_____ 8. A recession is declared once GDP declines for a period of one year or more (four consecutive quarters).

_____ 9. The unemployment rate indicates the percentage of the total labor force that is not working and has no intention of seeking work.

_____ 10. Seasonal unemployment occurs during specific seasons in certain industries such as agriculture.

_____ 11. Cyclical unemployment occurs when there is a mismatch between available jobs and the skills of available workers in an industry or a region.

>lg 3   **What is inflation, how is it measured, and what causes it?**

_____ 12. The situation in which the average of all prices of goods and services is falling is called inflation.

_____ 13. Demand-pull inflation occurs when the demand for goods and services is greater than supply.

_____ 14. Cost-push inflation occurs when increases in production costs push up the prices for final goods and services.

_____ 15. The PPI measures the prices paid by consumers for finished goods produced in the United States and foreign countries.

>lg 4   **How does the government use monetary policy and fiscal policy to achieve its macroeconomic goals?**

_____ 16. Monetary policy refers to the government's program for controlling the level of taxes that its citizens pay and the level of government expenditures.

_____ 17. Changes in the money supply and interest rates affect both the level of economic activity and the rate of inflation.

_____ 18. When following a contractionary monetary policy, the Fed will tighten the money supply by selling government securities or raising interest rates.

_____ 19. When following an expansionary monetary policy, the Fed will allow the money supply to grow by selling government securities.

_____ 20. Fiscal policy is the government's program of changing the money supply and interest rates to control economic growth.

_____ 21. Crowding out is a phenomenon that involves the government taking more money from the private sector and using the funds for public sector expenditures.

_____ 22. A federal deficit occurs when the government spends more for programs than it collects in taxes.

>lg 5   **What are the basic microeconomic concepts of demand and supply, and how do they establish prices?**

_____ 23. Unlike macroeconomics, microeconomics is concerned with how prices and quantities of goods and services behave in free markets.

_____ 24. Demand is the quantity of a good or service that people are willing to buy at various prices.

_____ 25. As prices move higher, suppliers will tend to supply less of a product to the market.

_____ 26. A shift in the demand or supply curve for a particular product might take place if income, availability of substitutes, expectations, and the number of buyers changes.

>lg 6   **What are the four types of market structure?**

_____ 27. A primary characteristic of perfect competition is a small number of firms in a very large market.

_____ 28. An important element of perfect competition is that buyers and sellers in the market have good information about prices, sources of supply, etc.

_____ 29. Since pure monopoly involves a market structure where one firm accounts for all industry sales, it is relatively simple for other firms to enter the market.

_____ 30. In monopolistic competition, firms sell similar items and use advertising in an attempt to distinguish them.

_____ 31. Since products are not the same under monopolistic competition, sellers do not have to justify price differences to customers.

_____ 32. Oligopolies have been known to illegally coordinate their pricing and output decisions.

>lg 7 **Which trends are reshaping micro and macro environments?**

_____ 33. Customer value is the customer's perception of the ratio of benefits to the sacrifice necessary to obtain those benefits.

_____ 34. Although it usually results in increased costs to businesses that use it, relationship management is often required in order to maintain customer relationships.

_____ 35. Strategic alliances often result in reducing the number of suppliers as well as drawing on supplier expertise in developing new products that can meet quality, cost, and delivery standards of the marketplace.

ENHANCE YOUR VOCABULARY

Abundant	Plentiful; an ample quantity
Accelerated	To hasten the progress or development of; to speed up
Acquisition	Something acquired or gained
Aggregate	The whole sum or amount
Allocate	To apportion for a specific purpose
Burden	Something oppressive or worrisome; duty, responsibility
Commodity	An economic good; something useful or valued
Coveted	To wish for enviously
Emerged	Come out into view
Emissions	Substances discharged into the air (as by automobile engine or smokestack)
Fiscal	Of or relating to financial matters
Lodging	A place to live; dwelling
Ratio	The relationship in quantity, amount, or size between two or more things; proportion
Swapped	Exchanged one thing for another
Venture	An undertaking involving chance, risk, or danger; a speculative business enterprise

Directions: Select the definition in Column B that best defines the word in Column A.

Column A	Column B
_____ 1. Emissions	a. Plentiful
_____ 2. Swapped	b. A speculative business enterprise
_____ 3. Ratio	c. Substances discharged into the air
_____ 4. Fiscal	d. To speed up
_____ 5. Coveted	e. Proportion

_____ **6.** Emerged   **f.** The whole sum or amount
_____ **7.** Aggregate   **g.** Exchanged one thing for another
_____ **8.** Venture   **h.** Of or relating to financial matters
_____ **9.** Accelerated   **i.** To wish for enviously
_____ **10.** Abundant   **j.** Come out into view

REVIEW YOUR KEY TERMS

Directions: Select the definition in Column B that best defines the word in Column A.

Column A   **Column B**

_____ **1.** Purchasing power

a. The combination of policies, laws, and choices made by a nation's government to establish the systems that determine what goods and services are produced and how they are allocated.

_____ **2.** Demand-pull inflation

b. The study of how a society uses scarce resources to produce and distribute goods and services.

_____ **3.** Cost-push inflation

c. Unemployment that is caused by a mismatch between available jobs and the skills of available workers in an industry or region; not related to the business cycle.

_____ **4.** Purchasing power

d. The subarea of economics that focuses on the economy as a whole by looking at aggregate data for large groups of people, companies, or products.

_____ **5.** Strategic alliance

e. A decline in GDP that lasts for at least two consecutive quarters.

_____ **6.** Relationship management

f. The subarea of economics that focuses on individual parts of the economy such as households or firms.

_____ **7.** Customer value

g. The movement of inputs and outputs among households, businesses, and governments; a way of showing how the sectors of the economy interact.

_____ **8.** Oligopoly

h. An increase in a nation's output of goods and services.

_____ **9.** Contractionary policy

i. Short-term unemployment that is not related to the business cycle.

_____ **10.** Economic system

j. The condition when all people who want to work and can work have jobs.

_____ **11.** Macroeconomics

k. The percentage of the total labor force that is actively looking for work but is not actually working.

_____ **12.** Expansionary policy

l. Upward and downward changes in the level of economic activity.

_____ **13.** Economics

m. The situation that occurs when government spending replaces spending by the private sector.

_____ **14.** Monopolistic competition

n. An index of the prices paid by producers and wholesalers for various commodities such as raw materials, partially finished goods, and finished products.

_____ **15.** Circular flow

o. A government's programs for controlling interest rates and the amount of money circulating in the economy.

_____ **16.** Producer price index (PPI)

p. The central banking system of the United States.

_____ 17. Microeconomics

_____ 18. Monetary policy

_____ 19. Economic growth

_____ 20. Barriers to entry

_____ 21. Business cycles

_____ 22. Federal Reserve System

_____ 23. Inflation

_____ 24. Full employment

_____ 25. Unemployment rate

_____ 26. Fiscal policy

_____ 27. Frictional unemployment

_____ 28. Crowding out

_____ 29. Pure monopoly

_____ 30. Structural unemployment

_____ 31. Cyclical unemployment

_____ 32. Market structure

_____ 33. Seasonal unemployment

_____ 34. Federal budget deficit

_____ 35. Perfect (pure) competition

_____ 36. National debt

_____ 37. Demand

_____ 38. Savings bonds

q. Unemployment that occurs when a downturn in the business cycle reduces the demand for labor throughout the economy.

r. An index of the prices of a market basket of goods and services purchased by typical urban consumers.

s. Unemployment that occurs during specific seasons in certain industries.

t. The situation in which the average of all prices of goods and services is rising.

u. The use of monetary policy by the Fed to increase the growth of the money supply.

v. Inflation that occurs when the demand for goods and services is greater than the supply.

w. The government's use of taxation and spending to affect the economy.

x. Inflation that occurs when increases in production costs push up the prices of final goods and services.

y. The use of monetary policy by the Fed to tighten the money supply by selling government securities or raising interest rates.

z. The point at which quantity demanded equals quantity supplied.

aa. The condition that occurs when the federal government spends more for programs than it collects in taxes.

bb. The accumulated total of all of the federal government's annual budget deficits.

cc. A market structure in which many firms offer products that are close substitutes and in which entry is relatively easy.

dd. Government bonds of relatively small denominations.

ee. Factors, such as technological or legal conditions, that prevent new firms from competing equally with a monopoly.

ff. The quantity of a good or service that people are willing to buy at various prices.

gg. A market structure in which a single firm accounts for all industry sales and in which there are barriers to entry.

hh. A graph showing the quantity of a good or service that a business will make available at various prices.

ii. A graph showing the quantity of a good or service that people are willing to buy at various prices.

jj. A market structure in which a large number of small firms sell similar products, buyers and sellers have good information, and businesses can be easily opened or closed.

kk. The number of suppliers in a market.

ll. The quantity of a good or service that businesses will make available at various prices.

_____ **39.** Equilibrium

mm. A cooperative agreement between business firms; sometimes called a strategic partnership.

_____ **40.** Demand curve

nn. The practice of building, maintaining, and enhancing interactions with customers and other parties in order to develop long-term satisfaction through mutually beneficial partnerships.

_____ **41.** Supply curve

oo. The customer's perception of the ratio of benefits (functionality, performance, durability, design, ease of use, and serviceability) to the sacrifice (of money, time, and effort) necessary to obtain those benefits.

_____ **42.** Supply

pp. The value of what money can buy.

_____ **43.** Consumer price index (CPI)

qq. A market structure in which a few firms produce most or all of the output and in which large capital requirements or other factors limit the number of firms.

CRITICAL THINKING ACTIVITIES

1. P.O.V. (Point of View)

Directions: In this exercise you will be asked to provide your personal opinion regarding some of the topics discussed in the chapter. At the completion of this exercise, your instructor may wish to poll the entire class regarding their responses.

a. Your book describes inflation as the situation in which the average of all prices of goods and services is *rising*. The opposite of inflation is deflation – the situation in which the average of all prices of goods and service is *falling*. Deflation would probably be better than inflation, because lower prices would allow all of us to purchase more goods and services.

Agree _____   Disagree _____

Explain:

_____

_____

_____

_____

_____

b. Borrowing by the United States Government to pay for services that it must buy has contributed to the national debt. In fact, the government often borrows more than it collects from taxes. Since the debt is spent on goods and services, it can only lead to greater prosperity for the country.

Agree _____   Disagree _____

Explain

_____

_____

_____

_____

_____

2. Using the Internet

Directions: Go to **http://www.mortgagemart.com/cpi.html.**

    a. What is the Consumer Price Index?
    b. What is the average CPI?
    c. What categories of items are included in the determination of the CPI?

3. Writing Skills

Directions: Write a paragraph on inflation. Tell the reader what it means and how it affects the economy. Also, discuss the effect of inflation on the working American and the retired American. Include at least a total of three words or definitions from Enhance Your Vocabulary and Review Your Key Words (Shown earlier in this chapter.)

NOTES ON CHAPTER 2

Chapter 3

Competing in the Global Marketplace

OUTLINE

I. The Importance of Global Business to the United States

II. Measuring Trade Between Nations
- A. Exports and Imports
- B. Balance of Trade
- C. Balance of Payments
- D. The Changing Value of Currencies

III. Why Nations Trade
- A. Absolute Advantage
- B. Comparative Advantage

IV. Barriers to Trade
- A. Natural
- B. Tariff
- C. Nontariff Barriers

V. Fostering Global Trade
- A. Antidumping laws
- B. The Uruguay Round and the World Trade Organization
- C. The World Bank and International Monetary Fund

VI. International Economic Communities
- A. North American Free Trade Agreement (NAFTA)
- B. The European Union
- C. The Euro

VII. Participating in the Global Marketplace
- A. Exporting
- B. Licensing
- C. Contract Manufacturing
- D. Joint Ventures
- E. Direct Investment
- F. Countertrade

VIII. Threats and Opportunities in the Global Marketplace
- A. Political Considerations
- B. Cultural Differences
- C. Economic Environment

IX. The Impact of Multinational Corporations

X. Capitalizing on Trends in Business
   A. Market Expansion
   B. Resource Acquisition
   C. Competition
   D. Technological Change
   E. Government Action

XI. Applying This Chapter's Topics

MULTIPLE CHOICE

Directions: Place the letter of the response that best completes the questions that follow in the blank space at the left.

>lg 1

Why is global trade important to the United States?

_____ 1. Global vision refers to:
   a. businesses that fail to recognize opportunities in global markets
   b. the ability to foresee an opportunity in the global satellite TV market
   c. recognition and reaction to business opportunities and being able to effectively function in foreign markets
   d. the use of television to attract customers in foreign markets

_____ 2. Global vision includes:
   a. being aware of threats from foreign competitors in all markets
   b. effectively using international distribution networks to get raw materials and move finished products to the customer
   c. recognizing and reacting to international business opportunities
   d. all of these answers are correct

_____ 3. Of the following countries, which depends least on international commerce:
   a. United States   c. Great Britain
   b. France   d. Germany

>lg 2

How is global trade measured?

_____ 4. Goods and services made in one country and sold to others are known as:
   a. deficits   c. surpluses
   b. exports   d. imports

_____ 5. Goods and services that are brought in from other countries are known as:
   a. deficits   c. surpluses
   b. exports   d. imports

_____ 6. A nation's balance of trade is the difference between its:
   a. total payments and total receipts from other countries
   b. quantity of goods imported and exported during a certain time
   c. value of exports and imports during a certain time
   d. none of these answers are correct

_____ 7. A nation's balance of payments is the difference between its:
   a. total payments and its total receipts from other countries
   b. quantity of goods imported and exported during a certain time
   c. value of exports and imports during a certain time
   d. none of these answers are correct

_____ **8.** Devaluation of a currency involves:
    a. raising its value in relation to other currencies
    b. letting a currency float upward in response to supply and demand
    c. running a trade surplus
    d. lowering the value of a nation's currency relative to other currencies

>lg 3   Why do nations trade?

_____ **9.** A country has an absolute advantage when it:
    a. can resell a product that another country can't sell
    b. can produce and sell a product at a lower cost than any other country or is the only country that can produce it
    c. absolutely cannot produce a product or does not possess the technology to develop it
    d. develops products for sale that it can sell cheaply

_____ **10.** The principle of comparative advantage states that a country should:
    a. avoid selling products that another country also sells
    b. resell used products whenever possible
    c. emphasize the sale of high technology items
    d. specialize in those products that it can produce most cheaply and trade those products for items that other countries can produce most cheaply

>lg 4   What are the barriers to international trade?

_____ **11.** Distance, language, and culture represent:
    a. tariff barriers to trade   **c.** natural barriers to trade
    b. national barriers to trade   **d.** protective barriers to trade

_____ **12.** Protective tariffs are intended to:
    a. increase imports   **c.** decrease imports
    b. increase exports   **d.** decrease exports

_____ **13.** An argument in favor of imposing tariffs is the:
    a. infant-industry argument   **c.** preparedness argument
    b. job-protection argument   **d.** all of these answers are correct

_____ **14.** Embargoes are intended to:
    a. increase imports   **c.** decrease imports
    b. increase exports   **d.** decrease exports

>lg 5   How do governments and institutions foster world trade?

_____ **15.** The practice of charging a lower price for a product in foreign markets than in the firm's home market is known as:
    a. embargoing   **c.** dumping
    b. tariffing   **d.** protectionism

_____ **16.** The most ambitious world trade agreement ever negotiated is known as the:
    a. Uruguay Round   **c.** International Monetary Fund
    b. WTO   **d.** North American Free Trade Agreement

_____ **17.** The International Monetary Fund:
    a. is also known as the World Bank
    b. operates as a lender of last resort for troubled nations
    c. accepts deposits from citizens of member nations
    d. makes loans without regard to making recipients change unacceptable economic policies

>lg 6   What are international economic institutions?

_____ **18.** An agreement to give trade advantages to one nation (or several nations) over others is known as a(n):
- **a.** embargo
- **b.** export quota
- **c.** nontariff union
- **d.** preferential tariff

_____ **19.** A free trade zone:
- **a.** reduces duties or rules among trade partners but not others
- **b.** eliminates duties or rules for all nations that seek to trade within it
- **c.** does not allow import or export tariffs
- **d.** is used to overcome natural barriers to international trade

_____ **20.** The North American Free Trade Agreement (NAFTA):
- **a.** increased tariffs on goods produced in the United States for shipment to Mexico
- **b.** reduced tariffs and other restrictions on trade between the United States, Canada, and Mexico
- **c.** guarantees rising prosperity for people in the United States, Canada, and Mexico
- **d.** none of these answers are correct

_____ **21.** The European Union was formed as a result of the:
- **a.** Uruguay Round
- **b.** WTA
- **c.** Maastricht Treaty
- **d.** NAFTA

>lg 7   How do companies enter the global marketplace?

_____ **22.** When a company decides to enter the global market the least risky and complicated method is:
- **a.** importing
- **b.** licensing
- **c.** exporting
- **d.** protectionism

_____ **23.** When a company decides to enter the global market through an agreement with a firm in a foreign market, the method is known as:
- **a.** importing
- **b.** licensing
- **c.** exporting
- **d.** protectionism

_____ **24.** When a domestic firm buys part of a foreign company or joins with a foreign company to create a new entity, it is known as:
- **a.** a joint venture
- **b.** protectionism
- **c.** exporting
- **d.** importing

_____ **25.** International trade, which involves a form of barter, is called:
- **a.** importing
- **b.** protectionism
- **c.** direct investment
- **d.** countertrade

>lg 8   What threats and opportunities exist in the global marketplace?

_____ **26.** The possibility of expropriation and confiscation of a foreign company's assets should cause the firm to:
- **a.** assess the hostility of the political climate in a country
- **b.** determine socially acceptable behavior
- **c.** look at the local economic infrastructure
- **d.** develop a comprehension of local languages

_____ 27. Nationalism is primarily a(n):
a. economic consideration
b. problem of infrastructure
c. political and cultural matter
d. factor that can be ignored if the product being sold is popular

>lg 9   **What are the advantages of multinational corporations?**

_____ 28. Multinational corporations can:
a. often overcome trade problems
b. sidestep regulatory problems
c. shift production and labor from one place to another to reduce costs
d. all of these answers are correct

_____ 29. The following is a multinational corporation:
a. General Electric
b. Microsoft
c. Coca-Cola
d. all of these are multinational corporations

>lg 10   **What are the trends in the global marketplace?**

_____ 30. A primary goal of the expansion of operations to global markets allows corporations to:
a. expand their domestic business
b. take advantage of the economies of large scale operations
c. tap domestic resources for distribution in world markets
d. adhere to government requirements

_____ 31. Government action around the world has had the effect of:
a. decreasing world trade through the imposition of tariffs
b. increasing world trade by significantly lowering trade barriers
c. increasing world trade by significantly raising domestic taxes
d. decreasing world trade by setting up trading partnerships

TRUE/FALSE

Directions: Place a T or an F in the space provided at the left of each question to indicate whether it is True or False.

>lg 1   **Why is global trade important to the United States?**

_____ 1. Global vision means recognizing and reacting to international business opportunities, being aware of threats from foreign competitors, and using international distribution networks to sell products and services to consumers.

_____ 2. Global financial turmoil usually limits opportunities for the purchase of foreign businesses at reasonable prices.

_____ 3. As a result of increased efficiencies, American firms are not being threatened by foreign competition in the United States.

_____ 4. Sales of American products in foreign markets account for approximately one third of U.S. corporate profits and twenty percent of domestic economic growth.

>lg 2   How is global trade measured?

_____ **5.** Exports include products made for sale in foreign markets but are held for sale in the domestic market.

_____ **6.** Although the United States is the largest importer of foreign goods, it is not the largest exporter of goods to foreign countries.

_____ **7.** A country that exports more than it imports is said to have a favorable balance of payments.

_____ **8.** A country that imports more than it exports is said to have an unfavorable balance of trade or a trade deficit.

_____ **9.** If a country's currency depreciates, more of that country's currency is needed to buy another country's currency and vice versa.

_____ **10.** Devaluation of a currency raises the value of other currencies relative to the currency that has been devalued.

>lg 3   Why do nations trade?

_____ **11.** A country has an absolute advantage when it can produce and sell a product at a higher price than other countries that make the same product.

_____ **12.** The principle of comparative advantage states that international businessmen should compare prices of imported goods before deciding which ones to purchase.

_____ **13.** The opposite of free trade is protectionism, in which a nation protects home industries from outside competition by creating artificial barriers to trade.

>lg 4   What are the barriers to international trade?

_____ **14.** The advent of technology has virtually eliminated all natural barriers to international free trade.

_____ **15.** A tariff is a tax imposed by a nation on imported goods. A protective tariff makes imports less attractive to buyers relative to domestic products.

_____ **16.** An import quota is a nontariff barrier to trade that limits the quantity of a certain good that can be imported.

_____ **17.** An embargo can only be imposed on a product that is to be exported.

_____ **18.** Exchange controls require a company earning foreign exchange from its exports to sell the foreign exchange to a control agency such as a central bank.

>lg 5   How do governments and institutions foster world trade?

_____ **19.** The policy known as dumping is usually suspected when variations in the price of a product in different foreign markets can be explained by the difference in the cost of serving the markets.

_____ **20.** Predatory dumping involves the attempt to gain control of a foreign market by destroying competitors with impossibly low prices.

_____ **21.** Although the World Bank and the IMF are instrumental in fostering international trade, they cannot require the nations that they help to modify the practices that caused them to face financial crises.

>lg 6   **What are international economic communities?**

_____   22. A free trade zone allows anyone who enters it to take advantage of lowered duties and eased restrictions related to imports and exports.

_____   23. A customs union sets up a free-trade area and specifies a uniform tariff structure for members' trade with nonmember nations.

_____   24. In a common market, a preferential tariff is imposed in order to restrict members for violating trade rules and restrictions.

_____   25. The creation of the European Union, as a result of the Maastrict Treaty, called for economic and monetary coordination, including a common currency and an independent central bank, with the United States and Canada.

_____   26. As a result of the creation of the European Union, most of its members have agreed to the conversion of their currencies into the Euro.

>lg 7   **How do companies enter the global market place?**

_____   27. Exporting is the most complicated method by which a firm can enter the global marketplace.

_____   28. Licensing and joint ventures are methods that are commonly used by American firms to manufacture and distribute their products in foreign markets.

_____   29. Direct foreign investment involves active ownership of a foreign company or of overseas manufacturing or marketing facilities.

_____   30. Countertrade involves the purchase or sale of foreign goods at trade fairs where business is conducted "over-the-counter."

>lg 8   **What threats and opportunities exist in the global marketplace?**

_____   31. Nationalism, values, language differences, customs, and traditions have largely become insignificant factors in relation to international trade because technology has served to wipe them out.

_____   32. The basic institutions and public facilities upon which an economy's development depends are known as infrastructure.

>lg 9   **What are the advantages of multinational companies?**

_____   33. Although a multinational corporation may operate in many countries around the world, it will always have one location that is its worldwide headquarters.

_____   34. Two major disadvantages of multinational corporations are their inability to sidestep regulatory problems and their inability to shift production from one location to another as market conditions change.

>lg 10   **What are the trends in the global marketplace?**

_____   35. The size of domestic markets is often an impediment to business expansion in foreign markets.

_____   36. Currently, governments around the world have attempted to lower barriers to world trade by "leveling the playing field" for sellers.

ENHANCE YOUR VOCABULARY

Affluence	A plentiful supply of material goods; wealth
Bilateral	Having two sides; affecting reciprocally two nations or parties
Bolsters	To support with; reinforce; to give a boost to
Displaced	To remove from the usual or proper place; to remove from a home or office
Embraced	To clasp in the arms; hug; to take in as a part
Exclusive	Limited to possession, control or use by a single individual or group
Fostering	To nurture; to encourage
Loopholes	A means of escape; an ambiguity or omission in the text through which the intent of a statute, contract, or obligation may be evaded
Pact	An agreement or covenant between two or more parties
Plausible	Appearing worthy of belief
Propel	To drive forward or onward by or as if by means of a force that imparts motion
Quintessentially	The essence of a thing in its purest and most concentrated form
Rebates	A return or refund of a part of a payment
Saturated	Full of moisture
Scenario	An outline of a play; an account of a possible course of events
Void	To make empty or vacant

Directions: Select the definition in Column B that best defines the word in Column A.

	Column A		Column B
_____	1. Fostering	a.	To make empty or vacant
_____	2. Rebates	b.	Full of moisture
_____	3. Pact	c.	Having two sides
_____	4. Void	d.	An agreement
_____	5. Quintessentially	e.	To hug; take in
_____	6. Saturated	f.	Appearing worthy of belief
_____	7. Loopholes	g.	The essence of a thing
_____	8. Bilateral	h.	A return of a part of a payment
_____	9. Embrace	i.	To nurture; encourage
_____	10. Plausible	j.	Means of escape

REVIEW YOUR KEY TERMS

Directions: Select the definition in Column B that best defines the word in Column A.

	Column A		Column B
_____	1. Imports	a.	The ability to recognize and react to international business opportunities, be aware of threats from foreign competition, and effectively use international distribution networks to obtain raw materials and move finished products to customers.
_____	2. Absolute advantage	b.	Goods and services produced in one country and sold in other countries.
_____	3. Embargo	c.	A lowering of the value of a nation's currency relative to other currencies.

_____ **4.** Uruguay Round

_____ **5.** Balance of payments

_____ **6.** Maastricht Treaty

_____ **7.** Joint venture

_____ **8.** World Trade Organization

_____ **9.** Licensing

_____ **10.** World Bank

_____ **11.** Tariff

_____ **12.** Infrastructure

_____ **13.** Balance of trade

_____ **14.** Contract manufacturing

_____ **15.** Global vision

_____ **16.** Exporting

_____ **17.** North American Free Trade Agreement (NAFTA)

_____ **18.** Trade deficit

_____ **19.** Protective tariffs

_____ **20.** Countertrade

_____ **21.** Exports

_____ **22.** Trade surplus

d. An unfavorable balance of trade that occurs when a country imports more than it exports.

e. The situation when a country can produce and sell a product at a lower cost than any other country or when it is the only country that can provide the product.

f. The difference between the value of a country's exports and the value of its imports during a certain time.

g. A favorable balance of trade that occurs when a country exports more than it imports.

h. A summary of a country's international financial transactions showing the difference between the country's total payments to and its total receipts from other countries.

i. A tariff that is lower for some nations than for others.

j. The concept that each country should specialize in the products that it can produce most readily and cheaply and trade those products for those that other countries can produce most readily and cheaply.

k. The policy of permitting the people of a country to buy and sell where they please without restrictions.

l. An organization established by the Uruguay Round in 1994 to oversee international trade, reduce trade barriers, and resolve disputes among member nations.

m. The policy of protecting home industries from outside competition by establishing artificial barriers such as tariffs and quotas.

n. A 1994 agreement by 117 nations to lower trade barriers worldwide.

o. A tax imposed on imported goods.

p. A total ban on imports or exports of a product.

q. The practice of charging a lower price for a product in foreign markets than in the firm's home market.

r. Laws that require a company earning foreign exchange (foreign currency) from its exports to sell the foreign exchange to a control agency, such as a central bank.

s. An agreement in which a domestic firm buys part of a foreign firm or joins with a foreign firm to create a new entity.

t. Tariffs that are imposed in order to make imports less attractive to buyers than domestic products are.

u. An international organization, founded in 1945, that promotes trade, makes short-term loans to member nations, and acts as a lender of last resort for troubled nations.

v. An organization of 15 European nations (as of 1999) that works to foster political and economic integration in Europe; formerly called the European Community.

_____ 23. Devaluation

    w. The practice of selling domestically produced goods to buyers in another country.

_____ 24. Protectionism

    x. An international bank that offers low-interest loans, as well as advice and information, to developing nations.

    y. A tariff that is lower for some nations than for others.

_____ 25. Direct foreign investment

    z. A trade agreement among Argentina, Brazil, Paraguay, and Uruguay that eliminates most tariffs among the member nations.

_____ 26. International Monetary Fund (IMF)

    aa. The practice in which a foreign firm manufactures private-label goods under a domestic firm's brand name.

_____ 27. Free-trade zones

    bb. A 1993 agreement creating a free-trade zone including Canada, Mexico, and the United States.

_____ 28. Dumping

    cc. The legal process whereby a firm agrees to allow another firm to use a manufacturing process, trademark, patent, trade secret, or other proprietary knowledge in exchange for the payment of a royalty.

_____ 29. Principle of comparative advantage

    dd. A 1993 treaty concluded by the members of the European Community (now the European Union) that outlines plans for tightening bonds among the members and creating a single market; officially called the Treaty on European Union.

_____ 30. Free trade

    ee. An area where the nations allow free, or almost free, trade among each other while imposing tariffs on goods of nations.

_____ 31. Mercosur

    ff. Active ownership of a foreign company or of manufacturing or marketing facilities in a foreign country.

_____ 32. Multinational corporations

    gg. The basic institutions and public facilities upon which an economy's development depends.

_____ 33. European Union (EU)

    hh. Corporations that move resources, goods, services, and skills across national boundaries without regard to the country in which their headquarters are located.

_____ 34. Nationalism

    ii. A form of international trade in which part or all of the payment for goods or services is in the form of other goods and services.

_____ 35. Preferential tariff

    jj. A sense of national consciousness that boosts the culture and interests of one country over those of all other countries.

_____ 36. Exchange controls

    kk. Goods and services that are bought from other countries.

CRITICAL THINKING ACTIVITIES

1. P.O.V. (Point of View)

Directions: In this exercise you will be asked to provide your personal opinion regarding some of the topics discussed in the chapter. At the completion of this exercise, your instructor may wish to poll the entire class regarding their responses.

    a. The United States has consistently run trade deficits for many years. This increases our debt to foreign countries. Perhaps the best way for us to reduce this debt would be for the United States to impose protectionists measures such as import quotas, increased tariffs, and strict customs regulations.

Agree _____   Disagree _____

Explain:

_____

_____

_____

_____

b. The strength of such institutions as the World Bank and the International Monetary Fund lies in their ability to serve as a "lender of last resort" for underdeveloped nations. In this capacity, they can always be relied on to step in to resolve financial crises in these countries.

Agree _____   Disagree _____

Explain:

_____

_____

_____

_____

2. Using the Internet

Directions: The value of trade between countries is an important component of economic growth. To better understand its magnitude, go to **http://www.census.gov/foreign-trade** and click on top trading partners.

   a. Who are the top five trading partners of the United States in the current month?
   b. List the top five trading partners with whom the United States has a trade surplus in the current month along with the dollar value of the surplus with each country.
   c. List the top five trading partners with whom the United States has a trade deficit in the current month along with the dollar value of the deficit with each country.
   d. What is the total dollar value of the surplus/deficit for the current month?
   e. What is the significance of this data?

3. Writing Skills

Directions: You are an international businessman. You have been asked by the president of an international business society to give a talk on how governments and institutions can foster world trade. Using at least 10 words or terms from Enhance Your Vocabulary and/or Review Your Key Terms , first outline, then write your speech.

NOTES ON CHAPTER 3

Chapter 4

Making Ethical Decisions and Managing a Socially Responsible Business

OUTLINE

MULTIPLE CHOICE

Directions: Place the letter of the response that best completes the questions that follow in the blank space at the left.

>lg 1

What philosophies and concepts shape personal ethical standards and what are the stages of ethical development?

_b_ 1. The set of moral standards for judging whether something is right or wrong is known as:
    a. professionalism
    b. ethics
    c. morale
    d. philosophy

_C_   2. The philosophy that focuses on the consequences of an action taken by a person or an organization is known as:
    a. ethics   **c.** utilitarianism
    b. morale   **d.** professionalism

_a_   3. The notion that "people should act so as to generate the greatest good for the greatest number" is derived from
    a. individual rights legislation   **c.** ethical dilemma philosophy
    b. professional behavior theory   **d.** utilitarianism

_a_   4. The term "human rights" implies that:
    a. certain rights such as freedom and the pursuit of happiness are conveyed at birth and cannot be taken away
    b. the government has the right to take basic rights away through legislation
    c. external circumstances dictate the level of rights afforded to individuals
    d. they cannot be taken away even under the most difficult circumstances

_C_   5. The modern concept of justice has come to mean:
    a. the legal system is incapable of providing justice
    b. life is not "fair" to most individuals
    c. an equitable distribution of the burdens and rewards that society offers
    d. all societies must agree on what is reasonably fair

_a_   6. The level of personal ethical behavior that is childlike, calculating, self-centered, and based on possible immediate reward or punishment falls into the:
    a. preconventional stage   **c.** maturation stage
    b. conventional stage   **d.** postconventional stage

_b_   7. The level of personal ethical behavior that involves adopting the viewpoint of society, including loyalty and obedience, is known as the:
    a. preconventional stage   **c.** maturation stage
    b. conventional stage   **d.** postconventional stage

_d_   8. The level of personal ethical behavior where people are concerned less about how others might see them and more about how they see and judge themselves is known as the:
    a. postconventional stage   **c.** maturation stage
    b. conventional stage   **d.** postconventional stage

>lg 2   **How can managers influence organizational ethics?**

_d_   9. Of the following, which represents an ethical business activity:
    a. taking unfair advantage
    b. refusing to seek personal gain
    c. giving false impressions
    d. divulging proprietary information

_C_   10. Of the following, which represents an unethical business activity:
    a. abiding by organizational rules
    b. reporting the embezzlement of funds
    c. humiliating an employee in the presence of customers
    d. disclosing safety defects in a new product

_d_   11. The following is a question that "The Three Question Test" requires be asked when an employee attempts to determine the most ethical response to a problem:
    a. Is it legal?   **c.** How does it make me feel?
    b. Is it balanced?   **d.** all of these answers are correct

>lg 3   What are the techniques for creating employee ethical awareness?

a   **12.** By providing employees with the knowledge of what their firm expects in terms of their responsibilities and behavior toward fellow employees, customers, and suppliers, the firm is establishing:
   a. a code of ethics
   b. the "Front Page of the Newspaper Test"
   c. the "Three Question Test"
   d. an ethical dilemma

d   **13.** A typical code of ethics can be contained in a:
   a. lengthy and extremely detailed document
   b. summary of goals, policies, priorities
   c. document that is hung on an office wall or printed on cards to be carried by employees
   d. all of these answers are correct

>lg 4   What is social responsibility?

b   **14.** Social responsibility is the:
   a. legal obligation that a company must accept when is sells goods and services
   b. concern of a business for the welfare of society as a whole
   c. need for a company to maximize its profit
   d. non-voluntary, legal response of a business to an ethical crisis

b   **15.** At the highest level of the "Pyramid of Corporate Social Responsibility" business firms are encouraged to meet their:
   a. ethical responsibilities   **c.** legal responsibilities
   b. philanthropic responsibilities   **d.** economic responsibilities

d   **16.** At the base of the "Pyramid of Corporate Social Responsibility" business firms are encouraged to meet their:
   a. ethical responsibilities   **c.** philanthropic responsibilities
   b. legal responsibilities   **d.** economic responsibilities

C   **17.** According to Peter Drucker we should look first at corporate:
   a. philanthropy and economics   **c.** legality and responsibility
   b. legality and economics   **d.** ethics and responsibility

>lg 5   How do businesses meet their social responsibilities to various stakeholders?

C   **18.** Stakeholders are:
   a. only corporate stockholders
   b. groups that only seek a stake in corporate decision making in order to earn profits
   c. those individuals or groups to whom a business has a responsibility
   d. those who cannot be readily identified when assessing corporate responsibility

a   **19.** Firms that allow employees to make decisions on their own and suggest solutions to company problems are said to be practicing:
   a. empowerment   **c.** stakeholding
   b. corporate discrimination   **d.** internal promotion

d   **20.** Activities that drive customers away from businesses include:
   a. empowerment   **c.** ethics
   b. shareholding   **d.** lapses in customer service

C   **21.** Corporate philanthropy includes:
   a. employing senior citizens because they possess special skills
   b. providing internships for students to serve as a pool of future employees
   c. making cash contributions, donations of equipment, and products
   d. none of these answers are correct

b   **22.** Social investing:
   a. is synonymous with corporate philanthropy
   b. involves individuals limiting their investments to securities that fit their beliefs about ethical and social responsibility
   c. is limited to those industries that are involved in social issues
   d. is limited to businesses that operate in a socialist economic system

>lg 6   **What are the global and domestic trends in ethics and social responsibility?**

a   **23.** Strategic giving involves:
   a. linking philanthropy closely to a corporation's missions and goals
   b. a long term commitment to a charity
   c. a short term commitment to a charity
   d. limiting donations to equipment or products

C   **24.** Multinational corporations:
   a. impose their sense of corporate responsibility on the countries in which they operate
   b. bring management from their country to change the attitudes of local managers
   c. must balance conflicting interests of stakeholders when making decisions regarding social responsibility
   d. none of these answers are correct

C   **25.** Global information technology (IT) will continue to:
   a. influence governments
   b. restructure corporations
   c. create world networks
   d. all of these answers are correct

TRUE/FALSE

Directions: Place a T or an F in the space provided to the left of each question to indicate whether it is True or False.

>lg 1   **What philosophies and concepts shape personal ethical standards and what are the stages of ethical development?**

F   **1.** The notion that, "people should act so as to generate the greatest good for themselves" is known as utilitarianism.

T   **2.** When an action affects the majority adversely, it is considered to be morally wrong.

T   **3.** Legal rights, as opposed to human rights, are guaranteed by law and can never be disregarded.

T   **4.** The concept of justice would include the right to "equal pay for equal work."

I   5. Preconventional ethics assume that individuals will respond to punishment or reward as opposed to a response based on the notion of what is right or wrong.

T   6. Conventional ethics moves from viewing the expectations of society to the egocentric point of view.

I   7. At the postconventional level business people are concerned less with how they see and judge themselves than with how others might judge them.

>lg 2

How can managers influence organizational ethics?

I   8. "Is it legal?" "Is it balanced?" "How does it make me feel?"-are questions that a manager can use to determine the most ethical response to an ethical problem.

I   9. The "front page of the newspaper test" refers to a technique used by managers for keeping potential conflicts of interest and ethical problems out of the press.

>lg 3

What are the techniques for creating employee ethical awareness?

I   10. Formal training and "games" have been used by many companies to develop an awareness of questionable business activities on the part of their employees.

I   11. Leaders and managers establish patterns of behavior that determine what is and is not acceptable within an organization.

F   12. Companies have not developed a code of ethics for their employees because each ethical problem requires a different response.

I   13. A code of ethics will always have a positive influence on employee ethical decision-making behavior.

>lg 4

What is social responsibility?

I   14. Social responsibility is the concern of businesses for the welfare of society as a whole, including obligations beyond those required by law or union contract.

F   15. Social responsibility is involuntary and includes investors, workers, suppliers, consumers, and communities.

I   16. The "Pyramid of Corporate Social Responsibility" ranks philanthropic responsibility as the highest level of the corporate social responsibility triangle.

I   17. Peter Drucker believes that we should look first at what an organization can do for society and next at what it does to society.

F   18. Corporations have been known to act irresponsibly, yet their actions were considered legal.

>lg 5

How do businesses meet their social responsibilities to various stakeholders?

F   19. Stakeholders are individuals who seek to purchase control of a company in order to influence ethical behavior.

F   20. Empowerment is a form of behavior by management that involves attempting to directly control employee behavior when faced with a problem.

F   21. Although a corporation provides a community with jobs, goods, and services, it has minimal responsibility to the general public with whom it has little contact.

I   22. Corporate philanthropy includes cash contributions, donations of equipment and products, and support for the volunteer efforts of corporate employees.

T **23.** Milton Friedman proposed the notion that the only social responsibility of business is to make a profit for its shareholders.

F **24.** Social investing occurs when investors limit their investments to securities that fit within widely held beliefs about ethical and social responsibility.

>lg 6 **What are the global and domestic trends in ethics and social responsibility?**

T **25.** Strategic giving links philanthropy to a corporate mission or goal, and targets donations to regions of the country where the company operates.

F **26.** There is unanimous agreement as to which organizations should be targeted for corporate strategic giving.

T **27.** Multinational corporations often must balance conflicting interests of stakeholders when making decisions regarding social responsibility.

ENHANCE YOUR VOCABULARY

Avant-garde	A group active in the invention and application of new techniques in a given field, especially in the arts
Cognizant	Knowledgeable of something especially through personal experience
Credo	Set of fundamental beliefs
Dilemma	Unpleasant or difficult choice
Disgruntled	To make discontented, cross, angry
Divulging	Disclosing (a secret); revealing
Embezzling	Appropriating (as property entrusted to one's care) fraudulently to one's own use; to steal
Generate	To bring into existence; produce
Nuances	A subtle distinction or variation
Pending	Deciding; impending
Permeates	To diffuse through or penetrate something; to pass through the pores of
Philanthropy	Goodwill to fellowmen
Sashayed	A dance in which partners sidestep in a circle around each other; to strut or move about in a conspicuous manner
Shoddy	Hastily or poorly done; inferior; shabby
Trailblazer	One that blazes a trail to guide others; pathfinder; pioneer

Directions: Select the definition in Column B that best defines the word in column A.

	Column A		Column B
h	1. Generate	a.	Hastily or poorly done; shabby
f	2. Credo	b.	Mindful
a	3. Shoddy	c.	A group active in the invention and application of new techniques
e	4. Disgruntled	d.	Pathfinder; pioneer
i	5. Sashayed	e.	To make discontented, cross
c	6. Avant-garde	f.	Set of fundamental beliefs
j	7. Dilemma	g.	Not yet decided; impending
d	8. Trailblazer	h.	To bring into existence; produce
b	9. Cognizant	i.	To move about conspicuously
g	10. Pending	j.	Unpleasant or difficult choice

REVIEW YOUR KEY TERMS

Directions: Select the definition in Column B that best defines the word in Column A.

Column A

cc. 1. Statutory law

g. 2. Arbitration

ee. 3. Judiciary

e. 4. Mediation

c. 5. Business law

6. Bankruptcy

7. Trademark

8. Tort

9. Laws

10. Common law

aa. 11. Uniform Commercial Code

a. 12. Contract

bb. 13. Appellate Courts

2. 14. Property taxes

m. 15. Antitrust regulation

h. 16. Express contract

d. 17. Administrative law

Column B

a. An agreement that sets forth the relationship between parties regarding the performance of a specified action; creates a legal obligation and is enforceable in a court of law.

b. The rules of conduct in a society, created and enforced by a controlling authority, usually the government.

c. The body of law that governs commercial dealings.

d. The rules, regulations, and orders passed by boards, commissions, and agencies of government.

e. A method of settling disputes in which the parties submit their case to an impartial third party but are not required to accept the mediator's decision.

f. The failure by one party to a contract to fulfill the terms of the agreement without a legal excuse.

g. A method of settling disputes in which the parties agree to present their case to an impartial third party and are required to accept the decision.

h. A contract in which the terms are specified in either written or spoken words.

i. A form of protection established by the government for creators of works of art, or other intellectual property; gives the creator the exclusive right to use, produce, and sell the creation during the lifetime of the creator and for 50 years thereafter.

j. A contract that depends on the acts and conduct of the parties to show agreement; the terms are not specified in writing or orally.

k. A form of protection established by the government for inventors; gives an inventor the exclusive right to manufacture, use, and sell an invention for 17 years.

l. Taxes that are imposed on specific items such as gasoline, alcoholic beverages, airline tickets, and guns.

m. Laws that prevent companies from entering into agreements to control trade through a monopoly.

n. The body of unwritten law that has evolved out of judicial (court) decisions rather than being enacted by a legislature; also called case law.

o. The employer's share of Social Security taxes and federal and state unemployment taxes.

p. The removal of rules and regulations governing business competition.

q. A social movement that seeks to increase the rights and powers of buyers vis-à-vis sellers.

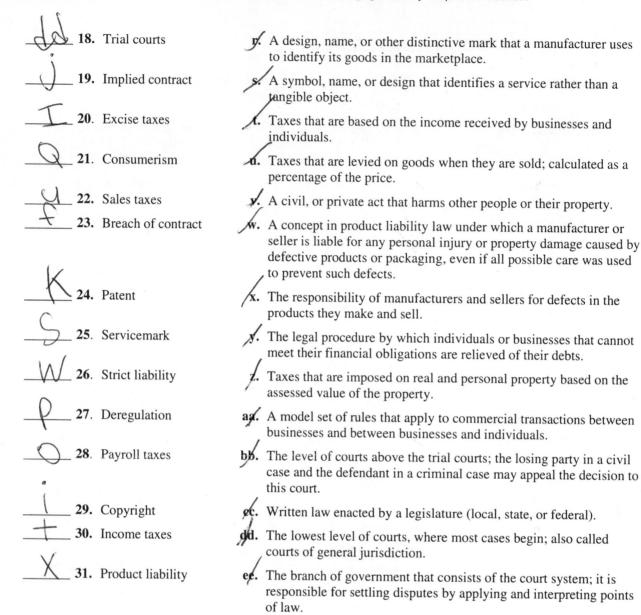

_dd_ **18.** Trial courts

_j_ **19.** Implied contract

_I_ **20.** Excise taxes

_Q_ **21.** Consumerism

_U_ **22.** Sales taxes

_t_ **23.** Breach of contract

_K_ **24.** Patent

_S_ **25.** Servicemark

_W_ **26.** Strict liability

_P_ **27.** Deregulation

_O_ **28.** Payroll taxes

_i_ **29.** Copyright

_t_ **30.** Income taxes

_X_ **31.** Product liability

r. A design, name, or other distinctive mark that a manufacturer uses to identify its goods in the marketplace.

s. A symbol, name, or design that identifies a service rather than a tangible object.

t. Taxes that are based on the income received by businesses and individuals.

u. Taxes that are levied on goods when they are sold; calculated as a percentage of the price.

v. A civil, or private act that harms other people or their property.

w. A concept in product liability law under which a manufacturer or seller is liable for any personal injury or property damage caused by defective products or packaging, even if all possible care was used to prevent such defects.

x. The responsibility of manufacturers and sellers for defects in the products they make and sell.

y. The legal procedure by which individuals or businesses that cannot meet their financial obligations are relieved of their debts.

z. Taxes that are imposed on real and personal property based on the assessed value of the property.

aa. A model set of rules that apply to commercial transactions between businesses and between businesses and individuals.

bb. The level of courts above the trial courts; the losing party in a civil case and the defendant in a criminal case may appeal the decision to this court.

cc. Written law enacted by a legislature (local, state, or federal).

dd. The lowest level of courts, where most cases begin; also called courts of general jurisdiction.

ee. The branch of government that consists of the court system; it is responsible for settling disputes by applying and interpreting points of law.

CRITICAL THINKING ACTIVITIES

1. P.O.V. (Point of View)

Directions: In this exercise you will be asked to provide your personal opinion regarding some of the topics discussed in the chapter. At the completion of this exercise, your instructor may wish to poll the entire class regarding their responses.

    a. Much is said about the social responsibility of business and its need to concern itself with the welfare of society. Yet, socially responsible behavior on the part of businesses can result in higher prices for goods and services. Therefore, business should concern itself with providing only goods and services, and consumers will ultimately decide which firms will succeed through the purchase of their offerings. In this way, responsible firms will succeed while less responsible firms will be forced out of business.

Agree _✓_   Disagree ___

Explain:

If business follow through with pursueing with economic responsibility, ethical responsibility philanthropic responsibility, social responsibility and follow through with the obligations of social responsibility then the business will suceed.

b. *Caveat emptor*, "let the buyer beware," is a term that is used widely when discussing the social responsibility of business. It essentially means that customers are responsible for making sure that what they purchase is exactly what they want. As long as a company operates within the framework of legally permissible activities, it is not important that it also concern itself with the impact of its behavior on society.

Agree ___   Disagree _✓_

Explain:

If a business does not operate with proper behavior on society then business will fail and consumers, customers and citizens will ignore them and may protest against them.

2. Using the Internet

customers, employees, business partners + government demand that corporations take an active role in social, environmental & community concern.

Directions: Corporate citizenship is an important issue related to the social responsibility of business. Click on **http://www.corporatecitizenship.net/**

An economic & social force touching many stakeholders.

a. Explain the concept of corporate citizenship.

To increase profits so long as it stays within the rules of the game, which is to say engages in open & free competition without deception or fraud.

b. What role do business ethics play in corporate activities?

c. What is a social audit. *Is encouragement of businesses in becoming more involved in driving up standards of adult literacy & numeracy encouraging.*

d. Describe community involvement.

The Government **e.** What is corporate governance?

commitment to social + environmental responsibility is reflected across a whole range of publications + projects activities are very wide-ranging.

(It is suggested that you click on other links in order to gain greater understanding of these issues).

3. Writing Skills

Directions: Companies wishing to raise the ethical awareness of employees, often do so through ethics training. You are a corporate consultant who does training. Plan a training program using ethical dilemmas.

Training program

• what do you do when you work as a maintenance worker and you have to clean and unclog a back up toilet and you dont really want to do it, but it part of your job. You either do the job and get paid for it or quit the job and let someone else deal with it.

• When a boss invites to have sex with him in order to give you a raise or promote you to a higher position and knows that you really need the extra cash, you either report him of sexual harassment or do as he wishes because you desperately in need of the extra cash.

NOTES ON CHAPTER 4

Chapter 5

Forms of Business Ownership

OUTLINE

MULTIPLE CHOICE

Directions: Place the letter of the response that best completes the questions that follow in the blank space at the left.

>lg 1

What are the three main forms of business organization, and what factors should a company's owners consider when selecting a form?

_d_ **1.** Most businesses fall into the following form of ownership:
   a. sole proprietorship   **c.** corporation
   b. partnership   **d.** all of these are correct

_d_ **2.** The percent of total business sales generated by corporations is about:
   a. 73%   **c.** 20%
   b. 7%   **d.** 90%

>lg 2

What are the advantages and disadvantages of sole proprietorships?

_b_ **3.** A sole proprietorship is:
   a. often owned and operated by more than one individual
   b. established, owned, operated, and often financed by one individual
   c. usually taxed at higher rates by the government
   d. virtually identical to a partnership

_d_ **4.** An advantage of forming a sole proprietorship is:
   a. ease of raising capital
   b. unlimited liability
   c. extensive managerial expertise
   d. taxes are often lower than for other forms of business

_a_ **5.** Limited managerial expertise is considered a disadvantage in a(n):
   a. sole proprietorship   **c.** partnership
   b. corporation   **d.** S corporation

>lg 3

Why would a new business venture choose to operate as a partnership, and what downside would the partners face?

_c_ **6.** An association of two or more persons who agree to operate a business together for a profit is known as a(n):
   a. sole proprietorship   **c.** partnership
   b. corporation   **d.** S corporation

_c_ **7.** A limited partnership has:
   a. corporate and limited partners
   b. proprietary and limited partners
   c. general and limited partners
   d. only limited partners

_d_ **8.** A disadvantage of forming a partnership is:
   a. unlimited liability
   b. possible conflicts between partners
   c. sharing of profits
   d. all of these answers are correct

>lg 4 **How does the corporate structure provide advantages and disadvantages to a company, and what are the major types of corporations?**

_b_   9.   A business which operates as a legal entity with an existence and life separate from its owners is known as a:
- **a.** sole proprietorship   **c.** partnership
- **b.** corporation   **d.** limited partnership

_a_   10.   The charter under which a corporation operates is issued to it by the:
- **a.** state in which it is formed
- **b.** federal government
- **c.** city in which it has its world headquarters
- **d.** county government where it operates

_d_   11.   The ownership of a corporation is held by its:
- **a.** directors   **c.** management
- **b.** stakeholders   **d.** stockholders

_b_   12.   The board of directors of a corporation are:
- **a.** appointed by outside officers   **c.** elected by inside directors
- **b.** elected by stockholders   **d.** officers hired to run the corporation

_d_   13.   The following is an advantage of a corporation:
- **a.** limited liability   **c.** unlimited life
- **b.** ease of transferring ownership   **d.** all of these are correct

_a_   14   A major disadvantage of a corporation is:
- **a.** double taxation of profits   **c.** ease of transferring ownership
- **b.** limited liability   **d.** unlimited life

_a_   15.   An S corporation has the advantage of being organized like a corporation, but is taxed like a:
- **a.** partnership   **c.** cooperative
- **b.** sole proprietorship   **d.** joint venture

>lg 5 **Does a company have any business options besides sole proprietorship, partnership, and corporation?**

_c_   16.   Cooperatives generally exist where:
- **a.** certain specialized goods or services cannot be provided by corporations
- **b.** people with dissimilar interests wish to form a business venture
- **c.** people with similar interests join together to reduce costs and gain economic power
- **d.** suppliers are at odds as to how to best distribute similar products

_c_   17.   Cooperatives do not pay any taxes because they:
- **a.** possess limited liability
- **b.** have an elected board of directors
- **c.** distribute all profits to members
- **d.** do not have administrative staffs

_c_   18.   When two or more companies form an alliance to pursue a specific project, usually for a specific time period, it is known as a:
- **a.** joint proprietorship   **c.** joint venture
- **b.** joint corporation   **d.** joint partnership

>lg 6   Why is franchising growing in importance?

_b_   **19.** Franchising is a form of business that:
  a. is one of the slower growing segments of the economy
  b. provides a way to own a business without starting from scratch
  c. generally sells products of inferior quality
  d. all of these answers are correct

_d_   **20.** The franchisor provides:
  a. capital   **c.** legal services
  b. employees   **d.** the product concept

_d_   **21.** The franchisee purchases:
  a. a proven product   **c** training in managing the franchise
  b. proven operating methods   **d.** all of these answers are correct

_a_   **22.** Although franchisors give up a share of profits to their franchisees, they receive ongoing payments in the form of:
  a. royalties   **c.** reimbursements
  b. rebates   **d.** recalls

>lg 7   Why would a company use mergers and acquisitions to grow?

_a_   **23.** A merger occurs when:
  a. two or more firms combine to form one new company
  b. a joint venture begins
  c. a corporation or investor group buys a company
  d. two joining firms seek to increase their operating costs

_c_   **24.** An acquisition occurs when:
  a. two or more firms combine to form one new company
  b. a joint venture begins
  c. a corporation or investor group buys a company
  d. two joining firms seek to increase their operating costs

_b_   **25.** A horizontal merger takes place when:
  a. a corporation or investor group buys a company
  b. companies at the same stage in the same industry merge to reduce costs
  c. a company buys a firm in the same industry that is involved in a later stage of the production or sales process
  d. suppliers buy out other suppliers' inventories

_c_   **26.** A vertical merger takes place when:
  a. a corporation or investor group buys a company
  b. companies at the same stage in the same industry merge to reduce costs
  c. a company buys a firm in the same industry that is involved in an earlier or later stage of the production process
  d. suppliers buy out other suppliers' inventories

_c_   **27.** A conglomerate merger brings together:
  a. companies in related businesses to reduce risk
  b. companies in different geographic regions to reduce risk
  c. companies in unrelated businesses to reduce risk
  d. none of these answers are correct

d 28. An LBO results when:
   a. conglomerates dissolve their working arrangements with suppliers
   b. a vertical merger occurs
   c. a horizontal merger occurs
   d. large amounts of borrowed money are used to purchase the stock of a company by outside investors or a corporation's management

>lg 8

What trends will affect business organizations in the future?

C 29. In order to differentiate themselves from other franchises, established franchises have:
   a. limited their product offerings
   b. offered fewer outlets for their products or services
   c. begun to practice cross-branding
   d. all of these answers are correct

C 30. In order to meet the product and service needs of consumers more franchises are:
   a. limiting their product offerings
   b. opening fewer outlets
   c. catering to niche markets
   d. developing joint venture corporations

TRUE/FALSE

Directions: Place a T or an F in the space provided to the left of each question to indicate whether it is True or False.

>lg 1

What are the three main forms of business organization, and what factors should a company's owners consider when selecting a form?

T 1. Most businesses fall into one of three major ownership categories: sole proprietorships, partnerships, and government agencies.

F 2. Corporations account for the majority of all businesses in the United States.

F 3. Corporations generate about 90 percent of total business sales and profits in the United States.

>lg 2

What are the advantages and disadvantages of sole proprietorships?

T 4. A sole proprietorship is a business that is established, owned, operated, and often financed by one person.

F 5. An advantage of a sole proprietorship is that it requires a huge time commitment and often dominates an owner's life.

T 6. Two advantages of sole proprietorships are that they are easy and inexpensive to form and the owner keeps all of the profits that the business earns.

T 7. Unlimited liability for a sole proprietor is a disadvantage because the owner is personally liable for all of the debts of the business.

F 8. A disadvantage of sole proprietorship is that tax laws allow the owner to deduct any losses from other types of personal income.

>lg 3

Why would a new business venture choose to operate as a partnership, and what downside would the partners face?

T 9. A partnership is an association of two or more persons who agree to operate a business together for profit.

T 10. Law firms, accounting firms, and real estate companies are often set up as partnerships.

F 11. In a general partnership, the limited partners do not share in the profits.

T 12. Limited partners agree not to take part in day-to-day management of a firm but share equally in its financial responsibility with the general partners.

T 13. Ease of formation, availability of capital, diversity of skills, experience, and relative freedom from government control are advantages of partnerships.

F 14. Conflicts between partners are not a disadvantage of partnerships because the partnership agreement clearly states individual responsibilities.

>lg 4

How does the corporate structure provide advantages and disadvantages to a company, and what are the major types of corporations?

T 15. Although stockholders own a corporation, it is a legal entity with an existence and life separate from them.

T 16. Over 70 percent of all corporations have sales under $500,000.

F 17. Nevada's pro-corporate policies have made it the state of incorporation for close to 50 percent of the Fortune 500.

F 18. A firm must become incorporated in the state in which is has its main office.

F 19. Shareholders differ from stockholders in that shareholders own shares while stockholders own stock in the corporation.

T 20. The board of directors of a corporation *sets* major corporate goals and policies, *elects* corporate officers, and *oversees* the firm's operation and finances.

T 21. A key advantage of a corporation is that it has limited liability. If it goes bankrupt, creditors look only to the assets of the corporation for payment.

F 22. Double taxation of profits is an advantage that corporations have long sought to maintain.

T 23. Limited Liability Corporations (LLC's) have the same liability protection as corporations but can choose to be taxed as a partnership or corporation.

>lg 5

Does a company have any business organization options besides sole proprietorship, partnership, and corporation?

F 24. Seller cooperatives are similar to flea markets wherein sellers agree to gather together to sell their products in one place at the same time.

F 25. A joint venture involves two or more individuals joining to purchase a small retail outlet, such as a tavern, and to operate it together.

>lg 6

Why is franchising growing in importance?

T 26. A franchisee is an individual or company that sells the goods or services of a franchisor in a certain geographic area.

T

27. A franchise agreement outlines the rules for running a franchise including inventory levels, equipment, sales and service levels, and operating rules.

F

28. An advantage of franchising to the franchisor is that the franchisee gains some control over the operation of the franchise.

>lg 7

Why would a company use mergers and acquisitions to grow?

F

29. A merger takes place when a corporation or investor group buys a corporation and the identity of the merged corporation is lost.

F

30. In an acquisition two or more firms combine to form one new company.

T

31. In a vertical merger, a company buys a firm in its same industry that is involved in an earlier stage of the production or sales process.

T

32. In a horizontal merger, companies at the same stage in the same industry merge to reduce costs.

>lg 8

What trends will affect business organizations in the future?

F

33. Cross-branding is not practiced today in the field of franchising.

F

34. Financial rather than strategic mergers are expected to dominate the field of mergers and acquisitions as companies jockey for position and competitive advantage.

T

35. Cross-border mergers have become more commonplace for businesses that operate in the global marketplace.

ENHANCE YOUR VOCABULARY

Clashes	Hostile encounters; sharp conflicts
Collaboration	To work jointly with others
Curtail	To make less; to reduce the length of
Feasibility	Capable of being accomplished or brought about; possible
Fluctuates	Shifts back and forth uncertainly
Gourmet	A connoisseur of food and drink
Horticulture	The science and art of growing fruits, vegetables, flowers, or ornamental plants
Hybrid	A person whose background is a blend of two diverse cultures or traditions; something that has two different types of components performing essentially the same function
Kiosks	Open summerhouses or pavilions; small structures with one or more open sides that is used to vend merchandise (as newspapers)
Patronize	Provide aid or support for; to adopt an air of condescension toward; treat haughtily
Plummeted	To drop sharply and abruptly
Portfolio	A hinged cover or case for carrying papers; the securities held by an investor
Prospective	Likely to come about; expected
Restrictive	Limiting
Royalties	Shares of the product or profit; payments made to an author or composer for each copy of a work sold or to an inventor for each article sold under a patent

Directions: Select the definition in Column B that best defines the word in Column A.

	Column A	Column B
g	1. Plummeted	a. To work jointly with others
e	2. Gourmet	b. Limiting
a	3. Collaboration	c. Shares of the product or profit
d	4. Portfolio	d. The securities held by an investor
c	5. Royalties	e. A connoisseur of food and drink
h	6. Patronize	f. Treat haughtily
b	7. Clashes	g. To drop sharply and abruptly
b	8. Restrictive	h. A hostile encounter; a sharp conflict
j	9. Curtail	i. Likely to come about
f	10. Prospective	j. To make less

REVIEW YOUR KEY TERMS

Directions: Select the definition in Column B that best defines the word in Column A.

	Column A	Column B
n	1. Sole proprietorship	a. A merger of companies at different stages in the same industry; done to gain control over supplies of resources or to gain access to different markets.
i	2. Limited liability company (LLC)	b. In a franchising arrangement, the individual or company that sells the goods or services of the franchisor in a certain geographic area.
m	3. S corporation	c. A partnership in which all partners share in the management and profits. Each partner can act on behalf of the firm and has unlimited liability for all its business obligations.
o	4. Corporation	d. The owners of a corporation, who hold shares of stock that provide certain rights; also known as shareholders.
a	5. Vertical merger	e. The purchase of a corporation by another corporation or by an investor group.
k	6. Limited partnership	f. An association of two or more persons who agree to operate a business together for profit.
f	7. Partnership	g. A group of people elected by the stockholders to handle the overall management of a corporation, such as setting corporate goals and policies, electing corporate officers, and overseeing the firm's operations and finances.
t	8. Horizontal merger	h. A form of business organization based on a business arrangement between a franchisor, which supplies the product concept, and the franchisee, who sells the goods or services of the franchisor in a certain geographic area.
b	9. Franchisee	i. A hybrid organization that offers the same liability protection as a corporation but may be taxed as either a partnership or a corporation.
e	10. Acquisition	j. The combination of two or more firms to form a new company, which often takes on a new corporate identity.

_____ V **11.** Joint venture

_____ q/k **12.** Leveraged buyout (LBO)

_____ o **13.** Stockholders

_____ C **14.** General partnership

_____ r **15.** Limited partners

_____ l **16.** Conglomerate merger

_____ P **17.** General partners

_____ g/c **18.** Board of directors

_____ W **19.** Co-operatives

_____ h **20.** Franchising

_____ j **21.** Merger

_____ S **22.** Franchisor

_____ u **23.** Franchise agreement

k. A partnership with one or general partners, who have unlimited liability, and one or more limited partners, whose liability is limited to the amount of their investment.

l. A merger of companies in unrelated businesses; done to reduce risk.

m. A hybrid entity that is organized like a corporation, with stockholders, directors, and officers, but taxed like a partnership, with income and losses flowing through to the stockholders and taxed as their personal income.

n. A business that is established, owned, operated, and often financed by one person.

o. A legal entity with an existence and life separate from its owners, who therefore are not personally liable for the entity's debts. It is chartered by the state in which it is formed and can own property, enter into contracts, sue and be sued, and engage in business operations under the terms of its charter.

p. Partners who have unlimited liability for all of the firm's business obligations, and who control its operations.

q. A corporate takeover financed by large amounts of borrowed money; can be done by outside investors or by a company's own management.

r. Partners whose liability for the firm's business obligations is limited to the amount of their investment. They do not participate in the firm's operations.

s. In a franchising arrangement, the company that supplies the product concept to the franchisee.

t. A merger of companies at the same stage in the same industry; done to reduce costs, expand product offerings, or reduce competition.

u. A contract setting out the terms of a franchising arrangement, including the rules for running the franchise, the services provided by the franchisor, and the financial terms. Under the contract, the franchisee is allowed to use the franchisor's business name, trademark, and logo.

v. An alliance formed by two or more companies to pursue a specific project, usually for a specific time period.

w. Legal entities typically formed by people with similar interests, such as customers or suppliers, to reduce costs and gain economic power. It has limited liability, an unlimited life span, and an elected board of directors; all profits are distributed to the member-owners in proportion to their contributions.

CRITICAL THINKING ACTIVITIES

1. P.O.V. (Point of View)

Directions: In this exercise you will be asked to provide your personal opinion regarding some of the topics discussed in the chapter. At the completion of this exercise, your instructor may wish to poll the entire class regarding their responses.

a. Corporations possess limited liability. They exist apart from their owners and therefore allow owners and managers to escape responsibility for many of their actions, some of which are not socially responsible. A suggestion has been made to change the laws of incorporation in many states so that limited liability no longer exists. It is felt that this would force corporations to be socially responsible because they would face financial and perhaps criminal penalties for their actions.

Agree _____   Disagree _✓_

Explain:

LLC is a hybrid organization. LLCs are not Corporations, like S corporations they appeal to small businesses; LLCs are easy to set up & are not subject to many restrictions, LLCs provide the same liability protection as Corporations but offer the option of being taxed as a partnership or a corporation.

b. The double taxation of profits that exists for corporations is unfair. Why should individuals have to pay taxes twice on the same money? Efforts should be made to eliminate them.

Agree _✓_   Disagree _____

Explain:

In addition, any profits paid to stockholders as dividends are also taxed as personal income. Double taxation of corporate profits is a major disadvantage for some small corporations.

2. Using the Internet

Directions: Franchising is an interesting way for individuals to gain ownership of a business. Click on **http://www.franchising.org** to develop an understanding of this area.

a. What resources are available for franchisees? *Build a website for franchise starting at $1,000 including opportunities. Database help make documents for franchising. Database search franchises by zip code, search engine registration and help completing manuals & advise on international franchising.*

b. Select two options, such as the American Franchise Association or Bison and provide an in-depth description of the information that is offered to franchisees.

Featuring the best franchise and business opportunities in a highly profitable, top-rated franchise structures. Bison provides a long list of franchising links.

c. What resources are available for franchisors?

d. Select two options, such as Franchise Business International or the American Business Group and provide and in-depth description of the information that is offered to franchisors. *This group helps franchisors market in the U.S. & abroad. Very highly recommended by their readers. Its an awesome company with very high standards & tremendous references!*

3. Writing Skills

Directions: First outline, then write a short essay on the advantages and disadvantages of partnerships.

Chapter 6

Entrepreneurship: Starting and Managing Your Own Business

OUTLINE

I. Entrepreneurship Today
    A. Entrepreneur or Small Business Owner?
        1. Classic Entrepreneurs
        2. Multipreneurs
        3. Intrapreneurs
    B. Why Become an Entrepreneur?
    C. Types of Entrepreneurs

II. Characteristics of the Successful Entrepreneur
    A. The Entrepreneurial Personality
    B. `Managerial Ability and Technical Knowledge

III. Small Business
    A. What is a Small Business?
    B. Advantages of Small Businesses
    C. Disadvantages of Small Businesses
    D. The Small Business Administration
        1. Financial Assistance Programs
        2. Management Assistance Programs

IV. Starting Your Own Business
    A. First Steps
        1. Finding the Idea
        2. Choosing a Form of Organization
    B. Developing the Business Plan
    C. Financing the Business
    D. Risks of Business Ownership

V. Managing Your Own Business
    A. Using Outside Consultants
    B. Hiring and Retaining Employees
    C. Operating Internationally

VI. Capitalizing on Trends in Business
    A. Home Based Businesses
    B. Ownership Trends
        1. You're Never Too Young
        2. Women on the Move
        3. Minority Businesses Branch Out
    C. The Internet Explosion

VII. Applying This Chapter's Topics

MULTIPLE CHOICE

Directions: Place the letter of the response that best completes the questions that follow in the blank space at the left.

>lg 1   **Why do people become entrepreneurs and what are the different types of entrepreneurs?**

_____   1. Entrepreneurs are individuals who are said to possess:
       a. vision   **c.** creativity
       b. drive   **d.** all of the above are correct

_____   2. The difference between small business owners and entrepreneurs is that small business owners:
       a. possess less individual drive
       b. do not have flexibility in planning for financing
       c. are more likely to accept the status quo
       d. take a longer term view than do entrepreneurs

_____   3. Micropreneurs generally:
       a. seek to start small and plan to enlarge their operations greatly
       b. plan to start small and stay small
       c. start their business without regard to their personal satisfaction
       d. have the same goals as growth oriented entrepreneurs

_____   4. Entrepreneurs who start a series of companies are known as:
       a. macropreneurs   **c.** multipreneurs
       b. intrapreneurs   **d.** none of these answers are correct

_____   5. Entrepreneurs who don't own their own companies but apply their creativity, vision, and risk taking within a large corporation are known as:
       a. macropreneurs   **c.** multipreneurs
       b. intrapreneurs   **d.** micropreneurs

>lg 2   **Which characteristics do successful entrepreneurs share?**

_____   6. Entrepreneurs tend to:
       a. take more vacation time
       b. have more time to take vacations
       c. succeed based upon having a great concept for a product or service
       d. *be* the company

_____   7. A 12-year study of executives indicated that the following characteristic was common among entrepreneurs:
       a. opinionated   **c.** aggressive
       b. focused   **d.** all of the above are correct

_____   8. The distinguishing characteristic of an entrepreneur is:
       a. the ability to manage the company that implements the idea
       b. having a concept that can potentially be brought to reality in the form of a product or service
       c. being able to leave problems at the office at the end of the business day
       d. elegating responsibility and being able to work fewer hours than other company managers

_____ 9. By being self-confident, entrepreneurs are said to be able to:
   a. spot trends
   b. be competitive
   c. act in a decisive manner and have faith in their ability to resolve problems
   d. make personal sacrifices to achieve their goals

_____ 10. By being committed, entrepreneurs are said to be able to:
   a. spot trends
   b. be competitive
   c. act in a decisive manner and have faith in their ability to resolve problems
   d. make personal sacrifices to achieve their goals

>lg 3 **How do small businesses contribute to the U.S. economy?**

_____ 11. The percentage of small businesses in the United States that have fewer than 100 employees is:
   a. 20%   **c.** 50%
   b. 98%   **d.** 37.5%

_____ 12. A major reason for the increase in small business formation is:
   a. large corporations no longer represent job security or offer as many fast-track career opportunities
   b. many small business owners gain great personal satisfaction from their work
   c. outsourcing, which has created opportunities for smaller companies
   d. all of the above are correct

_____ 13. A major characteristic that is used when classifying a business as being "small" is:
   a. it has a strong influence in its industry
   b. it is nationally based
   c. being owned by an individual or a small group of investors
   d. that its management can be controlled by a large conglomerate

>lg 4 **What are the advantages and disadvantages facing owners of small businesses?**

_____ 14. Small businesses are able to serve specialized markets because:
   a. they can provide their goods and services cost effectively
   b. the complexity of a firm is not a factor in entering these markets
   c. personal service is not a factor in the sale of products they sell
   d. small firms tend to focus on goods and services with an established demand and the potential for high sales is not a factor for them

_____ 15. Small businesses owners often:
   a. lack the necessary skills to respond quickly to change
   b. have a wide variety of financing readily available to them
   c. have been exempt from new federal, state, and local regulations
   d. none of these answers are correct

_____ 16. Small business owners often:
   a. have a fairly easy time finding investment funds
   b. pay interest rates that are lower than larger firms
   c. find dealing with newly added government rules and regulations burdensome
   d. find that technical skills are easily converted into management expertise

>lg 5   **How does the Small Business Administration help small businesses?**

_____ **17.** The Small Business Administration:
  a. is designed to provide financial assistance only to startup firms
  b. is a private organization which operates for a profit
  c. returns all profits from operations to local small businesses
  d. assists small businesses in the areas of management, federal contracts, and speaking on their behalf when needed

_____ **18.** Small Business Investment Companies:
  a. are government operated investment companies that assist small businesses
  b. are privately owned and provide long term funding for small businesses
  c. operate as not-for-profit organizations which make loans to small businesses
  d. lend money to the SBA which then channels the funds to small businesses

_____ **19.** The Service Corps of Retired Executives and the Active Corps of Executives:
  a. invest directly in small businesses
  b. operate small businesses when owners lack the proper training and skills
  c. provide free management consulting for small business owners
  d. have been prevented by the courts from counseling small business owners

>lg 6   **What are the first steps to take if you are starting your own firm?**

_____ **20.** The first step in starting a business is:
  a. self assessment
  b. finding the idea
  c selecting the form of business organization
  d. business planning

_____ **21.** The written document that details the idea for a new business is known as a(n):
  a. self assessment   **c.** idea and problem diary
  b. business plan   **d.** organization form

_____ **22.** Writing a business plan:
  a. allows you to immediately get caught up in the day-to-day operations of the business
  b. will eliminate the need for the type of analysis that requires you to make marketing decisions
  c. can reduce the need to take a critical look at operations
  d. should focus on the uniqueness of a business and explain why customers will be attracted to it

_____ **23.** The most common use of business plans is to:
  a. outline day-to-day business operations
  b. state marketing strategies
  c. persuade lenders and investors to finance the venture
  d. provide a description of operations to potential retailers or wholesalers

_____ **24.** Equity is:
  a. money raised through the sale of stock in a business
  b. borrowed money that must be repaid with interest over a stated period of time
  c. synonymous with debt
  d. repaid with interest to stockholders

_____ 25. Debt is:
    a. money raised through the sale of stock in a business
    b. borrowed money that must be repaid with interest over a stated period of time
    c. synonymous with equity
    d. repaid with interest to stockholders

_____ 26. Angel investors are:
    a. investment firms that specialize in financing small high-growth firms in return for an ownership interest and a voice in management
    b. individuals or groups of experienced investors who provide funding for startup businesses
    c. companies that handle the sale of equity instruments
    d. companies that handle the sale of debt instruments

_____ 27. Venture capital is:
    a. financing obtained from investment firms that specialize in financing small high-growth firms in return for an ownership interest and a voice in management
    b. an individual or group of experienced investors who provide debt funding for startup businesses
    c. a city or locality that handles the sale of equity instruments
    d. none of these answers are correct

>lg 7   Why does managing a small business present special challenges for the owner?

_____ 28. The main job of a small business owner is to:
    a. to obtain financing for operations
    b. find a prime location to place the physical operations of the business
    c. carry out the business plan through all areas of the business
    d. seek out markets for the product or service

_____ 29. Some aspects of a small business can be outsourced. This means that:
    a. outside sources of raw materials can be obtained to maintain manufacturing processes
    b. sales of products can be made to outside firms when business is slow
    c. some aspects of the business can be contracted out to specialists
    d. sources of outside funding can be obtained from venture capitalists

>lg 8   What trends are shaping the small business environment?

_____ 30. A trend that has contributed to the rising popularity of working at home is the:
    a. high cost of technology
    b. lack of former corporate executives in times of high employment with whom small business owners can consult
    c. the stigma attached to running a business from home
    d. the availability of low-cost technology including voice mail and computers

_____ 31. Among the ownership trends related to entrepreneurship:
    a. more young people indicate a desire to start their own businesses
    b. women start businesses at twice the national rate of business formation
    c. firms owned by minorities are a high growth sector of the economy
    d. all of these answers are correct

TRUE/FALSE

Directions: Place a T or an F in the space provided to the left of each question to indicate whether it is True or False.

>lg 1   **Why do people become entrepreneurs and what are the different types of entrepreneurs?**

_____ 1. Approximately 16 percent of all nonagricultural workers in the U.S. are involved in either full or part-time entrepreneurial activities.

_____ 2. All small business owners are considered to be entrepreneurs since they take risks to create a new business or greatly change the scope and direction of an existing firm.

_____ 3. Small business owners generally take a long-term view of a business while entrepreneurs are more likely to deal with the status quo.

_____ 4. Classic entrepreneurs can also be micropreneurs, in that they start their own companies based upon innovative ideas but plan to limit the size of their operations.

_____ 5. Growth oriented entrepreneurs want to limit the growth of their businesses so that they don't rival major corporations.

_____ 6. Multipreneurs are entrepreneurs who start a series of companies.

_____ 7. Entrepreneurs who expand their business operations to global markets are known as intrapreneurs.

_____ 8. Corporations that create supportive environments for intrapreneurship retain their most innovative employees along with ownership of products that they develop.

_____ 9. The desire to control one's own destiny has been cited as a major reason for the popularity of entrepreneurship.

>lg 2   **Which characteristics do successful entrepreneurs share?**

_____ 10. Most entrepreneurs are typically indecisive and lack confidence in their ability to resolve problems.

_____ 11. The ability to follow trends set by other firms and copy their product designs is a significant trait of entrepreneurs.

_____ 12. Despite being entrepreneurial, an individual must possess the business skills to run a successful business.

_____ 13. Once a new venture demonstrates significant growth, it is important for entrepreneurs to broaden their roles rather than hire others to do the additional tasks.

>lg 3   **How do small businesses contribute to the U.S. economy?**

_____ 14. Although there has been growth in small business in the U.S., the overwhelming majority employ more than 100 people.

_____ 15. It is estimated that U.S. small businesses in the aggregate would rank fourth among the world's economic powers in terms of the total value of goods and services produced.

_____ 16. Among the characteristics that would classify a business as "small" is that it is based locally and is not a dominant company in its industry.

>lg 4   What are the advantages and disadvantages facing owners of small businesses?

_____ 17. As a result of their small size, small businesses are not able to react quickly to changing market forces.

_____ 18. Owner-managers of small businesses, through their direct relationship with customers, get feedback on how well their firms are meeting customer needs.

_____ 19. Limited managerial skills are more than offset by small company size when small businesses attempt to respond quickly to changes in the marketplace.

_____ 20. Small businesses are exempt from federal, state, and local regulations and reporting requirements, thereby enhancing their ability to function without outside interference.

>lg 5   How does the Small Business Administration help small businesses?

_____ 21. The SBA offers financial assistance to qualified small businesses that cannot obtain financing on reasonable terms through normal lending channels.

_____ 22. Small Business Investment Companies are owned and operated by the federal government hoping to provide long term funding for small businesses.

>lg 6   What are the first steps to take if you are starting your own firm?

_____ 23. Self-assessment is the first step that an individual should take when considering whether to go into a business of his/her own.

_____ 24. Starting a firm in a field or industry other than the one in which an individual has experience is recommended, since the transfer of knowledge from one field to another is common.

_____ 25. It is more important to get a business up and running than to select whether it should be a sole proprietorship, partnership, or corporation.

_____ 26. A business plan helps business owners take an objective and critical look at their business venture and set goals that will help them manage its growth and performance.

_____ 27. Getting involved in day-to-day business operations does away with the need for a business plan since the plan has little to do with actual operations.

_____ 28. Once a business is up and running, the business plan becomes a little used document whose primary purpose was to convince investors to provide funding for the business.

_____ 29. A significant factor that can be a source of difficulty for a small business is rapid growth, which can place a strain on finances.

>lg 7   Why does managing a small business present special challenges for the owner?

_____ 30. The main job of a small business owner is to carry out the business plan through all areas of the business from personnel to production and maintenance.

_____ 31. Outsourcing involves the use of outside employment firms to locate new full-time employees to perform tasks that cannot be done by the current workforce.

_____ **32.** The availability of workers interested in joining small firms has grown to the extent that they are willing to forego comfortable working conditions, flexible hours, etc.

_____ **33.** Export managing companies serve the needs of small businesses that wish to sell their goods abroad by purchasing goods at a discount from the firm and then reselling them abroad.

>lg 8 **What trends are shaping the small business environment?**

_____ **34.** Today, most entrepreneurs are starting their second or third careers by deciding to venture out on their own.

_____ **35.** Firms owned by minorities are a high growth sector of the small business field.

ENHANCE YOUR VOCABULARY

Aggregate	The whole sum or amount
Clause	A separate section of writing; a distinct article in a document; a group of words containing a subject and predicate
Credibility	The quality or power of inspiring belief; capacity for belief
Dissuade	To advise against something
Hotbeds	An environment that favors rapid growth or development
Potential	Something that can develop or become actual; promise
Resounding	Producing or characterized by resonant sound; impressively sonorous; emphatic
Shun	To avoid deliberately and habitually
Status quo	The same; the existing state of affairs
Unscrupulous	Unprincipled

Directions: Select the definition in Column B that best defines the word in Column A.

	Column A		Column B
_____ **1.**	Shun	**a.**	An environment that favors rapid growth
_____ **2.**	Credibility	**b.**	Unprincipled
_____ **3.**	Potential	**c.**	A group of words
_____ **4.**	Status quo	**d.**	Something that can develop
_____ **5.**	Hotbeds	**e.**	The existing state of affairs
_____ **6.**	Dissuade	**f.**	To avoid deliberately
_____ **7.**	Unscrupulous	**g.**	The whole sum or amount
_____ **8.**	Clause	**h.**	To advise against something
_____ **9.**	Aggregate	**i.**	Sonorous; emphatic
_____ **10.**	Resounding	**j.**	Capacity for belief

REVIEW YOUR KEY TERMS

Directions: Select the definition in Column B that best defines the word in Column A.

Column A	Column B
_____ **1.** Intrapreneurs	**a.** Individual investors or groups of experienced investors who provide funding for start-up businesses.

_____ **2.** Small Business Administration (SBA)

    b. A business that is independently owned, is owned by an individual or a small group of investors, is based locally (although it may serve a larger market), and is not a dominant company in its industry.

_____ **3.** Business plan

    c. People with vision, drive, and creativity who are willing to take the risk of starting a new business or of greatly changing the scope and direction of an existing firm.

_____ **4.** Small business

    d. Financing obtained from investment firms that specialize in financing small, high-growth companies and receive an ownership interest and a voice in management in return for their money.

_____ **5.** Entrepreneurs

    e. A form of business financing consisting of borrowed funds that must be repaid with interest over a stated time period.

_____ **6.** Small Business Investment Companies (SBICs)

    f. Entrepreneurs who apply their creativity, vision, and risk taking within a large corporation, rather than starting a company of their own. They enjoy a high degree of autonomy while receiving a regular salary and financial backing from their employer.

_____ **7.** Venture capital

    g. A government agency that helps people start and manage small businesses, helps small business owners win federal contracts, and speaks on behalf of small business.

_____ **8.** Angel investors

    h. Privately owned and managed investment companies that are licensed by the Small Business Administration and provide long-term financing for small businesses.

_____ **9.** Debt

    i. A form of business financing consisting of funds raised through the sale of stock in a business.

_____ **10.** Equity

    j. A formal written statement that describes in detail the idea for a new business and how it will be carried out; includes a general description of the company, the qualifications of the owner(s), a description of the product, an analysis of the market, and a financial plan.

CRITICAL THINKING ACTIVITIES

1. P.O.V. (Point of View)

Directions: In this exercise you will be asked to provide your personal opinion regarding some of the topics in the chapter. At the completion of this exercise, your instructor may wish to poll the class regarding their responses.

    a. Your brother is disenchanted with his position as an advertising artist and has told you that he plans to leave his job to open a small business. He knows that he has an excellent reputation and is known as an outstanding artist. He also has a friend in the advertising industry who will provide him with a loan to start the business These three factors (reputation, talent, and start-up financing) are most important if he is to succeed at his new endeavor. He has asked you for your opinion regarding his plans.

        Agree _____   Disagree _____

Explain

_____

_____

_____

_____

b. The distinction between small business owners and entrepreneurs is not clearly understood. Small business owners typically remain so because the industries in which they operate are not open to change and innovation, while entrepreneurs are well versed in technical fields that are constantly changing.

Agree _____   Disagree _____

·Explain

_____

_____

_____

_____

2. Using the Internet

Directions: Creating a business plan is crucial for the success of a new business. It is a formal document that is used to guide management towards achieving specific goals. Assuming that you have an idea for a new product or service, go to **http://www.bplans.com** and click on Sample plans and then click on Select a Business Plan and review at least three plans.

a. Click through the executive summary and read the mission statement for each company that you have chosen. List the factors that are common to each plan.
b. Write a brief executive summary for your business plan.
c. Write a management summary for your business.

3. Writing Skills

Directions: Write a short essay describing the personal characteristics of a successful entrepreneur. Tell the reader whether you think you have these characteristics by giving examples of things you have done. If you possess these characteristics, what kind of business would you like to own? If you don't think you have these characteristics, what field of work would you like to be involved in, and what personal characteristics do you believe you need for your chosen field?

Chapter 7

Management and Leadership in Today's Organization

OUTLINE

MULTIPLE CHOICE

Directions: Place the letter of the response that best completes the questions that follow in the blank space at the left.

What is the role of management?

C _____ **1.** Management is the process of:
   a. operating a business for a large organization
   b. building a new business from scratch based upon a creative idea
   c. development, maintenance, and allocation of resources to attain organizational goals
   d. none of these answers are correct

 2. One of the four key functional areas of the management process is:
   a. coordinating   **c.** reporting
   b. controlling   **d.** budgeting

What are the four types of planning?

 3. Planning is:
   a. guiding an organization to a goal
   b. deciding what needs to be done to achieve organizational objectives, as well as identifying how, by whom, and when it will be done
   c. stating what the purpose of the organization is and the reason for its existence
   d. the process of coordinating and allocating a firm's resources in order to carry out its plan

 4. Tactical plans:
   a. have a shorter (less than one year) time frame than strategic plans
   b. create specific standards, methods, policies, and procedures that are used in specific functional areas of the organization
   c. identify alternative courses of action for very unusual or crisis situations
   d. state the purpose of the organization and its reason for existing

C _____ **5.** Contingency plans:
   a. have a shorter (less than one year) time frame than strategic plans
   b. create specific standards, methods, policies, and procedures that are used in specific functional areas of the organization
   c. identify alternative courses of action for very unusual or crisis situations
   d. state the purpose of the organization and its reason for existing

 6. Operational plans:
   a. have a shorter (less than one year) time frame than strategic plans
   b. create specific standards, methods, policies, and procedures that are used in specific functional areas of the organization
   c. identify alternative courses of action for very unusual or crisis situations
   d. state the purpose of the organization and its reason for existing

 7. Mission statements:
   a. have a shorter (less than one year) time frame than strategic plans
   b. create specific standards, methods, policies, and procedures that are used in specific functional areas of the organization
   c. identify alternative courses of action for very unusual or crisis situations
   d. state the purpose of the organization and its reason for existing

C   **8.** Top level management:
a. implement strategic plans   c. develop strategic plans
b. carry out tactical plans   d. design and carry out operational plans

a   **9.** Middle management and supervisory management:
a. carry out tactical plans
b. design and carry out operational plans
c. are responsible for beginning the implementation of strategic plans
d. all of these answers are correct

>lg 3   **What are the primary responsibilities of managers in organizing activities?**

a   **10.** Grouping jobs and employees is known as:
a. departmentalization   c. delegation
b. division of labor   d. specialty training

b   **11.** Dividing up tasks to be performed by employees is known as:
a. departmentalization   c. delegation
b. division of labor   d. specialty training

C   **12.** Assigning authority and responsibilities to individuals in the organization is known as:
a. departmentalization   c. delegation
b. division of labor   d. specialty training

>lg 4   **How do leadership styles influence corporate culture?**

d   **13.** The process of guiding and motivating others toward the achievement of organizational goals is known as:
a. organizing   c. controlling
b. operating   d. leading

d   **14.** Legitimate power is derived from:
a. extensive knowledge in one or more areas
b. personal charisma, respect, and admiration
c. the ability to threaten negative outcomes
d. an individual's position in an organization

C   **15.** Coercive power is derived from:
a. extensive knowledge in one or more areas
b. personal charisma, respect, and admiration
c. the ability to threaten negative outcomes
d. an individual's position in an organization

b   **16.** Referent power is derived from:
a. extensive knowledge in one or more areas
b. personal charisma, respect, and admiration
c. the ability to threaten negative outcomes
d. an individual's position in an organization

a   **17.** Consensual leaders:
a. encourage discussion about issues and then require all parties involved to agree to the final decision
b. turn over all authority and control to subordinates
c. are synonymous with free-rein or laissez-faire leaders
d. tend to be directive in their leadership style

_a_ **18.** Empowerment means:
    a. giving employees increased autonomy and discretion to make their own decisions
    b. placing the power to make decisions in the hands of superiors
    c. maintaining a consistent policy with regard to power and leadership
    d. using umpires to call issues "the way they see them"

_d_ **19.** Of the following, which is relevant to determining corporate culture:
    a. attitudes   **c.** standards of behavior
    b. values   **d.** all of these answers are correct

>lg 5   **How do organizations control activities?**

_c_ **20.** Controlling is the:
    a. granting of autonomy and discretion to employees to make their own decisions
    b. leadership style of the managers of an organization which is indicative of its underlying philosophy or values
    c. process of assessing the organization's progress toward accomplishing its goals
    d. process of guiding and motivating others toward the achievement of organizational goals

_d_ **21.** The most effective performance standards state:
    a. a general objective that can be modified as needed
    b. a general objective that can only be modified under specific circumstances
    c. any behavioral objective within the framework of the firm's business mission
    d. a measurable behavioral objective that can be achieved in a specified time frame

_b_ **22.** An essential part of the process of control is:
    a. free rein leadership   **c.** laissez-faire leadership
    b. feedback   **d.** culture

>lg 6   **What roles do managers take on in different organizational settings?**

_c_ **23.** Decisional roles are based on:
    a. gathering information to distribute to those who need it
    b. interactions with other people
    c. making decisions about such things as resource allocation
    d. seeking opportunities

_a_ **24.** Decisions that are made to deal with unforeseen, infrequent, or very unusual circumstances are considered to be:
    a. nonprogrammed   **c.** informational
    b. interpersonal   **d.** reactionary

_a_ **25.** The final stage of the decision making process involves:
    a. follow up to see if the problem has been solved
    b. putting a plan into action
    c. selecting one or more alternatives
    d defining the problem

>lg 7

What set of managerial skills is necessary for managerial success?

___d___ **26.** Specialized areas of knowledge and expertise and the ability to apply that knowledge represent the manager's:
a. human relations skills   c. conceptual skills
b. autocratic skills   d. technical skills

___a___ **27.** The interpersonal skills that managers use to accomplish goals represent their:
a. human relations skills   c. conceptual skills
b. autocratic skills   d. technical skills

___C___ **28.** The skills that managers use to view the organization as a whole, understand how the various parts are interdependent, and assess how the organization relates to the outside environment represent their:
a. human relations skills   c. conceptual skills
b. autocratic skills   d. technical skills

>lg 8

What trends will affect management in the future?

___d___ **29.** Managers must provide workers with the following in order to guarantee a high level of employee participation:
a. clear explanations of results
b. behavioral boundaries
c. access to information
d. all of these are correct

___b___ **30.** The concept of "grassroots leadership" means:
a. not allowing "grass to grow under your feet" when making decisions
b. finding a way to empower frontline employees within the firm
c. using ideas like fertilizer in order to accomplish corporate goals
d. only middle and upper level managers can make decisions for the firm

---

TRUE/FALSE

Directions: Place a T or an F in the space provided to the left of each question to indicate whether it is True or False.

>lg 1

What is the role of management?

___F___ **1.** Management should be static and unchanging in order to maintain the effectiveness and efficiency of an organization.

___T___ **2.** Management is the process of guiding the development, maintenance, and allocation of resources to attain organizational goals.

___F___ **3.** Leadership is not a functional area for managers because it implies that there will be a conflict when all managers attempt to lead employees.

___T___ **4.** Planning, organizing, leading, and controlling are the four key functional areas of management.

___F___ **5.** Good management is conducted by performing each managerial function one at a time as opposed to carrying out any of them simultaneously.

>lg 2

What are the four types of planning?

_____T_____   **6.** In order for planning to be effective it requires extensive information about the external business environment in which a firm competes, as well as its internal environment.

_____T_____   **7.** Long term plans should be designed to support short-term plans.

_____F_____   **8.** Strategic planning involves creating short term (less than one year), broad goals for an organization and determining the resources needed to accomplish these goals.

_____T_____   **9.** The long-term mission of the organization is part of the strategic plan that is formulated by top-level management.

_____T_____   **10.** Tactical plans have a short time frame and support broader strategic goals.

_____F_____   **11.** Operational plans are designed to implement strategic plans and control their implementation.

_____T_____   **12.** Contingency plans identify alternative courses of action for very unusual or crisis situations.

>lg 3

What are the primary responsibilities of managers in organizing activities?

_____T_____   **13.** Organizing involves the process of coordinating and allocating a firm's resources in order to carry out plans.

_____F_____   **14.** The decision concerning which tasks are performed by which employees is usually left to the employees themselves as opposed to managers.

_____T_____   **15.** Managers can arrange the structural elements of the firm to maximize the flow of information and the efficiency of work processes.

_____F_____   **16.** Division of labor, departmentalization, and delegation are the responsibility of managers.

>lg 4

How do leadership styles influence a corporate culture?

_____F_____   **17.** Leadership only at the highest levels of management is important for organizations to function effectively.

_____T_____   **18.** Power rests in the ability of a manager to influence others to behave in a particular way.

_____F_____   **19.** Autocratic leaders solicit input from all members of a group and then allow group members to make a final decision through a voting process.

_____T_____   **20.** Laissez-faire leaders allow for very little input from subordinates and prefer to make decisions on their own.

>lg 5

How do organizations control activities?

_____F_____   **21.** Controlling means giving employees increased autonomy and discretion to make their own decisions.

_____T_____   **22.** A corporate reporting system that provides feedback can help managers control problems before they get out of hand.

_____F_____   **23.** Control systems provide a means of coordinating employee activities and integrating resources throughout the organization.

>lg 6

What roles do managers take on in different organizational settings?

___ **24.** Managerial roles fall into three basic categories: informational, interpersonal, and decisional.

___ **25.** A manager's interpersonal role might involve thinking like an entrepreneur and making decisions about resource allocation.

___ **26.** Because nonprogrammed decisions made by managers occur in unique and complex situations, there is rarely precedent for them.

>lg 7

What set of managerial skills is necessary for managerial success?

___ **27.** The three main types of managerial skills are: technical, human relations, and conceptual.

___ **28.** Technical skills are the interpersonal skills managers use to accomplish goals through the use of human resources.

___ **29.** Specialized areas of knowledge and expertise, and the ability to apply that knowledge, make up the manager's human resource skills.

___ **30.** Conceptual skills include the ability to view the organization as a whole, understand how the various parts are interdependent, and assess how the organization relates to its external environment.

>lg 8

What trends will affect management in the future?

___ **31.** According to Steve Miller, grassroots leadership means empowering frontline people, "to challenge them, to provide them with the resources they need, and then to hold them accountable."

___ **32.** The proliferation of information technology is not having a major impact on managers because they must be technologically proficient to attain the positions that they hold.

ENHANCE YOUR VOCABULARY

Allocation	Distribute; to set apart; designate
Charisma	A personal magic of leadership; a special magnetic charm
Collectible	An object that is collected by fanciers
Crucial	Important, significant
Customization	The building, fitting, or altering according to individual specifications
Intriguing	Engaging the interest to a marked degree; fascinating
Isolation	Solitude; aloneness
Looming	To appear in an impressively great or exaggerated form; to take shape as an impending occurrence
Redundancy	Superfluous repetition
Vagueness	Not clearly expressed; stated in indefinite terms

Directions: Select the definition in Column B that best defines the word in Column A.

	Column A		**Column B**
___	1. Redundancy	a.	Important, significant
___	2. Allocation	b.	A special magnetic charm
___	3. Vagueness	c.	Not clearly expressed

e	**4.** Collectible	**d.**	Distribute; to set apart
f	**5.** Looming	**e.**	An object that is collected by fanciers
b	**6.** Charisma	**f.**	Repetitious
a	**7.** Crucial	**g.**	Fitting, or altering according to individual specifications
j	**8.** Intriguing	**h.**	Solitude; aloneness
g	**9.** Customization	**i.**	To take shape as an impending occurrence
h	**10.** Isolation	**j.**	Fascinating

REVIEW YOUR KEY TERMS

Directions: Select the definition in Column B that best defines the word in Column A.

Column A

Column B

f **1.** Management

m **2.** Leadership style

z **3.** Middle management

a **4.** Supervisory management

X **5.** Planning

L **6.** Participative leadership

h **7.** Free-rein (laissez-faire) leadership

g **8.** Leadership

8 **9.** Power

r **10.** Empowerment

u **11.** Conceptual skills

kk **12.** Nonprogrammed decisions

a. The third level of managers, who make up the bottom of the managerial pyramid; design and carry out operational plans for the ongoing daily activities of the firm.

b. The process of coordinating and allocating a firm's resources in order to carry out its plans.

c. The process of beginning to implement a strategic plan by addressing issues of coordination and allocating resources to different parts of the organization; has a shorter time frame (less than one year) and more specific objectives than strategic planning.

d. The process of creating long-range (one to five years), broad goals for the organization and determining what resources will be needed to accomplish those goals.

e. Plans that identify alternative courses of action for very unusual or crisis situations; typically stipulate the chain of command, standard operating procedures, and communication channels the organization will use during an emergency.

f. The process of guiding the development, maintenance, and allocation of resources to attain organizational goals.

g. The process of guiding and motivating others toward the achievement of organizational goals.

h. A leadership style in which the leader turns over all authority and control to subordinates.

i. Directive leaders who prefer to make decisions and solve problems on their own with little input from subordinates, who are expected to implement solutions according to specific instructions.

j. A manager's ability to operate in diverse cultural environments.

k. A manager's specialized areas of knowledge and expertise, as well as the ability to apply that knowledge.

l. A leadership style in which the leader shares decision making with group members and encourages discussion of issues and alternatives; includes democratic, consensual, and consultative styles.

_____ **13.** Consultative leaders

_____ **14.** Expert power

_____ **15.** Tactical planning

_____ **16.** Democratic leaders

_____ **17.** Legitimate power

_____ **18.** Informational roles

_____ **19.** Global management skills

_____ **20.** Human relations skills

_____ **21.** Corporate culture

_____ **22.** Referent power

_____ **23.** Autocratic leaders

_____ **24.** Strategic planning

_____ **25.** Top management

_____ **26.** Operational planning

_____ **27.** Mission

_____ **28.** Organizing

_____ **29.** Reward power

_____ **30.** Mission statement

_____ **31.** Coercive power

m. The relatively consistent way that individuals in leadership positions attempt to influence the behavior of others.

n. A formal document that states an organization's purpose and reason for existing and describes its basic philosophy.

o. The ability to influence others to behave in a particular way.

p. Power that is derived from an individual's extensive knowledge in one or more areas.

q. Leaders who solicit input from all members of a group and then allow the members to make the final decision through a vote.

r. The process of giving employees increased autonomy and discretion to make decisions, as well as control over the resources needed to implement those decisions.

s. A manager's activities as a figurehead, company leader, or liaison.

t. The process of assessing the organization's progress toward accomplishing its goals; includes monitoring the implementation of a plan and correcting deviations from the plan.

u. A manager's ability to view the organization as a whole, understand how the various parts are interdependent, and assess how the organization relates to its external environment.

v. Leaders who confer with subordinates before making a decision, but who retain the final decision-making authority.

w. Power that is derived from an individual's ability to threaten negative outcomes.

x. The process of deciding what needs to be done to achieve organizational objectives, solve current problems, prevent future problems, or take advantage of opportunities; identifying when and how it will be done; and determining by whom it should be done.

y. An organization's purpose and reason for existing; its long-term goals.

z. The second level of managers in the hierarchy; includes division heads, departmental managers, and regional sales managers who design and carry out tactical plans in specific areas of the company.

aa. The highest level of managers; includes CEOs, presidents, and vice-presidents, who develop strategic plans and address long-range issues.

bb. Power that is derived from an individual's position in an organization.

cc. Leaders who encourage discussion about issues and then require that all parties involved agree to the final decision.

dd. The process of creating specific standards, methods, policies, and procedures that are used in specific functional areas of the organization; helps guide and control the implementation of tactical plans.

ee. Power that is derived from an individual's control over rewards.

_CC_ **32.** Consensual leaders

_t_ **33.** Controlling

_S_ **34.** Interpersonal roles

_jj_ **35.** Decisional roles

_k_ **36.** Technical skills

_e_ **37.** Contingency plans

ff. Power that is derived from an individual's personal charisma and the respect and/or admiration the individual inspires.

gg. A manager's activities as an information gatherer, an information disseminator, or a spokesperson for the company.

hh. The set of attitudes, values, and standards that distinguishes one organization from another.

ii. A manager's interpersonal skills that are used to accomplish goals through the use of human resources.

jj. A managers activities as an entrepreneur, resource allocator, conflict resolver, or negotiator.

kk. Responses to infrequent, unforeseen, or very unusual problems and opportunities where the manager does not have a precedent to follow in decision making.

CRITICAL THINKING ACTIVITIES

1. P.O.V. – (Point of View)

Directions: In this exercise you will be asked to provide your personal opinion regarding some of the topics discussed in the chapter. At the completion of this exercise, your instructor may wish to poll the class regarding their responses.

a. Little league baseball teams have always been managed by one person. Lately, parents have objected to this model because some children are excluded from playing, due to their limited skills, and the managers have focused on keeping the best players in the game and winning "at all costs." Parents of the weaker players have complained that this is unfair to their children. A proposal has been made to replace the single, on-field, manager, with an "on-field committee" that would make joint-decisions during games. It is believed that this approach will give everyone a fair chance to play.

Agree _✓_   Disagree _____

Explain

A manager with that has interpersonal skills and strong strategic planning.

b. Regardless of the task to be performed or the product or service being produced, "top-down" management is the best method for managing large organizations. This method allows for top management to know what is going on within the organization at all times.

Agree _✓_   Disagree _____

Explain

Because they are the ones who develop strategic plans and address long range issues.

2. Using the Internet

Directions: The American Management Association is an organization that was formed to assist management professionals. Click on **http://www.amanet.org** and peruse the web site.

a. What is the role of the American Management Association? *Is to provide a full range of management development & educational services to individuals, companies & government agencies worldwide including 486 of the fortune 500 companies.*

b. Provide a brief summary of its history.

AMA consolidated five closely related national organization. With this consolidation, the regents of the state University of N.Y. granted recognition to AMA as an educational institution.

c. What special services does the American Management Association offer managers?

c) Joint web sites on network to provide access to guidance issued by agencies. Information for employees who think they might like to tell community there already doing so.

d. Describe how the American Management Association could be of service to you in your career? *They offer research & print and online self-study courses to prepare you for future career.*

3. Writing Skills

Directions: Part of the planning process for a potential business involves writing a mission statement which basically states the purpose of the organization and its reason for existing. Select a business (profit or non-profit) and write a short mission statement for that business.

The Fortune Society (Freedom) = non-for-profit agency.

Mission:

Our mission is to rehabilitate ex-offenders to alternative incarceration and helping them to regain their self and cope with society. Their goals to rehabilitate misdemeanors and felonist, in counseling, education, training, career opportunities and job readiness programs. Their belief that there are alternatives to incarceration and there are chances in helping instead of conviction and incarceration. Also there are impatient programs for drug-offenders with supervision and daily drug screening.

NOTES ON CHAPTER 7

NOTES ON CHAPTER 7

Chapter 8

Designing Organizational Structure

OUTLINE

MULTIPLE CHOICE

Directions: Place the letter of the response that best completes the questions that follow in the blank space at the left.

>lg 1   **What are the five structural building blocks that managers use to design organizations?**

_____   **1.** A formal organization:
    a. is generally not required for a business to succeed in today's complex business environment
    b. limits the ability of managers to carry out a firm's plans and to achieve goals
    c. has well defined lines of authority, channels for information flow, and means of control
    d. does not reflect the order and design of relationships within a firm

_____   **2.** The degree to which tasks within an organization are subdivided into smaller jobs is known as:
    a. an organization chart
    b. departmentalization
    c. specialization
    d. division of labor

_____ 3. The process of dividing work into separate jobs and assigning tasks to workers is known as:
- **a.** an organization chart
- **b.** departmentalization
- **c.** specialization
- **d.** division of labor

>lg 2

What are the five types of departmentalization?

_____ 4. Grouping similar or associated tasks is known as:
- **a.** an organization chart
- **b.** departmentalization
- **c.** specialization
- **d.** division of labor

_____ 5. A visual representation of the structured relationships among tasks and the people given the authority to do these tasks is known as:
- **a.** functional departmentalization
- **b.** an organization chart
- **c.** product departmentalization
- **d.** geographic departmentalization

_____ 6. The levels of management within an organization that consist of top, middle, and supervisory management is called the:
- **a.** chain of command
- **b.** management hierarchy
- **c.** unity of command
- **d.** authority/power pyramid

_____ 7. An organization with a well-defined hierarchy will also have a clear:
- **a.** chain of command
- **b.** management hierarchy level
- **c.** geographic departmentalization policy
- **d.** management pyramid

_____ 8. Legitimate power, granted by an organization, which allows an individual to request action and expect compliance is known as:
- **a.** command
- **b.** delegation of authority
- **c.** span of control
- **d.** authority

_____ 9. Making employees accountable to their supervisor is known as:
- **a.** chain of command
- **b.** span of control
- **c.** delegation of authority
- **d.** authority

_____ 10. In deciding how many managers are needed at each level of the management hierarchy to effectively supervise the work performed within organizational units is known as:
- **a.** chain of command
- **b.** span of control
- **c.** delegation of authority
- **d.** authority

>lg 3

How can the degree of centralization/decentralization be altered to make an organization more successful?

_____ 11. The degree to which formal authority is concentrated in one area or level of the organization is known as:
- **a.** decentralization
- **b.** chain of command
- **c** delegation of authority
- **d.** centralization

_____ 12. Giving lower level personnel more responsibility and power to make and implement a decision by pushing decision-making authority down the organizational hierarchy is known as:
- **a.** decentralization
- **b.** chain of command
- **c.** authority
- **d.** centralization

_____ 13. A factor that should be considered by an organization when considering decentralization of decision making is the:
a. size of the organization
b. speed of change in its environment
c. employees' willingness to accept more authority
d. all of these answers are correct

>lg 4 How do mechanistic and organic organizations differ?

_____ 14. Job specialization, rigid departmentalization, many layers of management, narrow spans of control, centralized decision making, and a long chain of command are characteristics of:
a. mechanic organizations   c. mechanistic organizations
b. decentralization   d. organic organizations

_____ 15. A low degree of job specialization, loose departmentalization, few levels of management, wide spans of control, decentralized decision-making, and a short chain of command are characteristics of:
a. mechanic organizations   c. mechanistic organizations
b. tall organizations   d. organic organizations

_____ 16. A tall organization structure will usually occur in a(n):
a. mechanistic organization   c. central organization
b. organic organization   d. systematic organization

_____ 17. A flat organization structure will usually occur in a(n):
a. organic organization   c. systematic organization
b. central organization   d. mechanistic organization

>lg 5 What is the difference between line positions and staff positions?

_____ 18. An organization designed with direct, clear lines of authority and communication flowing from top managers downward is known as a:
a. line-and-staff organization   c. committee structure
b. matrix organization   d. line organization

_____ 19. An organization wherein authority and responsibility are held by a group rather than an individual is known as a:
a. line-and-staff organization   c. committee structure
b. matrix organization   d. line organization

_____ 20. An organization wherein two different forms of departmentalization, functional and product, that have complimentary strengths and weaknesses are brought together is known as a:
a. line-and-staff organization   c. committee structure
b. matrix organization   d. line organization

_____ 21. In a line organization:
a. staff positions provide specialized support services to managers
b. direct, clear lines of authority and communication flow from top managers downward
c. groups, rather than individuals, have authority and responsibility
d. individuals are brought together to work on a special project

_____ 22. A matrix organization structure is sometimes used in conjunction with a:
a. committee system   c. staff organization
b. line organization   d. line-and-staff organization

>lg 6　**What is the goal of reengineering?**

_____ 23. The reevaluation of the way a corporation does business as well as identifying and abandoning outdated rules and fundamental assumptions that guide current business operations is known as:
　　a. regrouping　　　　　　**c.** divestment
　　b. project management　　**d.** reengineering

_____ 24. Reengineering requires businesses to:
　　a. assess the effectiveness of current organization structures
　　b. focus less on planning and operate on instinct
　　c. hire a large number of employees
　　d. downsize

>lg 7　**How does the informal organization affect the performance of the company?**

_____ 25. The informal organization can:
　　a. help employees be more aware of what is happening in the workplace
　　b. transmit incorrect information
　　c. result in a conflict between group norms and a company's standards
　　d. all of these answers are correct

_____ 26. In order for a firm to effectively deal with the informal organization it is often advisable to:
　　a. ignore it because it does not, as a rule, influence employee behavior
　　b. accept it as the norm within the corporate environment
　　c. eradicate it so that it does not have a negative impact on the workplace
　　d. include informal leaders in the decision-making process

>lg 8　**What trends are influencing the way businesses organize?**

_____ 27. A network of independent companies linked by information technology to share skills, costs, and access to one another's markets is know as a(n):
　　a. line-and-staff organization　**c.** virtual corporation
　　b. matrix organization　　　　**d.** on-line organization

_____ 28. A characteristic of virtual corporations that can hamper successful operations is:
　　a. technology
　　b. expanded organizational boundaries
　　c. opportunism
　　d. excellence

TRUE/FALSE

Directions: Place a T or an F in the space provided to the left of each question to indicate whether it is True or False.

>lg 1　**What are the five structural building blocks that managers use to design organizations?**

_____ 1. Division of labor, departmentalization, and delegation accomplish the organizing, or structuring, process.

_____ 2. When jobs are grouped together so that similar or associated tasks and activities can be coordinated, division of labor has taken place.

_____ 3. Specialization is a visual representation of the structured relationships among tasks and the people given the authority to do those tasks.

>lg 2 **What are the five types of departmentalization?**

_____ 4. Functional departmentalization is based upon the primary functions performed within an organizational unit.

_____ 5. Process departmentalization is based upon the goods or services produced and sold by the organizational unit.

_____ 6. In a managerial hierarchy or management pyramid, each organizational unit is controlled and supervised by a manager in a lower unit.

_____ 7. The number of employees increases as one moves down the managerial hierarchy.

_____ 8. Unity of command guarantees that everyone will have a direct supervisor and will not be taking orders from a number of different supervisors.

_____ 9. The chain of command is determined by the firm's customers, which is based upon the primary and secondary type of customers served by the organizational unit.

_____ 10. Authority makes the employees accountable to their supervisors, including responsibility for outcomes.

_____ 11. Delegation of authority consists of legitimate power, granted by the organization and acknowledged by employees.

_____ 12. Span of control represents the number of employees that a manager directly supervises.

>lg 3 **How can the degree of centralization/decentralization be altered to make an organization more successful?**

_____ 13. Centralization is the process of pushing decision-making authority down the organizational hierarchy by giving lower-level personnel more responsibility and power to make and implement decisions.

_____ 14. Centralization lets top managers develop a broad view of operations and exercise tight financial controls as well as reduce costs by eliminating redundancy in the organization.

_____ 15. Benefits of decentralization include quicker decision making, increased levels of innovation and creativity, and greater flexibility.

>lg 4 **How do mechanistic and organic organizations differ?**

_____ 16. A relative low degree of job specialization, loose departmentalization, few levels of management, wide spans of control, decentralized decision-making, and a short chain of command characterize a mechanistic organization.

_____ 17. A mechanistic organization usually results in a tall organization structure.

_____ 18. A relatively high degree of job specialization, rigid departmentalization, many layers of management, narrow spans of control, centralized decision making, and a long chain of command characterize an organic organization.

_____ 19. An organic organization usually results in a flat organization structure.

>lg 5   **What is the difference between line positions and staff positions?**

_____ 20. In a line organization, staff positions provide specialized advisory and support services to line managers.

_____ 21. A line organization is often found in small entrepreneurial firms with its simple design, clear chain of command, and broad managerial control.

_____ 22. In a line-and-staff organization, those individuals in staff positions provide the administrative and support services that line employees need to achieve the firm's goals.

_____ 23. A committee structure is usually used as part of a larger line-and-staff organization.

_____ 24. The matrix structure brings together individuals from the same functional areas within a department to work on a special project.

>lg 6   **What is the goal of reengineering?**

_____ 25. Reengineering was developed by the major railroad companies as a method of changing from steam to diesel locomotives.

_____ 26. Reengineering involves the complete redesign of business structures and processes in order to improve operations.

_____ 27. A question that a company must first ask itself when considering reengineering is: "How did we do it in the old days?"

>lg 7   **How does the informal organization affect the performance of the company?**

_____ 28. The informal organization cannot help the formal organization to achieve its goals. It cannot be used to benefit the organization.

_____ 29. Group norms have been known to cause problems by conflicting with a company's standards.

_____ 30. The spread of information through the employee grapevine can result in resistance to change and low morale.

_____ 31. An excellent method for dealing with the informal organization is for managers to ignore it completely.

>lg 8   **What trends are influencing the way businesses organize?**

_____ 32. Technology, opportunism, excellence, trust, and no borders are all key attributes of a virtual corporation.

_____ 33. Ideally, the virtual corporation has a central office, a detailed organization chart, a structured hierarchy, and a high degree of vertical integration.

ENHANCE YOUR VOCABULARY

Anthropologist	One who studies the science of human beings
Autonomous	Existing or capable of existing independently
Collaborating	Working jointly with others; cooperating
Content	Substance, meaning, significance; the matter dealt with in a field of study; to appease to desires of

Drawback   A disadvantage or inconvenience

Exploit   To make productive use of; to make use of meanly or unjustly for one's own advantage

Interim   An intervening time; interval; temporarily

Mundane   Characterized by the practical and ordinary; commonplace; earthly

Reinvigorate   Repossessing vigor: full of physical or mental strength or active force; energetically

Streamline   To make simpler or more efficient; modernize

Directions: Select the definition in Column B that best defines the word in Column A.

	Column A		**Column B**
_____	1. Mundane	a.	One who studies the science of human beings
_____	2. Exploit	b.	Independent
_____	3. Interim	c.	The matter dealt with in a field of study
_____	4. Content	d.	To make simpler or more efficient; modernize
_____	5. Drawback	e.	To use unjustly for one's own advantage
_____	6. Reinvigorate	f.	A disadvantage or inconvenience
_____	7. Anthropologist	g.	Full of active force; energetically
_____	8. Collaborating	h.	An intervening time; temporarily
_____	9. Streamline	i.	Commonplace
_____	10. Autonomous	j.	Working with others

REVIEW YOUR KEY TERMS

Directions: Select the definition in Column B that best defines the word in Column A.

Column A

_____ 1. Organizing

_____ 2. Process departmentalization

_____ 3. Formal organization

_____ 4. Chain of command

_____ 5. Product departmentalization

_____ 6. Line-and-staff organization

_____ 7. Decentralization

_____ 8. Authority

Column B

a. Departmentalization that is based on the geographic segmentation of the organizational units; for example, U.S. marketing, European marketing, and Asian marketing.

b. The process of dividing work into separate jobs and assigning tasks to workers.

c. The levels of management within an organization; typically, includes top, middle, and supervisory management; also called the management pyramid.

d. The process of coordinating and allocating a firm's resources so that the firm can carry out its plans and achieve its goals.

e. The order and design of relationships within a firm; consists of two or more people working together with a common objective and clarity of purpose.

f. The line of authority that extends from one level of an organization's hierarchy to the next, from top to bottom, and makes clear who reports to whom.

g. The degree to which tasks are subdivided into smaller jobs.

h. An organizational structure with direct, clear lines of authority and communication flowing from the top managers downward. Managers have direct control over all activities, including administrative duties.

_____ 9. Division of labor

  i. Departmentalization that is based on the primary type of customer served by the organizational unit; for example, wholesale or retail purchasers.

_____ 10. Managerial hierarchy

  j. Departmentalization that is based on the goods or services produced or sold by the organizational unit; for example, outpatient emergency services, pediatrics, and cardiology.

_____ 11. Organization chart

  k. Departmentalization that is based on the production process used by the organizational unit; for example, lumber cutting and treatment, furniture finishing, and shipping.

_____ 12. Specialization

  l. Departmentalization that is based on the primary functions performed within an organizational unit; for example, marketing, finance, production, and sales.

_____ 13. Delegation of authority

  m. An organizational structure that includes both line and staff positions.

_____ 14. Line positions

  n. A network of independent companies linked by information technology to share skills, costs, and access to one another's markets; allows the companies to come together quickly to exploit rapidly changing opportunities.

_____ 15. Line organization

  o. Legitimate power, granted by the organization and acknowledged by employees, that allows an individual to request action and expect compliance.

_____ 16. Functional departmentalization

  p. An organizational structure that is characterized by a relatively low degree of job specialization, loose departmentalization, few levels of management, wide spans of control, decentralized decision making, and a short chain of command.

_____ 17. Span of control

  q. Positions in an organization held by individuals who are directly involved in the processes used to create goods and services.

_____ 18. Virtual corporation

  r. The assignment of some degree of authority and responsibility to persons lower in the chain of command; makes the person lower in the hierarchy accountable to the supervisor.

_____ 19. Customer departmentalization

  s. A visual representation of the structured relationships among tasks and the people given the authority to do those tasks.

_____ 20. Departmentalization

  t. The process of grouping jobs together so that similar or associated tasks and activities can be coordinated.

_____ 21. Geographic departmentalization

  u. The number of employees a manager directly supervises; also called span of management.

_____ 22. Organic organization

  v. An organizational structure that is characterized by a relatively high degree of job specialization, rigid departmentalization, many layers of management, narrow spans of control, centralized decision making, and a long chain of command.

_____ 23. Centralization

  w. Positions in an organization held by individuals who provide the administrative and support services that line employees need to achieve the firm's goals; for example, legal counseling, public relations, and human resource management.

_____ 24. Staff positions

  x. The network of connections and channels of communication based on the informal relationships of individuals inside an organization.

_____ 25 Mechanistic organization

y. The process of pushing decision-making authority down the organizational hierarchy, giving lower-level personnel more responsibility and power to make and implement decisions.

_____ 26. Informal organization

z. The degree to which formal authority is concentrated in one area or level of an organization.

_____ 27. Committee structure

aa. An organizational structure that combines functional and product departmentalization by bringing together people from different functional areas of the organization to work on a special project; sometimes used in conjunction with the traditional line-and-staff structure; also called the project management approach.

_____ 28. Reengineering

bb. An organizational structure in which authority and responsibility are held by a group rather than an individual typically found as part of a larger line-and-staff organization.

_____ 29. Matrix structure

cc. The complete redesign of business structures and processes in order to improve operations.

CRITICAL THINKING ACTIVITIES

1. P.O.V. – (Point of View)

Directions: In this exercise you will be asked to provide your personal opinion regarding some of the topics discussed in the chapter. At the completion of this exercise your instructor may wish to poll the entire class regarding their responses.

a. Roger and Daniel Lipton import and distribute small, food related items such as refrigerator magnets and can openers, to supermarkets throughout the Cleveland metropolitan area. Their father, who founded the company in 1940, organized the operations of the company following a product departmentalization model – individual sales people sold specific products. Now that the business is expanding throughout the Midwest, Danny wants to reorganize using functional departmentalization so that each salesperson can sell the entire product line to customers. Roger believes that this change will not work, because the current sales force has specific product knowledge which the new sales force will lack. He has vetoed Danny's plan and refuses to consider any change.

Agree _____   Disagree _____

Explain:

_____

_____

_____

_____

b. Danny, who is Roger's son, will soon be taking over the management of operations when Roger retires, although Roger will remain as Chairman of the firm's Board of Directors. Roger, like his father who founded the company, believes that most management decisions should be made by top-management. Danny, who has been pushing hard for the expansion of the business throughout the Midwest region and has plans to go national, disagrees with his father. He feels that in the chain of command, decision-making processes, and organization structure must be modified. Without changes such as these, Danny believes that expansion cannot take place.

Agree _____   Disagree _____

Explain

_____

_____

_____

_____

2. Using the Internet

Directions: The ability to review and analyze an organization chart can provide insight into the way in which an organization functions. Although there may be differences between what the chart indicates and how the organization truly operates, several issues can be addressed. Go to **http://www.southern-cities.com** and click on the following: Clients, City of Abbeville, City Government, and Organizational Charts.

  a. What is unique about this organization, especially at the level of top management?
  b. Describe the type of organizational structure that Abbeville has.
  c. What type(s) of departmentalization exists in Abbeville?

3. Writing Skills

Directions: Describe the differences between line positions and staff positions. What are the advantages and disadvantages of both? When you enter the workplace, which one would you rather have, and why?

Chapter 9

Managing Human Resources

OUTLINE

MULTIPLE CHOICE

Directions: Place the letter of the response that best completes the questions that follow in the blank spaces at the left:

>lg 1

What is the human resource management process?

_____ b _____ **1.** The process of hiring, developing, motivating, and evaluating employees to achieve organizational goals is known as:
    a. organizational strategy
    b. human resource management
    c. organizational objectives
    d. career management

_C_ **2.** The following form the basis for all human resource management decisions:
   a. job analysis and design
   b. human resource planning and forecasting
   c. organizational strategies and objectives
   d. performance planning and evaluation

_d_ **3.** The human resource management process includes:
   a. training and development
   b. human resource planning and development
   c. performance planning and evaluation
   d. all of these answers are correct

>lg 2   **How are human resource needs determined?**

_a_ **4.** A job description indicates the:
   a. tasks and responsibilities of a job
   b. skills, knowledge, and abilities needed to fill a job
   c. human resource plan of an organization
   d. forecast of a firm's human resource needs

_b_ **5.** A job specification indicates the:
   a. tasks and responsibilities of a job
   b. skills, knowledge, and abilities needed to fill a job
   c. human resource plan of an organization
   d. forecast of a firm's human resource needs

_C_ **6.** Those who prefer temporary employment, either part-time or full-time, are known as:
   a. internal workers   **c.** contingent workers
   b. demand workers   **d.** none of these answers are correct

>lg 3   **How do human resource managers find good people to fill the jobs?**

_d_ **7.** An internal search for job applicants usually means that a:
   a. person already in a position assumes more responsibility
   b. promotion will not take place
   c. job transfer will not take place
   d. person must change his or her job

_C_ **8.** Recruitment involves:
   a. utilizing a firm's skills inventory
   b. primarily using job fairs to find recruits
   c. attempting to find qualified applicants in the external labor market
   d. recruiting a search firm in the external market that will supply employees

_a_ **9.** Many firms are able to fill vacant positions internally by using their employee:
   a. skills inventory
   b. job fairs
   c. search firms
   d. none of these answers are correct

>lg 4   **What is the employee selection process?**

_b_ **10.** The process of determining which persons in the applicant pool possess the qualifications necessary to be successful on a job is called:
   a. skills inventory   **c.** recruitment
   b. selection   **d.** job specification

d **11.** The portion of the employee selection process that usually includes the completion of an application and a brief interview is known as the:
a. background and reference check
b. decision to hire stage
c. selection interview
d. initial screening

c **12.** The portion of the employee selection process that includes an in-depth discussion of an applicant's work experience, skills, and abilities, education, and career interests is known as the:
a. initial screening
b. background and reference check
c. selection interview
d. testing stage

>lg 5 **What types of training and development do organizations offer their employees?**

a **13.** Job rotation involves a(an):
a. reassignment of workers to several jobs over time
b. employee learning a job by doing it with the guidance from a supervisor or experienced coworker
c. heavy use of on-the-job instruction with classroom training
d. senior or experienced employee providing job and career related information to a protégé

b **14.** Vestibule training involves:
a. direct instruction and training on the job
b. a scaled down version of an assembly line or retail outlet that is used for training purposes
c. large scale mentoring
d. reassignment of workers to several jobs over time

b **15.** Programmed instruction is a form of:
a. on-the-job training   c. mentoring
b. off-the-job training   d. job rotation

>lg 6 **What is a performance appraisal?**

c **16.** A comparison of actual performance with expected performance is known as:
a. mentoring   c. performance appraisal
b. off-the-job training   d. job assessment

a **17.** Performance planning and appraisal include providing the employee with:
a. job objectives   c. deadlines
b. schedules   d. all of these answers are correct

d **18.** Decisions concerning pay raises, training needs, and advancement opportunities are most often part of:
a. job descriptions   c. deadlines
b. job specifications   d. performance appraisal

>lg 7   **How are employees compensated?**

__d__   19. In order to remain competitive, many firms generally like to pay their employees:
- **a.** below the going rate until the employee threatens resignation
- **b.** at the going rate to retain employees
- **c.** sat a rate consistent with the firm's financial condition, efficiency, employee productivity, and rates paid by competitors
- **d.** above the going rate to attract new employees

__a__   20. Salaries are most commonly paid to:
- **a.** managerial and professional employees
- **b.** technicians, machinists, and assembly-line workers
- **c.** salespeople
- **d.** pieceworkers

__d__   21. A cafeteria style benefit plan is:
- **a.** generally offered by firms in the food and food processing business
- **b.** a plan which reimburses salaried employees for their food expenditures while on the job
- **c.** a legally required benefit for employees who must work mandatory overtime through the lunch and dinner hours
- **d.** one which allows employees to mix and match benefits or selected items based on individual need

>lg 8   **What is organizational career management?**

__b__   22. A promotion is:
- **a.** a downgrade or reassignment to a position with less responsibility
- **b.** an upward move in an organization to a position with more authority, responsibility, and pay
- **c.** a temporary separation from a job arranged by an employer
- **d.** a horizontal move within the organization

__a__   23. A transfer is:
- **a.** a horizontal move within the organization
- **b.** an upward move in an organization to a position with more authority, responsibility and pay
- **c** a temporary separation from a job arranged by an employer
- **d.** a downgrade or a reassignment to a position with less responsibility

__c__   24. When a person is downgraded or reassigned to a position with less responsibility it is know as a:
- **a.** separation   **c.** demotion
- **b.** layoff   **d.** transfer

>lg 9   **What are the key laws and federal agencies affecting human resource management?**

__c__   25. The Americans with Disabilities Act (1990):
- **a.** requires employers to provide unpaid leave for childbirth, adoption, or illness
- **b.** treats pregnancy as a disability and prevents employment discrimination based on pregnancy
- **c.** prohibits employment discrimination based upon mental or physical disabilities
- **d.** protects workers' health and safety

a **26.** The Family Medical Leave Act (1993):
   a. requires employers to provide unpaid leave for childbirth, adoption, or illness
   b. treats pregnancy as a disability and prevents employment discrimination based on pregnancy
   c. prohibits employment discrimination based upon mental or physical disabilities
   d. protects workers' health and safety

d **27.** The Occupational Safety and Health Act (1970):
   a. requires employers to provide unpaid leave for childbirth, adoption, or illness
   b. treats pregnancy as a disability and prevents employment discrimination based on pregnancy
   c. prohibits employment discrimination based upon mental or physical disabilities
   d. protects workers' health and safety

>lg 10 **What trends are affecting human resource management?**

a **28.** An invisible barrier in many firms that prevents women, minorities, and others from advancing to high level management positions is known as:
   a. diversity   **c.** outsourcing
   b. the glass ceiling   **d.** none of these answers are correct

d **29.** Outsourcing as it relates to human resource management is:
   a. assigning human resource functions to individual departments
   b. always looking to outside sources for new employees
   c. filling jobs with individuals who are unlike those who held them before
   d. assigning various human resource functions to outside organizations

c **30.** The arrangement whereby employees work at home is known as
   a. outsourcing   **c.** telecommuting
   b. work diversity   **d.** commuting

TRUE/FALSE

Directions: Place a T or an F in the space provided to the left of each question to indicate whether it is True or False.

>lg 1 **What is the human resource management process?**

T **1.** Human resource strategies and objectives form the basis for making all organizational decisions.

T **2.** Human resource management is the process of hiring, developing, motivating, and evaluating employees to achieve organizational goals.

F **3.** Employee job changes, including disengagement, are not part of the human resource management process.

>lg 2 **How are human resource needs determined?**

T **4.** Human resource planning includes job analysis and forecasting the firm's people needs.

F **5.** The tasks and responsibilities required for a job are spelled out in a job specification.

F

I

6. The skills, knowledge, and abilities a person must possess to fill a job are listed in a job description.

7. An HR internal supply forecast determines the number of outside people the firm will need by some future time to fill positions within the firm.

>lg 3

How do human resource managers find good people to fill jobs?

I

≠

F

I

8. A skills inventory is required by employees of a firm in order for employees to be made aware of the special aptitudes they possess.

9. Recruitment is the attempt to find and attract qualified applicants in the external labor market.

10. Search firms are normally paid a fee of one to three months' salary by the person who is hired.

11. A job fair is typically a one-day event held at a convention center to bring together thousands of job seekers and hundreds of firms seeking employees.

>lg 4

What is the employee selection process?

F

I

≠

I

12. Employment testing takes place after employee selection is made in order to determine the job for the applicant.

13. Selection is the process of determining which persons in the applicant pool possess the qualifications necessary to be successful on the job.

14. The selection interview represents the firm's initial screening of an applicant and includes the completion of an application form.

15. The background and reference check takes place prior to the selection interview.

>lg 5

What types of training and development do organizations offer their employees?

F

I

≠

I

≠

16. Employee orientation is not part of employee training and development because it does not involve a learning situation in which an employee acquires knowledge or skills related to job performance.

17. Job rotation is part of on-the-job training where workers are reassigned to several jobs over time.

18. On-the-job training programs such as mentoring and apprenticeships are considered expensive ways to learn about employee performance.

19. Vestibule training takes place in a facility that simulates the real working environment.

20. Off-the-job training is less expensive than on-the-job training and allows for the immediate transfer of knowledge.

>lg 6

What is performance appraisal?

≠

I

21. Employee performance and appraisal are linked to job objectives, schedules, deadlines, as well as product and/or service quality requirements.

22. Performance appraisal is a comparison of actual performance with expected performance to assess an employee's contributions to the organization and to make decisions about training, compensation, promotion, and other job changes.

>lg 7

How are employees compensated?

23. The wages, salary, and benefits earned by an employee will always reflect the importance of their job.

24. Piecework and commission are forms of compensation that involve payment according to how much an employee produces or sells.

25. Unemployment compensation, which provides former employees with money for a certain period of time while they are unemployed, is also paid to strikers in some states.

>lg 8

What is organizational career management?

26. A promotion is a horizontal move within an organization at about the same organizational level.

27. A transfer involves an upward move in an organization to a position with more responsibility and pay.

28. A separation occurs when an employee is laid off, terminated, resigns, or retires.

29. As opposed to other types of separation, a layoff is permanent.

30. Resignation is undertaken voluntarily by an employee while an employer arranges termination.

>lg 9

What are the key laws and federal agencies affecting human resource management?

31. The Equal Employment Opportunity Commission enforces the Social Security Act.

32. The Equal Pay Act eliminates pay differentials based upon gender.

33. The Pregnancy Discrimination Act treats pregnancy as a non-medical problem and allows for layoffs as a result of pregnancy.

34. The Family and Medical Leave Act requires employers with more than 50 employees to provide unpaid leave of up to 12 weeks during any 12 month period to workers who have been employed for at least a year and work a minimum of 25 hours a week.

>lg 10

What trends are affecting human resource management?

35. Diversity refers to differences in the age, income, and business activities of employers.

36. Outsourcing is the assignment of various functions, such as human resources or accounting, to outside organizations when a glass ceiling exists within the organization.

ENHANCE YOUR VOCABULARY

Accelerate	To bring about at an earlier time; to hasten the progress or development of
Evolving	Developing; working out
Facilitating	Making a task easier
Implementing	Carrying out, accomplishing

Mentor	A trusted counselor or guide; tutor; coach
Modular	Constructed with standardized units or dimensions for flexibility and variety in use
Reimbursement	To pay back to someone
Sexual harassment	Uninvited and unwelcome verbal or physical conduct directed at an employee because of his or her sex
Surfaced	To come into public view; show up
Trends	Current style or preference

Directions: Select the definition in Column B that best defines the word in Column A.

Column A

1. Evolving
2. Reimbursement
3. Trends
4. Implementing
5. Modular
6. Facilitating
7. Accelerate
8. Mentor
9. Surfaced
10. Sexual harassment

Column B

a. Current style or preference
b. Developing; working out
c. A trusted counselor or coach
d. Uninvited and unwelcome conduct because of gender or sexual orientation
e. To pay back to someone
f. To hasten
g. Making easier
h. To come into public view; show up
i. Constructed for flexibility in use
j. Carrying out; accomplishing

REVIEW YOUR KEY TERMS

Directions: Select the definition in Column B to that best defines the word in Column A.

Column A

1. Employee orientation
2. Recruitment
3. Human resource management
4. Job specification
5. Programmed instruction
6. Selection interview
7. Job fair
8. On-the-job training
9. Apprenticeship
10. Performance appraisal

Column B

a. The process of hiring, developing, motivating, and evaluating employees to achieve organizational goals.
b. Activities that provide learning situations in which an employee acquires additional knowledge or skills to increase job performance.
c. Persons who prefer temporary employment, either part-time or full-time.
d. Training in which the employee learns the job by doing it with guidance from a supervisor or experienced co-worker.
e. Indirect compensation such as pensions, health insurance, and vacations.
f. Creating a strategy for meeting future human resource needs.
g. A study of the tasks required to do a particular job well.
h. Reassignment of workers to several different jobs over time so that they can learn the basics of each job.
i. An upward move in an organization to a position with more authority, responsibility, and pay.
j. A list of the tasks and responsibilities of a job.

_t_ 11. Demotion

_k_ 12. Telecommuting

_l_ 13. Separation

_v_ 14. Retirement

_h_ 15. Job rotation

_f_ 16. Human resource planning

_cc_ 17. Selection

_ff_ 18. Mentoring

_n_ 19. Layoff

_u_ 20. Outsourcing

_y_ 21. Termination

_ee_ 22. Affirmative action programs

_gg_ 23. Vestibule training

_r_ 24. Transfer

_s_ 25. Resignation

_dd_ 26. Diversity

_q_ 27. Job analysis

_b_ 28. Training and development

k. An arrangement in which employees work at home and are linked to the office by phone, fax, and computer.

l. The departure of an employee from the organization; can be a layoff, termination, resignation, or retirement.

m. The specific groups who have legal protection against employment discrimination; includes women, African Americans, Native Americans, and others.

n. A temporary separation of an employee from the organization; arranged by the employer, usually because business is slow.

o. A comparison of actual performance with expected performance to assess an employee's contributions to the organization in order to make decisions about training, compensation, promotion, and other job changes.

p. A list of the skills, knowledge, and abilities a person must have to fill a job.

q. Training that prepares a new employee to perform on the job; includes information about job assignments, work rules, equipment, and performance expectations, as well as about company policies, salary and benefits, and parking.

r. A horizontal move in an organization to a position with about the same salary and at about the same organizational level.

s. A permanent separation of an employee from the organization, done voluntarily by the employee.

t. The downgrading or reassignment of an employee to a position with less responsibility.

u. The assignment of various functions, such as human resources, accounting or legal work, to outside organizations.

v. The separation of an employee from the organization at the end of his or her career.

w. A form of on-the-job training that combines specific job instruction with classroom instruction; can last as long as four years and is typically found in skilled trades such as carpentry, plumbing, and electrical work.

x. A form of computer-assisted off-the-job training; consists of a self-paced, highly structured system in which trainees are presented with concepts and problems using a modular format.

y. A permanent separation of an employee from the organization, arranged by the employer.

z. The attempt to find and attract qualified applicants in the external labor market.

aa. An event, typically one day, held at a convention center to bring together thousands of job seekers and hundreds of firms searching for employees.

bb. An in-depth discussion of an applicant's work experience, skills and abilities, education, and career interests.

_C___ **29.** Contingent workers

_M___ **30.** Protected classes

_J___ **31.** Job description

_e___ **32.** Fringe benefits

_I___ **33.** Promotion

cc. The process of determining which persons in the applicant pool possess the qualifications necessary to be successful on the job.

dd. Employee differences in age, race and ethnicity, gender, educational background, and work experience.

ee. Programs established by organizations to expand job opportunities for women and minorities.

ff. A form of on-the-job training in which a senior manager or other experienced employee provides job- and career-related information to a protégé.

gg. A form of off-the-job training in which trainees learn about products, manufacturing processes, or selling in a scaled-down version of an assembly line or retail outlet.

CRITICAL THINKING ACTIVITIES

1. P.O.V. (Point of View)

Directions: In this exercise you will be asked to provide your personal opinion regarding some of the topics discussed in the chapter. At the completion of this exercise, your instructor may wish to poll the entire class regarding their responses.

a. The topic of Social Security has come up in recent discussions at your office. Senior members of your company, who earn high salaries and have extensive retirement benefits, have been polled anonymously and indicate that, even though they might not need them, they will apply for and accept full Social Security benefits. Younger employees are concerned that the Social Security Trust Fund, from which benefits are paid, will be bankrupt by the time they retire. "That's your problem," muttered one senior staff member. A newly hired coworker responded that, "Those who do not need benefits are not entitled to receive Social Security income."

Agree _____   Disagree _✓_

Explain:

Those who worked most of their life should be entitled to recieve social security income no matter what.

b. New Federal laws, including the Americans with Disabilities Act which prohibits discrimination based on mental or physical disabilities and the Family Medical Leave Act which requires employers to provide unpaid leave for childbirth, adoption, or illness, have gone too far in providing employment and protecting individuals. They have led to higher costs, prices, and workload for the rest of us. They should be repealed.

Agree _____   Disagree _✓_

Explain:

Because if a disabled, sick, pregnant, or adopting person work very hard at their job and need time off from work due to circumstances then they should be considered to take time off from work whether high cost, price or work load.

support the use of telecommuting & other alternative work option, excellent resource information for students of telecommuting or those with telecommuting proposal.

2. Using the Internet

Directions: Telecommuting is a growing area whereby employees work at home and are linked to their offices via an electronic device such as a computer. It has become popular for many reasons. Go to **http://www.telecommuting.about.com** and click on Facts and Figures. Then click on Resource Features, and/or Statistical Features, and/or Surveys-Research resources and write a report summarizing the status of telecommuting and its future.

3. Writing Skills

Directions: Write a short essay involving human resources (HR) which includes at least a total of 10 words from Enhance Your Vocabulary and Review Your Key Terms.

If you don't have a HR topic you would like to write about, choose your essay topic from among the following:

- **a.** Employee recruitment
- **b.** Employee selection
- **c.** Employee training and development
- **d.** Employee compensation and/or benefits
- **e.** Laws affecting human resources management

Human Resources (Employee training and development) offers employee orientation that prepares a new employee to perform on the job, includes information about job assignments, work rules, equipment, and performance expectations, as well as about company policies, salary and benefits, and parking. In addition, job specification will be offered which is a list of the skills, knowledge, and abilities a person must have to fill a job. Programmed Instruction that consists of a self paced, highly structured system in which trainees are presented with concepts and problems using a modular format.

Other offers to employees such as, job fair and on-the-job training to facilitate their needs and job rotation with reassignment of workers to several different jobs over time so that they can learn the basics of each job.

Other trainings are offered, such as mentoring and versatile training which, offers job & career-related information to a protege, and teaches about products, manufacturing processes, or selling in a scaled-down version of an assembly line or retail outlet.

Last and final are job analysis and promotion that is a study of the tasks required to do a particular job well, and an upward movement in an organization to a position with more authority, responsibility, and pay.

NOTES ON CHAPTER 9

Chapter 10

Motivating Employees and Creating Self-Managed Teams

OUTLINE

MULTIPLE CHOICE

Directions: Place the letter of the response that best completes the questions that follow in the blank space at the left.

>lg 1

What are the basic principles of Frederick Taylor's concept of scientific management?

_____ 1. Frederick Taylor's approach to improved performance was based on:
    a. letting workers decide what approach is best
    b. allowing worker committees to decide what approach is best
    c. providing workers with numerous rules and regulations as an incentive to work harder
    d. economic incentives and the premise that there is "one best way" to perform any job

_____ **2.** As a result of his efforts to develop an approach to improving performance, Taylor is known as the father of:
　　　　a. classical management　　　　**c.** incentive management
　　　　b. scientific management　　　　**d.** performance management

_____ **3.** Frederick Taylor's work led to:
　　　　a. specialization of labor and the assembly line
　　　　b. strikes and labor unrest
　　　　c. less cooperation between workers and managers
　　　　d. a pooling of work responsibilities between workers and managers

_____ **4.** The fundamental flaw in Taylor's scientific management was that:
　　　　a. all people are motivated to work because they enjoy it
　　　　b. economic factors have nothing to do with motivation
　　　　c. it assumed that all people are motivated by economic means
　　　　d. none of these answers are correct

>lg 2   **What did Elton Mayo's Hawthorne studies reveal about worker motivation?**

_____ **5.** The era of management that was focused on how human behavior and relations affect organizational performance was known as the:
　　　　a. classical era　　　　　　　　**c.** human relations era
　　　　b. era of scientific management　　**d.** systems era

_____ **6.** Engineers at the Hawthorne Western Electric Plant who were studying the effect of light conditions on worker performance found that:
　　　　a. only raising the level of light increased productivity
　　　　b. both raising and lowering the level of light lead to increased productivity
　　　　c. only lowering the level of light increased productivity
　　　　d. varying the level of light had no impact on productivity

_____ **7.** Elton Mayo explained the affect that was caused by varying the lighting levels at the Hawthorne Western Electric Plant as being the result of group:
　　　　a. indifference　　　　　　　　**c.** pride
　　　　b. apathy　　　　　　　　　　　**d.** loyalty

_____ **8.** An outcome of the studies conducted by Elton Mayo at the Western Electric Plant is known as the:
　　　　a. scientific management effect　　**c.** classical effect
　　　　b. human relations effect　　　　 **d.** Hawthorne effect

>lg 3   **What is Maslow's hierarchy of needs and how do these needs relate to employee motivation?**

_____ **9.** Abraham Maslow's theory of motivation contends that:
　　　　a. people act to satisfy their unmet needs
　　　　b. economic incentives are the primary motivators of individuals
　　　　c. scientific management is the basis for motivation
　　　　d. human relations have no impact on motivation

_____ **10.** According to Maslow's hierarchy of needs, the most basic human needs are:
　　　　a. self-actualization　　　　　　**c.** social
　　　　b. esteem　　　　　　　　　　　**d.** physiological

_____ **11.** According to Maslow's hierarchy, the highest level need is:
　　　　a. physiological　　　　　　　　**c.** esteem
　　　　b. social　　　　　　　　　　　**d.** self-actualization

>lg 4   **How are McGregor's Theory X and Y used to explain worker motivation?**

_____   **12.** Douglas McGregor's Theory X is based upon a:
            a. optimistic view of human nature
            b. neutral view of human nature
            c. negative view of human nature
            d. all of these answers are correct

_____   **13.** Douglas McGregor's Theory Y is based upon a:
            a. optimistic view of human nature
            b. neutral view of human nature
            c. negative view of human nature
            d. all of these answers are correct

_____   **14.** Managers who operate using Theory Y assumptions recognize:
            a. that people must be controlled, directed, or threatened with punishment in order to get them to make an effort
            b. individual differences and encourage workers to learn to develop their skills
            c. that the average person dislikes work and will avoid it if possible
            d. that the average person prefers to be directed, avoids responsibility, is relatively unambitious, and want security above all else

>lg 5   **What are the basic components of Herzberg's motivator-hygiene theory?**

_____   **15.** According to Herzberg's motivator-hygiene theory:
            a. motivating factors are intrinsic to a job and are dissatisfiers
            b. hygiene factors are extrinsic to a job and are satisfiers
            c. motivating factors are intrinsic to a job and are satisfiers
            d. hygiene factors are intrinsic to a job and are satisfiers

_____   **16.** Herzberg's studies of motivating and hygiene factors led him to the conclusion that:
            a. hygiene factors could never be managed to prevent dissatisfaction
            b. motivating factors had to be managed, but could never serve as a source of satisfaction
            c. hygiene factors ultimately lead to satisfaction
            d. proper management of hygiene factors could prevent employee dissatisfaction, but these factors could not serve as a source of satisfaction

_____   **17.** A criticism of Herzberg's work is that it:
            a. focused on job satisfaction which is different from motivation
            b. focused on motivation which is different from job satisfaction
            c. did not focus on job satisfaction or motivation
            d. placed too much emphasis on both job satisfaction and motivation

>lg 6   **What three contemporary theories on employee motivation offer insights into improving employee performance?**

_____   **18.** According to expectancy theory, employee motivation depends on:
            a. effort and performance
            b. performance and outcomes
            c. outcomes and individual needs
            d. all of these answers are correct

_____   **19.** Expectancy theory focuses on the probability of:
            a. extrinsic hygiene factors influencing individual behavior and outcomes
            b. the individual not valuing the outcome of an act or particular mode of behavior

     c. an individual acting in a certain way based upon their belief that what they do will have a particular outcome and the value that they place on the outcome

     d. strong motivating factors preceding the action being taken, regardless of its outcome

_____ **20.** A component of expectancy theory that focuses on employee rewards is called:

     a. equity   **c.** goal-setting

     b. valence   **d.** the ideal

_____ **21.** Equity theory focuses on:

     a. perceived valence

     b. perceived fairness in the way employees are treated

     c. employee expectancy

     d. the intention of an employee to work toward a goal as the primary source of motivation

_____ **22.** Goal setting theory is based upon:

     a. perceived valence

     b. perceived fairness in the way employees are treated

     c. employee expectancy

     d. the intention of an employee to work toward a goal as the primary source of motivation

>lg 7

How can managers redesign existing jobs to increase employee motivation and performance?

_____ **23.** Job enlargement is the:

     a. horizontal expansion of a job by increasing the number and variety of tasks that a person performs

     b. vertical expansion of an employee's job

     c. synonymous with job rotation or cross-training

     d. none of these answers are correct

_____ **24.** Job enrichment is the:

     a. horizontal expansion of a job by increasing the number and variety of tasks that a person performs

     b. vertical expansion of an employee's job

     c. synonymous with job rotation or cross-training

     d. none of these answers are correct

_____ **25.** Job sharing is the:

     a. horizontal expansion of a job by increasing the number and variety of tasks that a person performs

     b. vertical expansion of an employee's job

     c. scheduling option that allows two individuals to split their tasks, responsibilities, and work hours of one 40 hour job

     d. synonymous with job rotation or cross-training

>lg 8

What different types of teams are being used in organizations today?

_____ **26.** A strength of group decision making is that it:

     a. brings more information and knowledge to the decision process

     b. yields better results because it takes longer

     c. allows individuals in the group to dominate the process

     d. leads to no one individual being held responsible for the outcomes of the group

_____ 27. A work group that is made up of employees from about the same hierarchical level, but different functional areas of the organization is known as a:
a. problem solving team   c. cross-functional team
b. self-managed work team   d. synergy team

_____ 28. A work group that functions in a highly autonomously manner is known as a:
a. problem solving team   c. cross-functional team
b. self-managed work team   d. synergy team

>lg 9   What initiatives are organizations using today to motivate and retain employees?

_____ 29. According to an *Industry Week* article, the only way companies can stay competitive is by:
a. reintroducing scientific management
b. using Mayo's theories when dealing with human resources
c. adopting McGregor's Theory Y philosophies
d. unleashing the full creative power of people at all levels of the organization

TRUE/FALSE

Directions: Place a T or an F in the space provided to the left of each question to indicate whether it is True or False.

>lg 1   What are the basic principles of Frederick Taylor's concept of scientific management?

_____ 1. The study of human behavior in organizations, although somewhat useful, has not contributed a great deal to an understanding of motivation and job performance.

_____ 2. An essential factor, which contributes to the success of managers, is an understanding of human relations and how employees interact with one another.

_____ 3. The important element in understanding motivation is not what motivates individuals but rather how an organization can create a workplace that allows people to perform to the best of their abilities.

_____ 4. Taylor's scientific management held that improved employee performance was not based upon economic incentives, but rather on an understanding of the human element.

_____ 5. Taylor was convinced that productivity was linked to breaking down each task into separate movements and determining, thorough the use of scientific measurements, the one best way to perform each job.

>lg 2   What did Elton Mayo's Hawthorne Studies reveal about worker motivation?

_____ 6. The Hawthorne Studies demonstrated that Taylor's hypothesis—that workers responded mostly to economic incentives—was correct.

_____ 7. The Hawthorne Studies demonstrated that workers would respond to a change in the work environment as long as they perceive themselves as being singled out for a special project.

_____ 8. The Hawthorne Studies indicated that social needs are not a significant factor in influencing worker behavior.

>lg 3   **What is Maslow's hierarchy of needs and how do these needs relate to employee motivation?**

_____   9.   Maslow proposed a hierarchy of needs which state that the need for food and clothing are at the uppermost level and lead to high levels of motivation.

_____   10. Maslow's theory contends that people act to satisfy their unmet needs.

_____   11. The need for fulfillment, for living up to one's potential, and for using one's abilities to the utmost, fall into Maslow's physiological needs category.

_____   12. Self-actualization needs are those needs that could be characterized by the U.S. Army recruiting slogan, "be all that you can be."

>lg 4   **How are McGregor's Theories X and Y used to explain worker motivation?**

_____   13. Managers who operate under Theory X assumptions would probably assume that people enjoy work and will, under most circumstances, attempt to do the best job possible.

_____   14. Theory X managers are very directive, like to be in control, and show little confidence in employees.

_____   15. Theory Y managers assume that under most circumstances, workers will not try hard to accomplish organizational goals even if they believe that they will be rewarded for doing so.

_____   16. Managers who operate under Theory Y assumptions recognize individual differences and encourage workers to learn and develop their skills.

>lg 5   **What are the basic components of Herzberg's motivator-hygiene theory?**

_____   17. Hygiene factors are extrinsic element of the work environment.

_____   18. Motivating factors are primarily intrinsic job elements that lead to satisfaction.

_____   19. Herzberg was able to demonstrate that dissatisfaction was the opposite of satisfaction.

_____   20. Herzberg demonstrated that such factors as good working conditions would keep workers on the job, but not lead them to work harder. Yet, poor working conditions would lead employees to quit.

_____   21. Herzberg's findings have been used to explain job satisfaction as well as motivation.

>lg 6   **What three contemporary theories on employee motivation offer insights into improving employee performance?**

_____   22. Expectancy theory focuses on individual perceptions about how fairly they are treated compared with their coworkers.

_____   23. Equity theory focuses on the probability of a person acting a certain way based upon the strength of that individual's belief that the act will have a particular outcome and whether the individual values that outcome.

_____   24. Goal-setting theory is based upon the premise that an individual's intention to work toward a goal is the primary source of motivation.

_____   25. An important element of goal-setting theory is feedback because it helps an individual identify the gap between the real and the ideal.

>lg 7 **How can managers redesign existing jobs to increase employee motivation and performance?**

_____ **26.** Job enlargement is the vertical expansion of an employee's job.

_____ **27.** Job enrichment is the horizontal expansion of a job by increasing the number and variety of tasks that a person performs.

_____ **28.** Job rotation, also known as cross-training, involves shifting workers from one job to another.

_____ **29.** Job sharing is a scheduling option that allows two individuals to split tasks, responsibilities, and work hours of one 40-hour job.

_____ **30.** Variable-pay is offered to individuals who have personal expenses that vary from pay period to pay period.

>lg 8 **What different types of teams are being used in organizations today?**

_____ **31.** When group performance norms are high, group cohesiveness will have a negative impact on productivity.

_____ **32.** Work teams limit the ability of individuals to perform above expected norms thereby leading to a synergy which makes the performance of the team to be less than the sum of the team members' individual contributions.

_____ **33.** Problem-solving teams are typically made up of employees from the same department or area of expertise and from the same level of the organizational hierarchy.

_____ **34.** Cross-functional teams are made up of employees from about the same hierarchical level, but different functional areas of the organization.

>lg 9 **What initiatives are organizations using today to motivate and retain employees?**

_____ **35.** The ways in which companies are currently choosing to invest in their human resources include education and training, employee ownership, and work-life programs.

ENHANCE YOUR VOCABULARY

Array	A regular and imposing grouping or arrangement
Atrophy	Decrease in size or wasting away of a body part; degeneration
Coddling	Treating with extreme care; pampering
Compressed	Pressed together; flattened
Conveyed	Imparted or communicated by statement, suggestion, or appearance
Distort	To twist out of the true meaning or proportion
Forgo	To give up the enjoyment or advantage of; do without
Pessimistic	Gloomy; cynical
Prod	Prick; to incite to action
Secluded	Screened or hidden from view; sequestered; solitary

Directions: Select the definition in Column B that best defines the word in Column A.

Column A	Column B
_____ **1.** Atrophy	**a.** Gloomy
_____ **2.** Distort	**b.** Prick; to incite to action
_____ **3.** Array	**c.** Screened or hidden from view
_____ **4.** Forgo	**d.** Decrease in size or wasting away
_____ **5.** Coddling	**e.** To twist out of the true meaning or proportion
_____ **6.** Conveyed	**f.** Do without
_____ **7.** Prod	**g.** Communicated by statement or suggestion
_____ **8.** Secluded	**h.** A regular and imposing grouping or arrangement
_____ **9.** Compressed	**i.** Treating with extreme care
_____ **10.** Forgo	**j.** Pressed together; flattened

REVIEW YOUR KEY TERMS

Directions: Select the definition in Column B that best defines the word in Column A.

Column A	Column B
_____ **1.** Scientific management	**a.** A management style, formulated by Douglas McGregor, that is based on a relatively optimistic view of human nature; assumes that the average person wants to work, accepts responsibility, is willing to help solve problems, and can be self-directed and self-controlled.
_____ **2.** Job rotation	**b.** In Frederick Herzberg's motivator-hygiene theory, intrinsic job elements that lead to worker satisfaction; also called job satisfiers.
_____ **3.** Expectancy theory	**c.** The phenomenon that employees perform better when they feel singled out for attention or feel that management is concerned about their welfare; first identified by Elton Mayo from studies conducted at the Hawthorne Western Electric plant.
_____ **4.** Theory X	**d.** The vertical expansion of a job by increasing the employee's autonomy, responsibility, and decision-making authority.
_____ **5.** Goal-setting theory	**e.** A scheduling option that allows two individuals to split the tasks, responsibilities, and work hours of one 40-hour-per-week job.
_____ **6.** Hawthorne effect	**f.** In Frederick Herzberg's motivator-hygiene theory, extrinsic elements of the work environment that do not serve as a source of employee satisfaction or motivation, although proper management of these factors can prevent employee dissatisfaction; also called job dissatisfiers.
_____ **7.** Self-managed work teams	**g.** Teams of employees who are from about the same level in the organizational hierarchy but from different functional areas; for example, task forces, organizational committees, and project teams.
_____ **8.** Theory Y	**h.** A system of management developed by Frederick W. Taylor and based on four principles: developing a science for each element of a job, scientifically selecting and training workers, encouraging cooperation between workers and managers, and dividing work and responsibility between management and workers according to who can better perform a particular task.

_____ **9.** Equity theory

i. The horizontal expansion of a job by increasing the number and variety of tasks that a person performs.

_____ **10** Motivating factors

j. The shifting of workers from one job to another; also called cross-training.

_____ **11.** Maslow's hierarchy of needs

k. A theory of motivation that holds that the probability of an individual acting in a particular way depends on the strength of that individual's belief that the act will have a particular outcome and on whether the individual values that outcome.

_____ **12.** Hygiene factors

l. A theory of motivation developed by Abraham Maslow; holds that humans have five levels of needs and act to satisfy their unmet needs. At the base of the hierarchy are fundamental physiological needs, followed, in order, by safety, social esteem, and self-actualization needs.

_____ **13.** Job enlargement

m. A theory of motivation based on the premise that an individual's intention to work toward a goal is a primary source of motivation; holds that specific or difficult goals lead to higher performance than do more general or easier goals and that feedback on progress enhances performance.

_____ **14.** Job enrichment

n. A management style, formulated by Douglas McGregor, that is based on a pessimistic view of human nature and assumes that the average person dislikes work, will avoid it if possible, prefers to be directed, avoids responsibilitly, and wants security above all. Consequently, managers must constantly prod workers to perform and closely control their on-the-job behavior.

_____ **15.** Cross-functional teams

o. A theory of motivation that holds that worker satisfaction is influenced by employees' perceptions about how fairly they are treated compared with their coworkers.

_____ **16.** Work Groups

p. A system of paying employees in which a portion of an employee's pay is directly linked to an individual or organizational performance measure. Variable-pay programs include piece-rate pay plans, profit-sharing plans, gain-sharing plans, and bonuses.

_____ **17.** Problem-solving teams

q. Highly autonomous teams of employees who manage themselves without any formal supervision and take responsibility for setting goals, planning and scheduling work activities, selecting team members, and evaluating team performance.

_____ **18.** Job sharing

r. Groups of employees who not only coordinate their efforts, but also collaborate by pooling their knowledge, skills, abilities, and resources in a collective effort to attain a common goal; create synergy, causing the performance of the team to be greater than the sum of the members' individual efforts.

_____ **19.** Work teams

s. The degree to which group members want to stay in the group and tend to resist outside influences.

_____ **20.** Variable pay

t. Teams of employees from the same department or area of expertise and from the same level of the organizational hierarchy who meet regularly to share information and discuss ways to improve processes and procedures in specific functional areas.

_____ **21.** Group cohesiveness

u. Groups of employees who share resources and coordinate efforts so as to help members better perform their individual duties and responsibilities. The performance of the group can be evaluated by adding up the contributions of the individual group members.

CRITICAL THINKING EXERCISES

1. P.O.V. (Point of View)

Directions: In this exercise you will be asked to provide your personal opinion regarding some of the topics discussed in the chapter. At the completion of this exercise, your instructor may wish to poll the entire class regarding their responses.

    a. The best way to motivate workers is to provide them with instructions concerning the most efficient way to perform a task or job. With specific rules and expectations, workers know what is required of them and will be limited in the way in which they can deviate from workplace norms. In addition, workers will be motivated to perform at optimum levels if salaries are based on their output.

    Agree _____   Disagree _____

    Explain:

    _____

    _____

    _____

    _____

    b. When hired, workers should be made aware of the expectations that the employer has of them. By making expectations clear, the employer empowers the employee to conduct himself/herself in a way that will lead to positive outcomes. By making the employee aware of expectations at the outset, the possibility of poor performance can be eliminated.

    Agree _____   Disagree _____

    Explain:

    _____

    _____

    _____

    _____

2. Using the Internet

Directions: Employee motivation is essential for and organization to consistently achieve its goals. Click on **http://www.adamssixsigma.com** and describe how this company attempts to deal with employee motivation. Your answer should address the following questions:

    a. What is meant by strategic planning and goal setting?
    b. What is strategic process control?
    c. How can team building enhance employee motivation?

3. Writing Skills

Directions: As a manager, write an essay for other managers, briefly explaining McGregor's Theory X and Theory Y. Discuss the possible effects of these theories on worker motivation and retention.

Chapter 11

Understanding Labor-Management Relations

OUTLINE

MULTIPLE CHOICE

Directions: Place the letter of the response that best completes the questions that follow in the blank space at the left.

>lg 1   **What is the historical development of American labor unions?**

_____   1. A labor group that represents workers in dealing with management conducts:
    a. union organizing
    b. negotiations that lead to a labor agreement
    c. day-to-day administration of a labor agreement
    d. all of these answers are correct

_____   2. The process of negotiating labor agreements is known as:
    a. union organizing   **c.** collective bargaining
    b. contract administration   d. the labor-management process

_____   3. The first national labor union was the:
    a. American Federation of Labor
    b. Knights of Labor
    c. Congress of Industrial Organizations
    d. Federation of Organized Trades and Labor Unions

_____   4. The American Federation of Labor consisted of:
    a. craft groups from within the Knights of Labor
    b. industrial groups from within the Knights of Labor
    c. craft groups from within the Congress of Industrial Organizations
    d. industrial groups from within the Congress of Industrial Organizations

_____   5. The Congress of Industrial Organizations succeeded in organizing:
    a. craft workers   **c.** the AFL
    b. business workers   **d.** workers in mass-production industries

_____   6. A current trend in labor union representation is the formation of:
    a. trade unions   **c.** conglomerate unions
    b. craft unions   **d.** yellow-dog unions

>lg 2   **What role did federal law play in the development of the union-management relationship?**

_____   7. The Norris-LaGuardia Act of 1932 ended:
    a. union organizing as practiced by the CIO
    b. the use of injunctions by employers
    c. strike privileges afforded union members
    d. mandatory union membership

_____   8. The Wagner Act (National Labor Relations Act of 1935) encouraged:
    a. union formation
    b. the use of injunctions by employers
    c. yellow-dog contracts
    d. unfair labor practices

_____   9. The Wagner Act (National Labor Relations Act of 1935) established the:
    a. Norris-Laguardia Review Board
    b. Joint Council of Labor Review
    c. Occupational Safety and Health Administration
    d. National Labor Relations Board

_____ 10 The Taft-Hartley Act (Labor Management Relations Act of 1947) permitted:
   a. picketing by union members to block nonstriking employees from entering the workplace
   b. high fees charged by unions to members
   c. an 80 day cooling-off period that forces strikers back to work while management and labor negotiators try to resolve differences
   d. numerous injunctions to forestall strikes

_____ 11. The Taft-Hartley Act (Labor Management Relations Act of 1947) created the:
   a. Taft-Hartley Review Board
   b. Federal Mediation and Conciliation Service
   c. Occupational Safety and Health Administration
   d. National Labor Relations Board

_____ 12. The process wherein an individual is selected to hold talks with union and management negotiators and suggest compromises is called:
   a. negotiation   c. injunction
   b. mediation   d. arbitration

_____ 13. The Landrum-Griffin Act (Labor-Management Reporting and Disclosure Act of 1959) dealt with:
   a. labor management issues   c. yellow dog contracts
   b. workplace safety issues   d. nternal affairs of labor unions

>lg 3   What is the union organizing process?

_____ 14. In order for the National Labor Relations Board to conduct a union certification election, authorization cards must be presented from at least:
   a. 20 percent of employees   c. 40 percent of employees
   b. 30 percent of employees   d. 51 percent of employees

_____ 15. The employees who are eligible to vote for union certification are known as a:
   a. negotiating group   c. bargaining unit
   b. certification unit   d. authorizing group

>lg 4   What is the collective bargaining process and what key issues are included in the union contract?

_____ 16. A company where only union members can be hired is called a(n):
   a. open shop   c. closed shop
   b. bargaining unit   d. agency shop

_____ 17. A firm for which employees can work without having to join a union is called a(n):
   a. open shop   c. closed shop
   b. bargaining unit   d. agency shop

_____ 18. An agency shop:
   a. is one in which only union members can be hired
   b. does not require employees to join the union although they must pay the union a fee to cover its expenses in representing them
   c. allows employees to neither join the union nor pay dues or fees to the union
   d. requires a dues checkoff clause in order to exist

_____ 19. Right-to-work laws allow:
   a. states to require union membership
   b. employees to work at one firm while maintaining union membership at another firm

    c. the federal government determine who has the right-to-work at a job site

    d. states to determine whether employees can work at a unionized company without having to join the union

_____ **20.** A cost-of-living adjustment:

    a. allows for wage increases that are linked to changes in the cost of living

    b. provides lump-sum wage adjustments

    c. is a management prerogative

    d. is considered a supplementary unemployment benefit

>lg 5   How do employees file a grievance?

_____ **21.** A formal complaint, by an employee or by the union, that management has violated some part of the contract is called a(n):

    a. seniority benefit right   **c.** conciliation

    b. arbitration   **d.** grievance

_____ **22.** The process of settling a labor-management dispute by having a third party make a decision is called:

    a. conciliation   **c.** arbitration

    b. grievance   **d.** mediation

>lg 6   What economic tactics do unions and employers use in labor-management conflicts?

_____ **23.** A work stoppage conducted by a group of union members or an entire union which takes place without the approval of the national union, while a contract is still in effect is known as a:

    a. selective strike strategy   **c.** bulldog strike

    b. wildcat strike   **d.** lockout

_____ **24.** The union tactic of shutting down a critical plant that supplies parts to other plants is know as a:

    a. lockout   **c.** wildcat strike

    b. selective strike strategy   **d.** bulldog strike

_____ **25.** In order to keep customers and others form doing business with an employer a union might conduct a:

    a. boycott   **c.** corporate campaign

    b. mutual-aid program   **d.** mediation campaign

_____ **26.** The term used by union officials to describe anti-union strategies is called:

    a. union busting   **c.** scabbing

    b. mutual aid   **d.** corporate campaigning

_____ **27.** Scabs are:

    a. union officials who disrupt stockholder meetings of a company it wants to pressure

    b. synonymous with pickets

    c. employers who refuse to let workers enter a plant or building to work

    d. non-union employees hired to replace striking union members

>lg 7   What trends will affect American workers and labor-management relations?

_____ **28.** Firms that consist of two entities, one union and the other non-union are called:

    a. wildcat employers

    b. mutual-aid employers

    c. double-breasted employers

    d. scab employers

TRUE/FALSE

Directions: Place a T or an F in the space provided to the left of each question to indicate whether it is True or False.

>lg 1

What is the historical development of American labor unions?

_____ 1. Collective bargaining is the process of negotiating labor agreements that provide for compensation and working arrangements that are not always mutually acceptable to the union and management.

_____ 2. The Knights of Labor was formed after many of the craft groups within the American Federation of Labor were unhappy with its social reform policy and political activities.

_____ 3. The American Federation of Labor consisted of many craft unions, that is skilled workers in a single craft or occupation such as bricklaying, carpentry, or plumbing.

_____ 4. The Congress of Industrial Organizations was formed to compete with the American Federation of Labor and represent the disgruntled members of its craft unions.

_____ 5. In 1935, John L. Lewis took his union, the United Mine Workers, and a few other unions and left the American Federation of Labor, to form the Congress of Industrial Organizations.

_____ 6. In 1945, union members accounted for 32.5 percent of all employed Americans. Today union membership stands at about 15 percent of all employed Americans.

_____ 7. Conglomerate unions purchase major corporations in different industries and organize their workers into a single bargaining unit.

_____ 8. The AFL-CIO is an umbrella organization that represents about 85 percent of all rank-and-file union members.

>lg 2

What role did federal law play in the development of the union-management relationship?

_____ 9. An injunction is a federal, state, or local law that prohibits certain union activities.

_____ 10. The Wagner Act (National Labor Relations Act of 1935) made it illegal for an employer to refuse to bargain with a union about wages, hours, and other job conditions.

_____ 11. The National Labor Relations Board (NLRB), which enforces the provisions of the Wagner Act, is responsible for investigating charges of unfair labor practices of employers but not those of unions.

_____ 12. The Taft-Hartley Act (Labor-Management Relations Act of 1947) was enacted by Congress to address some of the protests made by management which claimed that the Wagner Act was too pro-labor.

_____ 13. The Federal Mediation and Conciliation Service helps management and unions to focus on issues and acts as a go-between to help resolve them.

_____ 14. The Landrum-Griffin Act (Labor-Management Reporting and Disclosure Act of 1959) prohibited federal, state, and local governments from interfering with the internal organizing and financial activities of union officers.

>lg 3

What is the union organizing process?

_____ 15. Union organizing involves the signing of authorization cards by workers, which prove the workers' interest in having the union represent them.

_____ 16. A union certification election involves the NLRB posting an election notice and defining the bargaining unit.

_____ 17. A decertification election allows the rank and file union members to vote out the management of their union.

>lg 4

What is the collective bargaining process and what key issues are included in the union contract?

_____ 18. A contract negotiated by the union and an employer, which is agreed to by the membership, remains a non-binding document.

_____ 19. The closed shop, agency shop, and open shop are all similar in that all workers in firms that have them must join the union in order to benefit from the provisions of the contract that has been negotiated.

_____ 20. Right-to-work laws mandate that those states that have them must unionize all firms that have negotiated contracts with more than one union.

_____ 21. A management rights clause might give the employer all rights to manage the business except as specified in the contract.

_____ 22. A lump-sum wage adjustment provides that each worker's base pay remains the same for the contract period, but each worker receives a bonus once or twice during the contract.

>lg 5

How do employees file a grievance?

_____ 23. A grievance is usually an informal complaint made by an employee that must be investigated by the union grievance officer.

_____ 24. Arbitration is the process of settling a labor-management dispute by having a third party, or panel, make a decision regarding the matter.

_____ 25. The arbitrator's decision, which is contained in the award document, is not reviewable and is binding.

>lg 6

What economic tactics do unions and employers use in labor-management conflicts?

_____ 26. A wildcat strike is a strike that is approved by the national union which takes place while a contract is still in effect.

_____ 27. A mutual-aid pact is an employer strategy that involves a firm receiving money from other companies in its industry to cover some of the income lost because of a strike.

_____ 28. A corporate campaign is an employer strategy whereby a firm tries to disrupt meetings of a union that it wants to pressure into a contract agreement.

>lg 7

What trends will affect American workers and labor-management relations?

_____ 29. The most notable trend in union activity will be to reverse the decline in their memberships and the efforts by employers to remain union-free.

_____ **30.** In order to avoid employing more union employees, some firms, known as single-breasted employers, have created second firms that hire nonunion workers who are paid less than union workers.

ENHANCE YOUR VOCABULARY

Antagonism	Actively expressed opposition or hostility
Anticipated	To foresee and deal with in advance; to give advance thought or treatment to
Coerce	To compel to an act or choice; to bring about by force or threat
Cohesive	The act or state of sticking together tightly; adhering
Disband	To break up the organization of; dissolve; disperse
Exclusive	A newspaper story at first printed by only one newspaper; An exclusive right (as to sell a particular product); not permitting others to participate
Galvanize	To stimulate or excite as if by an electric shock; to coat (iron or steel) with zinc
Jeopardizing	Exposing to danger or risk
Jurisdiction	The power, right, or authority to interpret and apply the law
Picketing	A person or persons usually outside of a place of employment during a strike to express grievance and discourage entry

Directions: Select the definition in Column B that best defines the word in Column A.

Column A

_____ **1.** Jeopardizing
_____ **2.** Galvanize
_____ **3.** Disband
_____ **4.** Picketing
_____ **5.** Coerce
_____ **6.** Antagonism
_____ **7.** Cohesive
_____ **8.** Exclusive
_____ **9.** Jurisdiction
_____ **10.** Anticipated

Column B

a. To bring about by force or threat
b. The right to interpret and apply the law
c. Exposing to danger or risk
d. A story printed by only one publication
e. Sticking; adhering
f. To stimulate; to coat with zinc
g. To break up; dissolve; disperse
h. Actively expressed opposition or hostility
i. To give advance thought or treatment to
j. People protesting outside their place of employment

REVIEW YOUR KEY TERMS

Directions: Select the definition in Column B that best defines the word in Column A.

Column A

_____ **1.** Labor union

_____ **2.** Industrial union

_____ **3.** Local union

Column B

a. An elected union official who represents union members to management when workers have complaints.

b. An organization that represents workers in dealing with management over disputes involving wages, hours, and working conditions.

c. A union that represents skilled workers in a single craft or occupation such as bricklaying, carpentry, or plumbing.

_____ 4. Knights of Labor

d. A national labor organization made up of numerous industrial unions; founded in 1935. In 1955, the CIO merged with the American Federation of Labor (AFL) to form the AFL-CIO.

_____ 5. National union

e. A method of attempting to settle labor disputes in which a specialist from the Federal Mediation and Conciliation Service serves as a mediator, holding talks with union and management negotiators and suggesting possible compromises.

_____ 6. National Labor Relations Board (NLRB)

f. A statute enacted in 1932 that barred the use of injunctions to prevent strikes and other union activities and made yellow-dog contracts unenforceable; also called the Anti-Injunction Act.

_____ 7. Collective bargaining

g. A branch or unit of a national union that represents workers at a specific plant or in a specific geographic area.

_____ 8. Craft union

h. A method of attempting to settle labor disputes in which a specialist from the Federal Mediation and Conciliation Service help management and the union focus on the issues and acts as a go-between.

_____ 9. Mediation

i. The process of negotiating labor agreements that provide for compensation and working arrangements mutually acceptable to the union and to management.

_____ 10. Shop steward

j. A union that represents a wide variety of workers in various industries.

_____ 11. Landrum-Griffin Act

k. State laws that allow employees to work at a unionized company without having to join the union.

_____ 12. Decertification election

l. A statute enacted in 1959 to regulate the internal affairs of unions; contains a bill of rights for union members, rules for electing union officers, and safeguards to keep unions financially sound; also called the Labor-Management Reporting and Disclosure Act.

_____ 13. Cost-of-living adjustment (COLA)

m. A company where only union members can be hired; made illegal by the Taft-Hartley Act.

_____ 14. American Federation of Labor (AFL)

n. A union that represents all of the workers in a particular industry, such as auto workers or steel workers.

_____ 15. Union certification election

o. A company where employees do not have to join the union or pay dues or fees to the union; established under right-to-work laws.

_____ 16. Open shop

p. A national labor organization made up of numerous craft unions; founded in 1881 by splinter groups from the Knights of Labor. In 1955, the AFL merged with the Congress of Industrial Organizations (CIO) to form the AFL-CIO.

_____ 17. Congress of Industrial

q. The first important national labor organization Organizations (CIO) in the United States; founded in 1869.

_____ 18. Injunction

r. Contracts in which employees agreed not to join a labor union as a condition of being hired.

_____ 19. Taft-Hartley Act

s. An agency established by the Wagner Act of 1935 to enforce the act and investigate charges of employer and union wrongdoing and supervise elections for union representatives.

_____ **20.** Wagner Act

_____ **21.** Conglomerate union

_____ **22.** Conciliation

_____ **23.** Yellow-dog contracts

_____ **24.** Norris-LaGuardia Act

_____ **25.** Bargaining unit

_____ **26.** Closed shop

_____ **27.** Right-to-work laws

_____ **28.** Give-backs

_____ **29.** Lockout

_____ **30.** Selective strike strategy

_____ **31.** Union shop

_____ **32.** Picketing

_____ **33.** Grievance

_____ **34.** Wildcat strike

_____ **35.** Agency shop

_____ **36.** Arbitration

t. A union that consists of many local unions in a particular industry, skilled trade, or geographic area and thus represents workers throughout an entire country.

u. A statute enacted in 1947 that defined unfair union practices, outlined the rules for dealing with strikes of major economic impact, broadened employer options for dealing with unions, and further defined the rights of employees as individuals; also known as the Labor-Management Relations Act.

v. A statute enacted in 1935 that established that employees have a right to organize and join labor unions and to engage in collective bargaining; also known as the National Labor Relations Act.

w. Benefits given up by a union; also called concession bargaining.

x. A court order barring certain union activities.

y. An election in which workers vote, by secret ballot, on whether they want to be represented by a union; conducted by the National Labor Relations Board.

z. A company where employees are not required to join the union but they must pay the union a fee to cover its expenses in representing them.

aa. The employees who are eligible to vote in a union certification election and who will be represented by the union if it is certified.

bb. An election in which workers vote, by secret ballot, on whether they want to continue to be represented by their union.

cc. A formal complaint, filed by an employee or by the union, charging that management has violated the contract.

dd. A union tactic conducted as part of a strike. Union members parade in front of the employer's plant carrying signs and trying to persuade nonstriking workers to stop working and customers and suppliers from doing business with the company.

ee. The process of settling a labor-management dispute by having a third party make a decision, which is binding on both the union and the employer.

ff. A union strategy in which a group of employees claim they cannot work because of illness, thereby disrupting the company.

gg. A strike by a group of union members or an entire local union without the approval of the national union while the contract is still in effect; often illegal because it violates the contract.

hh. A company where nonunion workers can be hired; but they must then join the union, usually with in 30 or 60 days.

ii. A provision in a labor contract that calls for wages to increase automatically as the cost of living rises (usually measured by the consumer price index).

jj. A union strategy of conducting a strike at a critical plant that supplies parts to other plants.

_____ **37.** Sick-out

kk. An employer tactic in a labor dispute in which the employer refuses to allow workers to enter a plant or building to work, which means that the workers do not get paid.

_____ **38.** Double-breasted employers

ll. A union strategy in which a union disrupts a corporation's relations with its shareholders or investors as a means of attacking the company. For example, a union might disrupt the shareholder meetings of a company it wishes to pressure or threaten to withdraw large sums of money from banks that do business with the company.

_____ **39.** Corporate campaign

mm. An agreement by companies in an industry to create a fund that can be used to help cover fixed costs of any member company whose workers go on strike.

_____ **40.** Strike replacements

nn. Firms that consist of two entities, one unionized and the other nonunionized.

_____ **41.** Union busting

oo. Nonunion employees hired to replace striking union members; also known as scabs.

_____ **42.** Mutual-aid pact

pp. The process by which a company avoids unionization by moving to another region of the country or shifting operations offshore.

CRITICAL THINKING ACTIVITIES

1. P.O.V. (Point of View)

Directions: In this exercise you will be asked to provide your personal opinion regarding some of the topics discussed in the chapter. At the completion of this exercise, your instructor may wish to poll the entire class regarding their responses.

    a. The owners of businesses are the risk takers in our country. As such, they invest their time and capital to develop their firms. In fact, most business do not succeed. In view of this fact, the money left over from operations should be kept by the owners and not shared with employees. Workers should consider themselves fortunate when they are gainfully employed. Most benefits that they receive should be determined by their employers.

        Agree _____   Disagree _____

        Explain:

        _____

        _____

        _____

        _____

    b. When a firm does poorly, the owners must absorb any losses. Workers continue to get paid at the negotiated salary rate. In order to avoid laying off coworkers when business is slow, all employees should agree to take lower salaries to in order to keep everyone employed.

        Agree _____   Disagree _____

Explain:

_____

_____

_____

_____

2. Using the Internet

Directions: The strength and membership of labor unions in the United States has been on the decline for a number of years. Many people believe that this trend can only erode the ability of workers to prosper in the 21st century. Political parties have sought to address this issue in order to gain support from organized labor. Go to **http://www.slp.org** and review the material presented at this website.

    a. Summarize the history, program, and organization of the Socialist Labor Party.

    b. Click on a number of links at the site and, after reviewing them, discuss whether or not you agree with their point of view and provide a justification for your answer.

3. Writing Skills

Directions: Your factory is threatened by a strike. Write a memo to your managers and supervisors describing the kinds of tactics the union might use. Discuss such ploys as slowdowns, sickouts, and various types of strikes. In your memo, remind your managers and supervisors that management also has ways of responding such as lockout, union busting, scabbing, etc. Discuss which methods you feel are appropriate and/or legal and which are not. Emphasize the importance of acting properly during a job action, and the possible consequences of inappropriate behavior.

NOTES ON CHAPTER 11

Chapter 12

Achieving World-Class Operations Management

OUTLINE

I. Production and Operations-An Overview

II. Production Planning
   A. Production Process
      1. Mass Production
      2. Mass Customization and Customization
      3. Converting Inputs to Outputs
      4. Production Timing
   B. Site Selection
      1. Availability of Production Inputs
      2. Marketing Factors
      3. Local Incentives
      4. Manufacturing Environment
      5. International Location Consideration
   C. Facility Layout
      1. Process Layout
      2. Product Layout
      3. Fixed-Position Layout
   D. Resource Planning
      1. Insourcing and Outsourcing
      2. Inventory Management
      3. Computerized Resource Planning
   E. Supply Chain Management
      1. Strategies for Supply Chain Management
      2. Improving Supplier Communications

III. Production and Operations Control
   A. Routing Production
   B. Scheduling
      1. Gantt Chart
      2. The Critical Path Method and PERT

IV. Improving Production and Operations
   A. Total Quality Management
   B. The Move Toward Lean Manufacturing
   C. Automation in Productions and Operations Management
      1. Computer-Aided Design and Manufacturing Systems
      2. Robotics
      3. Flexible Manufacturing Systems
      4. Computer-Integrated Manufacturing
   D. Technology and Automation in Non-Manufacturing Operations

MULTIPLE CHOICE

Directions: Place the letter of the response that best completes the questions that follow in the blank space at the left.

>lg 1

Why is production and operations management important in both manufacturing and service firms?

_____ 1. The creation of products and services is called:
   a. operations management **c.** production
   b. planning **d.** control

_____ 2. Managing the conversion of inputs, such as natural resources, raw materials, and capital into outputs, products and services is known as:
   a. control **c.** planning
   b. production **d.** operations management

_____ 3. In the 1980's, many U.S. industries, such as automotive, steel and electronics lost customers to foreign competitors because:
   a. U.S. customers wanted only low priced goods
   b. U.S. production systems could not provide the quality customers wanted
   c. U.S. goods were in high demand in foreign countries
   d. U.S. firms only produced high quality, high cost, products

_____ 4. The first decision that must be made in production and operations management is:
   a. production planning
   b. production control
   c. improving production and operations
   d. all of these answers are correct

_____ 5. During the production planning stage of production and operations management:
   a. decisions are made regarding where, when, and how production will occur
   b. more efficient methods of producing the firm's goods are developed
   c. scheduling, controlling quality and costs, and the actual day-to-day operations of running a factory or service facility are carried out
   d. sources of supply and raw materials are contacted for placement of orders and/or delivery

>lg 2

What types of production processes are used by manufacturers and service firms?

_____ 6. The ability to manufacture many identical products at once, without regard for the individual needs of customers, is called:
   a. mass customization **c.** mass production
   b. customization **d.** processing

_____ 7. Producing goods using mass production techniques, but only up to a point, and then tailoring the item to the needs of customers is:
   a. job shop processing **c.** processing
   b. mass production **d.** mass customization

_____ 8. Producing goods, one at a time, according to the specific needs or wants of customers is called:
   a. customization   **c.** mass production
   b. job shop processing   **d.** mass customization

_____ 9. The length of a production run that is relatively long and can last days, weeks, or even months, is called a(n):
   a. job shop process   **c.** intermittent process
   b. continuous process   **d.** bifurcated process

_____ 10. The length of a production run that is relatively short and is used to make batches of different products is known as a(n):
   a. job shop process   **c.** intermittent process
   b. continuous process   **d.** bifurcated process

>lg 3 **How do organizations decide where to put their production facilities? What choices must be made in designing the facility?**

_____ 11. A term used to describe land, labor, and other resources that determine site selection is:
   a. production outputs   **c.** incentives
   b. marketing factors   **d.** production inputs

_____ 12. A marketing factor that would lead a firm to place its operations at a particular location is:
   a. how the location will affect the firm's ability to serve its customers
   b. the cost of distributing products to customers
   c. how difficult it is to distribute products from the chosen location
   d. all of these answers are correct

_____ 13. Tax breaks offered by countries, states, and other localities that influence site selection are called:
   a. marketing incentives   **c.** input incentives
   b. manufacturing incentives   **d.** local incentives

_____ 14. When a product cannot be put on an assembly line or moved about in a plant, the recommended arrangement of work flow is a:
   a. fixed-position layout   **c.** process layout
   b. service layout   **d.** product layout

>lg 4 **Why are resource planning tasks like inventory management and supplier relations critical to production?**

_____ 15. The process of buying inputs from various sources is called:
   a. a bill of material   **c.** purchasing
   b. outsourcing   **d.** inventory management

_____ 16. The supply of goods that a firm holds for use in production or for sale to customers is called:
   a. material   **c.** outsourcing
   b. insourcing   **d.** inventory

_____ 17. Enterprise Resource Planning:
   a. incorporates a master schedule to ensure that the materials, labor, and equipment needed for production are available
   b. expands ERP to integrate information from other departments such as finance, engineering, and manufacturing

    c. incorporates information about the firm's suppliers and customers in the flow of data and unites all major departments into one software program

    d. none of these answers are correct

_____ **18.** Smoothing the entire sequence of securing inputs, producing goods, and delivering goods to customers is known as:

    a. outsourcing control   **c.** inventory management

    b. supply chain management **d.** insourcing

>lg 5   How do operations managers schedule and control production?

_____ **19.** The production scheduling and control technique that helps managers to identify dependent tasks along with the longest path through the interrelated activities that are necessary to complete a project according to a specific schedule, is called:

    a. a Gantt Chart   **c.** PERT

    b. CPM   **d.** TQM

_____ **20.** The production scheduling and control technique that helps managers identify critical tasks and assess how delays in certain activities will affect operations or production, which also assigns three time estimates for each activity, is called:

    a. a Gantt Chart   **c.** PERT

    b. CPM   **d.** TQM

_____ **21.** When Dr. W. Edwards Deming suggested the use of TQM as a company-wide goal, he was referring to the:

    a. need for all companies to incorporate the "culture" of producing quality into all aspects of corporate operations

    b. use of CPM and PERT in all manufacturing processes

    c. requirement that firms use Gantt charts and bar graphs to show the relationship between scheduled and actual production

    d. importance of scheduling in each step of the production process

>lg 6   How can quality management and lean manufacturing techniques help firms improve production and operations management?

_____ **22.** Streamlining production by eliminating steps in the production process that do not add benefits that customers are willing to pay for is called:

    a. lean manufacturing

    b. just-in-time

    c. the performance-evaluation-review-technique

    d. the critical-path-method

_____ **23.** A concept of inventory control developed by the Japanese and incorporated into lean production systems is known as:

    a. CPM   **c.** JIT

    b. PERT   **d.** PDQ

>lg 7   What roles do technology and automation play in manufacturing and service industry operation management?

_____ **24.** The use of computers to design and test new products and modify existing ones is known as:

    a. robotics   **c.** CIM

    b. CAD   **d.** CAM

_____ 25. The use of computers to develop and control the production process is known as:
    a. robotics   **c.** CIM
    b. CAD   **d.** CAM

_____ 26. Flexible manufacturing systems:
    a. use computers to design and test new products
    b. blend the use of computers, robots, machine tools, and materials and parts-handling to automate a factory
    c. use computers to develop and control production processes
    d. none of these answers are correct

_____ 27. Combining computerized manufacturing process with other computerized systems that control design, inventory, production, and purchasing is known as:
    a. CAD/CAM   **c.** CIM
    b. FMS   **d.** JIT

>lg 8   **What key trends are affecting the way companies manage production and operations?**

_____ 28. Modular production involves:
    a. developing a production system comprised of flexible tools and processes that can be quickly changed to produce new or different products
    b. shifting the use of manufacturing techniques to service-oriented firms
    c. using self-contained production units that include several machines and workers arranged in a compact, sequential order
    d. breaking a complex product, service, or process into smaller pieces that can be created independently and then combined quickly to make a whole

_____ 29. Agile manufacturing requires that a firm:
    a. develop a production system comprised of flexible tools and processes that can be quickly changed to produce new or different products
    b. shift the use of manufacturing techniques to service-oriented firms
    c. use self-contained production units that include several machines and workers arranged in a compact, sequential order
    d. break a complex product, service, or process into smaller pieces that can be created independently and then combined quickly to make a whole

_____ 30. Work cell design involves:
    a. developing a production system comprised of flexible tools and processes that can be quickly changed to produce new or different products
    b. shifting the use of manufacturing techniques to service-oriented firms
    c. using self-contained production units that include several machines and workers arranged in a compact, sequential order
    d. breaking a complex product, service, or process into smaller pieces that can be created independently and then combined quickly to make a whole

TRUE/FALSE

Directions: Place a T or an F in the space provided to the left of each question to indicate whether it is True or False.

>lg 1   **Why is production and operations management important in both manufacturing and service firms?**

_____ 1. Production turns outputs, such as natural resources, raw materials, human resources, and capital into inputs, products, and services.

_____ 2. Operations management is the process of managing the conversion of inputs into outputs, products, and services.

_____ 3. When a firm considers the competitive environment and its own strategic goals in order to find the best production methods, it is conducting production planning.

_____ 4. As a result of the expense involved in carrying it out, production planning mainly focuses on long-term product or service considerations of from three to five years.

>lg 2   **What types of production processes are used by manufacturers and service firms?**

_____ 5. Mass production and customization are virtually the same. They are terms used to describe the manufacture of identical goods at once.

_____ 6. In mass customization, mass production is used up to a point in the manufacturing process. Then a product is custom tailored to the needs or desires of individual customers.

_____ 7. In a continuous production process, short production runs are used to make batches of different products.

_____ 8. A continuous production process is best for high-volume, low-variety products with standardized parts.

_____ 9. An intermittent production process is best for low-volume, high-variety products such as those produced by mass customization or customization.

>lg 3   **How do organizations decide where to put their production facilities? What choices must be made in designing the facility?**

_____ 10. If other production facilities are located in a particular area, a firm is advised to locate its manufacturing facility elsewhere because of the strong competition that exists within the manufacturing base.

_____ 11. Local incentives, including those from countries, states, and cities have not served to attract manufacturing firms to specific locations that otherwise might have been selected.

_____ 12. Lower labor costs, fewer regulations, and proximity to new markets are all factors in determining whether to open a new production facility in a foreign location.

_____ 13. When large quantities of a product must be processed on an ongoing basis, the workstations or departments are arranged in a line with products moving along the line. The assembly process that is best suited to a product made this way is the product layout design.

_____ 14. The product layout assembly line design is best suited for products such as large aircraft and ships.

_____ 15. A fixed-position layout lets a product stay in one place while workers and machinery move to it as needed.

>lg 4   **Why are resource planning tasks like inventory management and supplier relations critical to production?**

_____ 16. The purchase of large components from another manufacturer is known as outsourcing.

_____ 17. A firm that maintains a perpetual inventory will always have an oversupply of raw materials and parts in reserve in order to deal with large "rush" orders.

_____ 18. Enterprise resource planning focuses internally and externally by incorporating data about a firm's suppliers and customers into the flow of data used for resource and inventory planning.

_____ 19. Supply chain management focuses on smoothing the transitions along the supply chain, with the ultimate goal of satisfying suppliers in the area of purchasing.

_____ 20. EDI is a useful tool in which two trading partners exchange information electronically either through a linked computer system or over the Internet.

>lg 5 **How do operations managers schedule and control production?**

_____ 21. Routing, the first stage in the production controlling process, involves specifying and controlling the time required for each step in the production process.

_____ 22. Both CPM and PERT are methods that help managers identify critical tasks and assess how delays in certain activities will affect operations or production.

_____ 23. Gantt charts assign three time estimates needed for the completion of each production or operations activity: optimistic, probable, and pessimistic.

>lg 6 **How can quality management and lean manufacturing techniques help firms improve production and operations management?**

_____ 24. Today, with the strong demand for consumer products, quality control has come to mean inspecting products before they leave the factory door.

_____ 25. TQM emphasizes that all employees involved with bringing a product or service to customers contribute to its quality and that improving operations in order to achieve greater efficiency leads to higher quality output.

_____ 26. Lean manufacturing means streamlining production so that extra benefits can be added to products without raising prices.

_____ 27. Under the JIT system, manufacturers determine what parts will be needed and when, and then order them so that they arrive "just in time."

>lg 7 **What roles do technology and automation play in manufacturing and service industry operation management?**

_____ 28. CAD/CAM systems are used by engineers to draw products and view them from different angles as well as develop and control the production process.

_____ 29. In modular production, firms strive to develop a production system comprised of flexible tools and processes that can be quickly changed to produce new or different products.

_____ 30. Agile manufacturing involves the adaptation of a firm to shifts in customer demand and technological changes that affect its products or services.

>lg 8 **What key trends are affecting the way companies manage production and operations management?**

_____ 31. Work cell design involves the creation of small, self contained, production units that include several machines and workers arranged in a compact, sequential order.

_____ 32. As a small part of the total production "picture," it is not necessary for employees to understand the role that they play in the manufacturing process.

ENHANCE YOUR VOCABULARY

Alter	To make different without changing into something else; castrate
Contamination	To soil, stain, corrupt or infect by contact or association
Divert	To turn aside; deviate
Forefront	The foremost part or place
Integral	Essential to completeness
Optimistic	To anticipate the best possible outcome; hopeful
Prototypes	An original model on which something is patterned; archetype
Revs up	To increase the number of revolutions per minute of
Robots	Machines that look like human beings and perform various acts; machines whose lack of capacity for human emotions is often emphasized
Skyrocketing	Causing a rapid increase; shooting up abruptly

Directions: Select the definition in Column B that best defines the word in Column A.

Column A

_____ 1. Prototypes
_____ 2. Forefront

_____ 3. Alter
_____ 4. Contamination

_____ 5. Robots
_____ 6. Optimistic
_____ 7. Revs up
_____ 8. Skyrocketing

_____ 9. Integral

_____ 10. Divert

Column B

a. To soil, stain, corrupt or infect by association
b. Machines that look like humans and perform tasks
c. Hopeful
d. To make different without changing into something else
e. Deviate
f. Essential to completeness
g. The foremost part or place
h. To increase, as in the number of revolutions per minute
i. An original model on which something is patterned
j. To shoot up abruptly

REVIEW YOUR KEY TERMS

Directions: Select the definition in Column B that best defines the word in Column A.

Column A

_____ 1. Production

_____ 2. Mass customization

_____ 3. Continuous process

_____ 4. Inventory management

Column B

a. A production process that uses short production runs to make batches of different products; generally used for low-volume, high-variety products.

b. A manufacturing firm that produces goods in response to customer orders.

c. The creation of products and services by turning inputs, such as natural resources, raw materials, human resources, and capital, into outputs.

d. A facility arrangement in which work flows according to the production process. All workers performing similar tasks are grouped together, and products pass from one workstation to another.

_____	**5.** Intermittent process	**e.**	The way a good is made.

_____ **6.** Operations management

f. A production process in which the basic input is broken down into one or more outputs (products).

_____ **7.** Customization

g. A production process that uses long production runs lasting days, weeks, or months without equipment shutdown; generally used for high-volume, low-variety products with standardized parts.

_____ **8.** Process layout

h. The determination of how much of each type of inventory a firm will keep on hand and the ordering, receiving, storing, and keeping track of inventory.

_____ **9.** Fixed-position layout

i. A list of the components and the number of each required to make a given product.

_____ **10.** Production planning

j. A production process in which the basic inputs are either combined to create the output or transformed into the output.

_____ **11.** Product layout (assembly-line)

k. A facility arrangement in which the product stays in one place and workers and machinery move to it as needed; used for products that are impossible to move, such as ships, airplanes, and construction projects.

_____ **12.** Perpetual inventory

l. The supply of goods that a firm holds for use in production or for sale to customers.

_____ **13.** Routing

m. A facility arrangement in which workstations or departments are arranged in a line with products moving along the line; used for a continuous or repetitive production process.

_____ **14.** Make-or-buy decision

n. Management of the production process.

_____ **15.** Supply chain

o. Streamlining production by eliminating steps in the production process that do not add benefits that customers are willing to pay for.

_____ **16.** Purchasing

p. The purchase of items from an outside source rather than making them internally.

_____ **17.** Production process

q. The process of buying production inputs from various sources; also called procurement.

_____ **18.** Materials requirement

r. The aspect of production control that involves setting out the work flow, the sequence of machines and operations through which the product or service progresses from start to finish.

_____ **19.** Quality control

s. The use of quality principles in all aspects of a company's production and operations.

_____ **20.** Electronic data interchange (EDI)

t. The determination by a firm of whether to make its own production materials or buy them from outside sources.

_____ **21.** Mass production

u. The aspect of operations management in which the firm considers the competitive environment and its own strategic goals in an effort to find the best production methods.

_____ **22.** Inventory

v. The ability to manufacture many identical goods at once.

_____ **23.** Supply chain management

w. A continuously updated list of inventory levels, orders, sales, and receipts.

_____ **24.** Job shop

x. The aspect of production control that involves specifying and controlling the time required for each step in the production process.

_____ **25.** Gantt charts

y. The process of creating standards for quality and then measuring all finished goods and services against those standards.

_____ **26.** Total quality management (TQM)

z. In the critical path method, the longest path is through the linked activities. If activities on the critical path are not completed on time, the project will fall behind schedule.

_____ **27.** Assembly process

aa. A computerized system of controlling the flow of resources and inventory. A master schedule is used to ensure that the materials, labor, and equipment needed for production are at the right places in the right amounts at the right times.

_____ **28.** Manufacturing Resource Planning II (MRPH)

bb. The electronic exchange of information between two trading partners; can be conducted via a linked computer system or over the Internet.

_____ **29.** Critical path

cc. Bar graphs plotted on a time line that show the relationship between scheduled and actual production.

_____ **30.** Outsourcing

dd. The entire sequence of securing inputs, producing goods, and delivering them to customers.

_____ **31.** Bill of material

ee. A complex computerized system that integrates data from many departments to control the flow of resources and inventory; can generate a production plan for the firm as well as management reports, forecasts, and financial statements.

_____ **32.** Enterprise resource planning

ff. The process of smoothing transitions along the (ERP) supply chain so that the firm can satisfy its customers with quality products and services; focuses on forging tighter bonds with suppliers.

_____ **33.** Scheduling

gg. A project management tool that is similar to the CPM method but assigns three time estimates for each activity (optimistic, most probable, and pessimistic); allows managers to anticipate delays and potential problems before they occur.

_____ **34.** Critical path method (CPM)

hh. A computerized resource planning system that includes information about the firm's suppliers and customers as well as data generated internally.

_____ **35.** Lean manufacturing

ii. A project management tool that enables a manager to determine the critical path of activities for a project—the activities that will cause the entire project to fall behind schedule if they are not completed on time. To do so, the manager constructs a diagram showing all of the activities required to complete the project, the relationships among them, and the order in which they must be completed.

_____ **36.** Program evaluation and review technique (PERT)

jj. A manufacturing process in which goods are mass-produced up to a point and then custom tailored to the needs or desires of individual customers.

_____ **37.** Process manufacturing

kk. The production of goods or services one at a time according to the specific needs or wants of individual customers. Each product or service produced is unique.

_____ **38.** Just-in-time (JIT)

ll. The combination of computerized manufacturing processes such as robots and flexible manufacturing systems with other computerized systems that control design, inventory, production, and purchasing.

_____ **39.** CAD/CAM systems

mm. The use of computers to design and test new products and modify existing ones.

_____ **40.** Flexible manufacturing system

nn. A system in which production inputs arrive just when they are needed for production rather than being stored on site. Inventory and products are "pulled" through the production process in response to customer demand.

_____ **41.** Computer-Integrated Manufacturing

oo. The use of computers to develop and control the production process.

_____ **42.** Computer-aided design (CAD)

pp. A system that combines automated workstations with computer-controlled transportation devices—automatic guided vehicles (AGVs)—that move materials between workstations and into and out of the system.

_____ **43.** Robotics

qq. Linked computer systems that combine the advantages of computer-aided design and computer-aided manufacturing. The system helps design the product, control the flow of resources, and operate the production process.

_____ **44.** Computer-aided manufacturing

rr. The technology involved in designing, constructing, and operating robots (computer-controlled machines that can perform tasks independently).

CRITICAL THINKING EXERCISES

1. P.O.V. (Point of View)

Directions: In this exercise you will be asked to provide your personal opinion regarding some of the topics discussed in the chapter. At the completion of this exercise, your instructor may wish to poll the entire class regarding their responses.

a. The increased use of computers and technology in the area of production and operations management, can only lead to the loss of jobs for workers. Once a firm decides to automate and computerize its operations, the reduced role played by employees can only result in the loss of employment at the firm as well as in the economy as a whole.

Agree _____   Disagree _____

Explain:

_____

_____

_____

_____

b. The primary criterion that is used when a factory location decision is to be made is the level of wages in the area. Other factors may play a role, but the significance of the impact of wages and salaries is the most important of all.

Agree _____   Disagree _____

Explain:

_____

_____

_____

_____

2. Using the Internet.

Directions: The production and distribution of materials known as intellectual property, such as books and recordings that are the result of the creative activities of individuals, can find their way into the marketplace through various routes. Go to **http://www.courier.com** and click on Book Manufacturing, then click on Services.

    a. Describe the type of services that this company provides

    b. How does their "fulfillment services program" provide streamlined operations management?

    c. Click on Investor Resources and describe the potential for investment opportunities in this firm.

3. Writing Skills

Directions: Site selection for a facility such as a factory or service office must be made early in the production and operations planning process. The location of the site is very important and the consequences of locating in the wrong place may be considerable. Write a letter to the Chamber of Commerce in the area you are considering for development. Include in this letter all of the questions that are relevant for this decision such as the availability and cost of labor, housing, tax breaks or consequences, etc.

Chapter 13

Understanding the Customer and Creating Goods and Services that Satisfy

OUTLINE

MULTIPLE CHOICE

Directions: Place the letter of the response that best completes the questions that follow in the blank space at the left.

>lg 1   **What are the marketing concept and relationship building?**

___b___   1. The marketing concept is:
   a. working to lower production costs in order to satisfy consumer demand
   b. identifying consumer needs and then producing the goods or services that will satisfy them while making a profit
   c. an exchange of something of value between two parties
   d. the ratio of benefits to the sacrifice necessary to obtain those benefits

___a___   2. Customer value is:
   a. the ratio of benefits to the sacrifice necessary to obtain those benefits
   b. identifying consumer needs and then producing the goods or services that will satisfy them while making a profit
   c. working to lower production costs in order to satisfy consumer demand
   d. an exchange of something of value between two parties

___c___   3. Customer satisfaction is:
   a. a response to lower production costs that results from a desire to satisfy the needs of customers
   b. the ratio of benefits to the sacrifice necessary to obtain those benefits
   c. the customer's feeling that a product has met or exceeded expectations
   d. a clear indicator of a customer's willingness to purchase a product

___c___   4. A strategy that focuses on forging long-term partnerships with customers is known as:
   a. exchange marketing
   b. product-oriented marketing
   c. relationship marketing
   d. customer value marketing

___d___   5. A benefit of relationship marketing is that it:
   a. leads to repeat sales
   b. can lead to referrals that lead to increases in sales, market share, and profit
   c. results in lower costs to serve existing customers
   d. all of these answers are correct

>lg 2   **How do managers create a marketing strategy?**

___b___   6. The continual collection and evaluation of environmental information with the goal of identifying future market opportunities and threats is known as:
   a. target marketing   c. competitive marketing
   b. environmental scanning   d. advantage marketing

___c___   7. The specific group of consumers toward which a firm directs its marketing efforts is called a:
   a. competitive market   c. target market
   b. advantage market   d. environmental market

a   **8.** A firm that has a cost-competitive advantage:
  - **a.** can produce a product or service at a lower cost than all its competitors while maintaining satisfactory profit margins
  - **b.** possesses a set of unique features in that the company and its products are perceived by the market as significant and superior to those of the competition
  - **c.** targets and effectively serves a single segment of the market within a limited geographical area
  - **d.** provides something unique that is valuable to buyers beyond simply offering a low price

d   **9.** A firm that has a differential competitive advantage:
  - **a.** can produce a product or service at a lower cost than all its competitors while maintaining satisfactory profit margins
  - **b.** possesses a set of unique features in that the company and its products are perceived by the market as significant and superior to those of the competition
  - **c.** targets and effectively serves a single segment of the market within a limited geographical area
  - **d.** provides something unique that is valuable to buyers beyond simply offering a low price

c   **10.** A firm that has a niche competitive advantage:
  - **a.** can produce a product or service at a lower cost than all its competitors while maintaining satisfactory profit margins
  - **b.** possesses a set of unique features in that the company and its products are perceived by the market as significant and superior to those of the competition
  - **c.** targets and effectively serves a single segment of the market within a limited geographical area
  - **d.** provides something unique that is valuable to buyers beyond simply offering a low price

>lg 3   **What is the marketing mix?**

b   **11.** A firm's marketing mix is its:
  - **a.** choice of brand name, packaging, colors, warranties, accessories, and service program
  - **b.** blend of product offerings, pricing, promotional methods, and distribution system
  - **c.** decision as to how many stores and which specific wholesalers and retailers will handle the product in a geographic area
  - **d.** personal selling, advertising, public relations, and sales promotion program

d   **12.** A firm's decision as to how many stores and which specific wholesalers and retailers will handle the product is called its:
  - **a.** marketing mix
  - **b.** promotion strategy
  - **c.** product strategy
  - **d.** distribution strategy

a   **13.** A product strategy includes:
  - **a.** choice of brand name, packaging, colors, warranties, accessories, and service program
  - **b.** blend of product offerings, pricing, promotional methods, and distribution system
  - **c.** decision as to how many stores and which specific wholesalers and retailers will handle the product in a geographic area
  - **d.** personal selling, advertising, public relations, and sales promotion program

b   **14.** Personal selling, advertising, and public relations are all part of a firm's:
    a. marketing mix   **c.** product strategy
    b. promotion strategy   **d.** distribution strategy

C   **15.** The application of marketing to social issues and causes is known as:
    a. interest marketing   **c.** social marketing
    b. political marketing   **d.** cooperative marketing

>lg 4

How do consumers make buying decisions?

a   **16.** The first step in the consumer buying decision-making process is:
    a. problem recognition   **c.** search for information
    b. evaluation of alternatives   **d.** a stimulus

C   **17.** The influences on consumer decision making that include perception, beliefs, values, and attitudes are called:
    a. social factors   **c.** individual factors
    b. business factors   **d.** antisocial factors

d   **18.** The influences on consumer decision making that include family, opinion leaders, social class, and culture are called:
    a. antisocial factors   **c.** business factors
    b. individual factors   **d.** social factors

b   **19.** A characteristic that distinguishes business-to-business markets from consumer markets is:
    a. making rational purchasing decisions on the part of businesses
    b. direct distribution of products to businesses
    c. intended use of products by businesses
    d. all of these answers are correct

>lg 5

What are the five basic forms of market segmentation?

b   **20.** The process of separating, identifying, and evaluating the layers of a market to design a marketing mix is known as:
    a. sales management
    b. market segmentation
    c. rational purchase decision making
    d. the consumer decision making process

a   **21.** Demographic segmentation:
    a. uses categories such as age, education, gender, income, and household size to differentiate among markets
    b. means segmenting markets by region of the country
    c. is market segmentation by personality or lifestyle
    d. is based on what a product will do rather than on consumer characteristics

c   **22.** Psychographic segmentation:
    a. uses categories such as age, education, gender, income, and household size to differentiate among markets
    b. means segmenting markets by region of the country
    c. is market segmentation by personality or lifestyle
    d. is based on what a product will do rather than on consumer characteristics

_d_   **23.** Benefit segmentation:
  a. uses categories such as age, education, gender, income, and household size to differentiate among markets
  b. means segmenting markets by region of the country
  c. is market segmentation by personality or lifestyle
  d. is based on what a product will do rather than on consumer characteristics

_b_   **24.** Geographic segmentation:
  a. uses categories such as age, education, gender, income, and household size to differentiate among markets
  b. means segmenting markets by region of the country
  c. is market segmentation by personality or lifestyle
  d. is based on what a product will do rather than on consumer characteristics

>lg 6   **How is marketing research used in marketing decision making?**

_d_   **25.** The most critical step in the marketing research process is:
  a. choosing a method of research
  b. collection of the data
  c. observation
  d. defining the marketing problem

_a_   **26.** Experimental marketing research involves:
  a. an investigator changing one or more variables and observing the effects of these changes on another variable
  b. an interviewer interacting with respondents, either in person, or by mail, to obtain facts, opinions, and attitudes
  c. monitoring respondents' actions without direct interaction
  d. none of these answers are correct

_b_   **27.** Secondary data is:
  a. changing one variable and observing the effects of the change on a second variable
  b. information that has already been collected for a project other than the current one, but which can be used to help solve it
  c. monitoring the actions of a second person without them being aware of it
  d. an interview of a second person by mail or in person in order to obtain facts

_a_   **28.** In the final stage of the marketing research process:
  a. data is analyzed in order to make interpretations and draw conclusions
  b. primary and secondary data are collected
  c. the results of surveys are tabulated
  d. a presentation tool, such as Power Point or Astound, is used to create tables and charts of data that are going to be presented

>lg 7   **What are the trends in understanding the consumer?**

_c_   **29.** DSS is:
  a. a presentation tool, such as Power Point or Astound, that is used to create tables and charts related to a marketing research project
  b. a survey tool used by researchers to support marketing decisions
  c. an interactive, flexible computerized information system that allows managers to make decisions quickly and accurately
  d. a technique used to gather direct statistical support for marketing research decisions

_d_   **30.** The creation of large computerized files of the profiles and purchasing patterns of potential customers is known as:
   a. the decision support system
   b. scavenger marketing
   c. systems for measuring and reporting about television (SMART)
   d. database or micromarketing

TRUE/FALSE

Directions: Place a T or an F in the space provided to the left of each question to indicate whether it is True or False.

 1

What are the marketing concept and relationship building?

_F_   **1.** Marketing is referred to as the *"right" principle*—the right of a manufacturer or service provider to perform the marketing function in accordance with their schedule. Time, place, price, and promotion are not relevant to them.

_F_   **2.** The major weakness of the marketing concept is that it does not allow for the producer to make a profit.

_F_   **3.** The marketing concept has a production orientation. Lower production costs, which lead to lower prices, take precedence over satisfying customer needs.

_T_   **4.** The ratio of benefits to the sacrifice necessary to obtain those benefits is known as customer value.

_T_   **5.** When companies focus on long-term partnerships with customers, they are conducting relationship marketing.

 2

How do managers create a marketing strategy?

_F_   **6.** Environmental scanning is the placement of security tags on all equipment, such as computers, so that their data banks cannot be stolen by employees and sold to competitors.

_F_   **7.** Target marketing is a strategy that lets a firm use its resources efficiently and focus its marketing strategy on those who are most likely to purchase its products.

_T_   **8.** A firm holds a cost-competitive-advantage when it delivers a product or service at a lower cost that all its competitors while maintaining satisfactory profit margins.

_T_   **9.** A differential competitive advantage tends to be shorter lasting than a cost-competitive-advantage because a differential advantage is subject to continual erosion.

_T_   **10.** A niche competitive advantage may be a viable option for a small firm because it can serve a market segment that is not crucial for a major competing firm.

 3

What is the marketing mix?

_T_   **11.** The blend of product offerings, pricing, promotional methods, and distribution systems that brings a specific group of consumers superior value is known as the marketing mix.

_F_   **12.** The four P's of marketing are based on performance, practicality, placement, and potential.

F   **13.** Demand for a product and the cost of producing it determines a firm's production strategy.

F   **14.** A promotion strategy would concern itself mainly with the number of stores and the specific wholesalers and retailers that handle a product in a geographic area.

T   **15.** Not-for-profit marketing helps certain groups, such as symphonies, museums, and other cultural organizations identify target markets and develop marketing mixes.

>lg 4

How do consumers make buying decisions?

T   **16.** *Individual factors* that affect the decision-making process include all interactions between a consumer and the external environment.

T   **17.** *Individual factors* are within the consumer and are unique to each person.

T   **18.** *Social factors* that affect the decision-making process include: family, opinion leaders, social class, and culture.

F   **19.** A significant factor that distinguishes a business-to-business purchase and a consumer purchase is that unlike businesses, consumers usually approach purchasing rather formally.

>lg 5

What are the five basic forms of market segmentation?

T   **20.** Market segmentation is the process of separating, identifying, and evaluating layers of a market to design a marketing mix.

T   **21.** Demographic segmentation uses categories such as age, education, gender, income, and household size to differentiate among markets.

F   **22.** Psychographic segmentation is based on what a product will do rather than on consumer characteristics.

T   **23.** Volume segmentation is based on the amount of the product that will be sold in various markets.

>lg 6

How is marketing research used in marketing decision making?

T   **24.** Marketing research is the process of planning, collecting, and analyzing data relevant to a marketing decision.

F   **25.** Survey research involves an investigator who changes one or more variables while observing the effects of those changes on another variable.

T   **26.** The fastest growing form of observation research is the use of cash registers with scanners that monitor respondents' actions without direct interaction.

T   **27.** Primary data are collected directly from the original source to solve the problem.

T   **28.** The final step in the marketing research process is for the researcher to prepare a report and to communicate its conclusions and recommendations to management.

>lg 7

What are the trends in understanding the consumer?

F   **29.** Brain science has allowed researchers to gain insights into how consumers perceive, think, and make decisions.

F   **30.** The main drawback to the use of DSS is that it does not provide interactive information that is necessary to make accurate marketing decisions.

31. An advantage of database marketing, also known as *micromarketing*, is that it can create a computerized form of the old-fashioned relationship that people used to have with the corner shopkeeper.

ENHANCE YOUR VOCABULARY

Aerial	Of, relating to, or occurring in the air or atmosphere; thin, lacking substance
Bias	To give a settled and often prejudiced outlook to; to apply a slight negative or positive voltage to
Brittle	Easily broken, cracked, or snapped; easily hurt or offended
Compelling	Forceful; demanding attention; convincing
Constituencies	A body of citizens entitled to elect a representative; the people involved in or served by an organization (as a business or institution)
Differentiable	To express the specific distinguishing quality of; discriminate
Equitable	Dealing fairly and equally with all concerned
Honed	To make more acute, intense, or effective
Option	The power or right to choose
Prodding	Thrusting a pointed instrument into; prick; stir
Resurrected	Raised from the dead; to bring to view, attention, or use again
Touted	Publicized as being of great worth
Viable	Capable of living; capable of working, functioning, or developing adequately
Vintage	Of old, recognized, and enduring interest, importance, or quality
Withering	Drying up or shriveling from; to lose freshness, strength or vitality; fade

Directions: Select the definition in Column B that best defines the word in Column A.

Column A	Column B
1. Constituencies	a. Of old and enduring interest
2. Differentiable	b. Occurring in the air; lacking substance
3. Withering	c. The people served by an organization
4. Bias	d. Drying up or fading
5. Brittle	e. Easily broken, cracked, or snapped
6. Vintage	f. To express the distinguishing quality of
7. Equitable	g. The power or right to choose
8. Compelling	h. Demanding attention; convincing
9. Option	i. To apply a slight negative or positive slant to
10. Aerial	j. Dealing fairly with all concerned

REVIEW YOUR KEY TERMS

Directions: Select the definition in Column B that best defines the word in Column A.

Column A	Column B
1. Exchange	a. The specific group of consumers toward which a firm directs its marketing efforts.

_____ cc _____ **2.** Customer satisfaction

_____ j _____ **3.** Competitive advantage

_____ u _____ **4.** Marketing mix

_____ h _____ **5.** Market segmentation

_____ e _____ **6.** Distribution strategy

_____ i _____ **7.** Secondary data

_____ g _____ **8.** Demographic segmentation

_____ l _____ **9.** Marketing research

_____ b _____ **10.** Marketing

_____ d _____ **11.** Cost competitive advantage

_____ ff _____ **12.** Cognitive dissonance

_____ z _____ **13.** Product strategy

_____ r _____ **14.** Promotion strategy

_____ k _____ **15.** Buyer behavior

_____ q _____ **16.** Marketing concept

_____ a _____ **17.** Target market

_____ o _____ **18.** Differential competitive advantage

_____ t _____ **19.** Geographic segmentation

b. The process of discovering the needs and wants of potential buyers and customers, and then providing goods and services that meet or exceed their expectations.

c. An approach in which a firm works to lower production costs without a strong desire to satisfy the needs of customers. The firm concentrates on mass production—maximizing the efficiency of its operations, increasing output, and ensuring uniform quality.

d. A firm's ability to produce a product or service at a lower cost than all other competitors in an industry while maintaining satisfactory profit margins.

e. The part of the marketing mix that involves choosing a brand name, packaging, colors, a warranty, accessories, and a service program for the product.

f. The process in which two parties give something of value to each other to satisfy their respective needs.

g. The differentiation of markets through the use of categories such as age, education, gender, income, and household size.

h. The process of separating, identifying, and evaluating the layers of a market in order to design a marketing mix.

i. Information that has already been collected for a project other than the current one, but which can be used to solve the current problem.

j. A set of unique features of a company and its products that are perceived by the target market as significant and superior to those of the competition; also called differential advantage.

k. The actions people take in buying and using goods and services.

l. The process of planning, collecting, and analyzing data relevant to a marketing decision.

m. The differentiation of markets based on what a product will do rather than on customer characteristics.

n. A firm's ability to target and effectively serve a single segment of the market within a limited geographic area.

o. A firm's ability to provide a unique product or service that offers something of value to buyers besides simply a lower price.

p. The process in which a firm continually collects and evaluates information about its external environment.

q. Identifying consumer needs and then producing the goods or services that will satisfy them while making a profit for the organization.

r. The part of the marketing mix that involves personal selling, advertising, public relations, and sales promotion of the product.

s. Information collected directly from the original source to solve a problem.

_____aa_ **20.** Survey research

_____v_ **21.** Volume segmentation

_____s_ **22.** Primary data

_____n_ **23.** Niche competitive advantage

_____dd_ **24.** Relationship marketing

_____c_ **25.** Production orientation

_____y_ **26.** Pricing strategy

_____w_ **27.** Four P's

_____x_ **28.** Customer value

_____p_ **29.** Environmental scanning

_____ee_ **30.** Psychographic segmentation

_____gg_ **31.** Observation research

_____m_ **32.** Benefit segmentation

_____ii_ **33.** Decision support system (DSS)

_____bb_ **34.** Experiment

_____jj_ **35.** Social marketing

_____hh_ **36.** Database marketing

t. The differentiation of markets by region of the country, city or county size, market density, or climate.

u. The blend of product offerings, pricing, promotional methods, and distribution systems that brings a specific group of consumers superior value.

v. The differentiation of markets based on the amount of the product purchased.

w. Product, price, promotion, and place (distribution).

x. The ratio of benefits to the sacrifice necessary to obtain those benefits, as determined by the customer; reflects the willingness of customers to actually buy a product.

y. The part of the marketing mix that involves establishing a price for the product based on the demand for the product and the cost of producing it.

z. The part of the marketing mix that involves deciding how many stores and which specific wholesalers and retailers will handle the product in a geographic area.

aa. A marketing research method in which an interviewer interacts with respondents, either in person or by mail, to obtain facts, opinions, and attitudes.

bb. A marketing research method in which the investigator changes one or more variables—price, packaging, design, shelf space, advertising theme, or advertising expenditures—while observing the effects of these changes on another variable (usually sales).

cc. The customer's feeling that a product has met or exceeded expectations.

dd. A strategy that focuses on forging long-term partnerships with customers by offering value and providing customer satisfaction.

ee. The differentiation of markets by personality or lifestyle.

ff. The condition of having beliefs or knowledge that are internally inconsistent or that disagree with one's behavior.

gg. A marketing research method in which the investigator monitors respondents' actions without interacting directly with the respondents; for example, by using cash registers with scanners.

hh. The creation of a large computerized file of the profiles and purchase patterns of customers and potential customers; usually required for successful micromarketing.

ii. An interactive, flexible, computerized information system that allows managers to make decisions quickly and accurately; used to conduct sales analyses, forecast sales, evaluate advertising, analyze product lines, and keep tabs on market trends and competitors' actions.

jj. The application of marketing techniques to social issues and causes.

CRITICAL THINKING EXERCISES

1. P.O.V. (Point of View)

Directions: In this exercise you will be asked to provide your personal opinion regarding some of the topics discussed in the chapter. At the completion of this exercise, your instructor may wish to poll the entire class regarding their responses.

a. In an effort to create a competitive or differential advantage, many companies overwhelm potential customers with information, leading to "mental gridlock." Service providers, such as cell phone companies and department stores, barrage consumers with so many confusing variations of products, services, and brands that many people cannot make meaningful purchasing decisions.

Agree ✓   Disagree ~~✗~~

Explain:

Some merchendise may consist of similarities in
product and price leaving customers confused and
unable to decide correctly or effectively.

b. Market segmentation, which is the process of separating, identifying, and evaluating the layers of a market to design a marketing mix, is merely another form of discrimination. Firms target products, such as cigarettes and expensive clothing, to individuals who can ill-afford to buy them. The government should step in to limit its use by firms.

Agree _____   Disagree ✓

2. Using the Internet

Directions: Marketing research is an important element in understanding consumer tastes. In the broadcast media, such as radio and television, advertisers are always interested in reaching as many people in their target audience as possible. Click on **http://www.nielsenmedia.com**.

a. What service(s) does this company provide and what is the top priority that they describe? → _They provide its service to a complex & highly competitive marketplace._

Their a research for television ratings & audience estimates which provide an estimate of audience size & competition

b. Click on Who They Are and What They Do. What are measurement activities do they carry out that are related to national and local markets?

Nielsen TV ratings provide an estimate of the audience for just about every program that can be seen on T.V.

c. Click on What TV Ratings Really Mean and discuss their relevance for advertisers.

3. Writing Skills

Directions: Write a short motivational speech to your marketing department discussing how consumers make buying decisions. Include and explain individual and social factors. Use at least three terms from Review Your Key Terms.

Consumers make buying decisions by guaranteeing customer satisfaction. In addition, producing a product or service at a lower cost then other competitors while maintaining satisfactory profit margins is considered a cost competitive advantage. A firms ability to target and effectively serve a single segment of the market within a limited geographic area is a niche competitive advantage, which all of the above include individual and social factors. That is factors within the consumer and are unique to each other that includes perceptions, beliefs and attitudes, values, learning, self concept, and personality.

NOTES ON CHAPTER 13

Also, the decision-making process and all interactions between a consumer and the external environment includes, opinions of leaders, social class and culture.

Chapter 14

Developing Quality Products at the Right Price

OUTLINE

MULTIPLE CHOICE

Directions: Place the letter of the response that best completes the questions that follow in the blank space at the left.

>lg 1   **What is a product and how is it classified?**

_____   1. A product is defined as:
   a. a good only, including its tangible attributes, that create value
   b. a service only, including its intangible attributes, that create value
   c. only tangible goods and services, regardless of their value creation
   d. any good or service, along with its perceived attributes and benefits, that create value for the customer

_____   2. Consumer nondurables:
   a. last for a long time
   b. are generally purchased first by industrial users and then resold to consumers
   c. are products that get used up
   d. are usually unknown to the potential buyer or are not actively sought by consumers

_____   3. Relatively inexpensive items that require little shopping effort are called:
   a. shopping products   **c.** specialty products
   b. convenience products   **d.** unsought products

_____   4. Products for which consumers shop long and hard and for which they refuse to accept substitutes are known as:
   a. shopping products   **c.** specialty products
   b. convenience products   **d.** unsought products

_____   5. Capital products are:
   a. usually large, expensive items with a long life span
   b. typically small, relatively inexpensive items that usually have a life span of less than one year
   c. products for which consumers search long and hard and for which they refuse to accept substitutes
   d. bought only after a brand-to-brand and store-to-store comparison of price, suitability, and style

>lg 2   **How does branding distinguish a product from its competitors?**

_____   6. A legally exclusive design, name, or other identifying mark associated with a company's brand is called a:
   a. product ID mark   **c.** servicemark
   b. patentmark   **d.** trademark

_____   7. Brand equity refers to:
   a. the value of company and brand names
   b. the product identifier for a company's products
   c. marks used to identify a company's products and services
   d. dominant consumer brand names

_____ 8. A brand so dominant in consumers' minds that is thought of immediately when a product category, use, attribute, or customer benefit is mentioned is called a:
   a. leader brand   **c.** master brand
   b. equity product   **d.** distinguished brand

_____ 9. Manufacturer brands:
   a. are sold nationally
   b. are owned by national or regional manufacturers and are widely distributed
   c. must be owned by nationwide or international manufacturers in order to fall into this brand category
   d. always carry the name of the wholesaler or retailer who carries them

>lg 3   What are the functions of packaging?

_____ 10. A product's packaging should:
   a. protect the product from breaking or spoiling
   b. be easy to ship, store, and stack on a shelf
   c. help promote the product by providing clear brand identification and information about the product's features
   d. all of these answers are correct

_____ 11. An express warranty:
   a. ranges from simple statements such as those about product content to extensive documentation that accompanies a product
   b. is an unwritten guarantee that a product is fit for the purpose for which it was sold
   c. means the manufacturer must meet certain minimum standards, within a reasonable amount of time and without charge and/or provide replacement for defective products after a reasonable attempt to repair them
   d. requires manufacturers to provide "speedy" refunds

_____ 12. An implied warranty:
   a. ranges from simple statements such as those about product content to extensive documentation that accompanies a product
   b. is an unwritten guarantee that a product is fit for the purpose for which it was sold
   c. means the manufacturer must meet certain minimum standards, within a reasonable amount of time and without charge and/or provide replacement for defective products after a reasonable attempt to repair them
   d. requires manufacturers to provide "speedy" refunds

_____ 13. A full warranty:
   a. ranges from simple statements such as those about product content to extensive documentation that accompanies a product
   b. is an unwritten guarantee that a product is fit for the purpose for which it was sold
   c. means the manufacturer must meet certain minimum standards, within a reasonable amount of time and without charge and/or provide replacement for defective products after a reasonable attempt to repair them
   d. requires manufacturers to provide "speedy" refunds

>lg 4   How do organizations create new products?

_____ 14. Line extension consists of:
   a. setting up a committee to generate new product ideas
   b. developing a new flavor, size, or model using an existing product category
   c. using venture teams for major new product development tasks
   d. isolating new product teams from day-to-day activities of the organization so that they can think and be creative

_____ 15. Bringing consumers together to find out how they feel about a product, concept, idea, or organization, involves using:
a. line extension groups
b. venture team groups
c. new product department team groups
d. focus groups

_____ 16. The individual who develops and implements a complete strategy and marketing program for a particular product or brand is called a:
a. test marketer
b. venture manager
c. conceptualizer
d. product manager

>lg 5

What are the stages of the product life cycle?

_____ 17. The pattern of sales and profits over time for a product or product category is known as the:
a. product management phase
b. focus group cycle
c. brainstorming phase
d. product life cycle

_____ 18. During the growth stage of the product life cycle:
a. sales rise at an increasing rate, profits are healthy, and many competitors enter the market
b. frequent production modifications are made, distribution is limited, and heavy promotion takes place
c. sales and profits fall
d. sales continue to mount—but at a decreasing rate

_____ 19. During the maturity stage of the product life cycle:
a. sales rise at an increasing rate, profits are healthy, and many competitors enter the market
b. frequent production modifications are made, distribution is limited, and heavy promotion takes place
c. sales and profits fall
d. sales continue to mount—but at a decreasing rate

_____ 20. During the decline stage of the product life cycle:
a. sales rise at an increasing rate, profits are healthy, and many competitors enter the market
b. frequent production modifications are made, distribution is limited, and heavy promotion takes place
c. sales and profits fall
d. sales continue to mount—but at a decreasing rate

>lg 6

What is the role of pricing in marketing?

_____ 21. The pricing objective where a firm seeks a target return on investment:
a. means producing a product as long as the revenue from selling it exceeds the cost of producing it
b. occurs where a price is set to give the company the desired profitability in terms of return on its money
c. usually includes offering the target market a high quality product so customers get a high return for the money they have spent
d. must include barter so that goods can be exchanged to avoid taxation of income from sales

_____ **22.** Value pricing means:

    a. offering the target market a high quality product so customers get a high return for the money they have spent

    b. providing a perceived value at the time a transaction is made

    c. maximizing the value of gross revenue from sales

    d. setting revenue targets based upon price so that a target return on investment can be realized

_____ **23.** Perceived value refers to:

    a. the expected satisfaction you will receive from a product based upon the price paid

    b. the actual satisfaction you will receive from a product once you own it

    c. the price you paid for a product

    d. all of these answers are correct

>lg 7   How are product prices determined?

_____ **24.** Markup is the:

    a. difference between selling price and profit after taxes

    b. expense that is incurred when a product is manufactured

    c. investment made in equipment that must be purchased to manufacture a product

    d. amount added to the cost to cover expenses and leave a profit

_____ **25.** The following influences markups:

    a. stock turnover   **c.** tradition

    b. competition   **d.** all of these answers are correct

_____ **26.** Total cost is:

    a. the selling price per unit times the number of units sold

    b. all fixed costs and variable costs

    c. selling price per unit minus the variable costs per unit

    d. total revenue minus total cost

_____ **27.** Total revenue is:

    a. the selling price per unit times the number of units sold

    b. all fixed costs and variable costs

    c. selling price per unit minus the variable costs per unit

    d. total revenue minus total cost

>lg 8   What strategies are used for pricing new products?

_____ **28.** A pricing strategy that involves offering new products at low prices in the hope of achieving a large sales volume is called:

    a. price skimming   **c.** penetration pricing

    b. bundling   **d.** odd-even pricing

_____ **29.** A pricing strategy that retailers believe signals to consumers that the price is at the lowest level possible is:

    a. bundling   **c.** odd-numbered pricing

    b. prestige pricing   **d.** penetration pricing

_____ **30.** The strategy of raising the price of a product so consumers will perceive it as being of higher quality is known as:

    a. bundling   **c.** odd-numbered pricing

    b. prestige pricing   **d.** penetration pricing

_____ 31. Grouping two or more products together and pricing them as a single product is called:

a. bundling
c. odd-numbered pricing
b. prestige pricing
d. penetration pricing

>lg 9   **What trends are occurring in products and pricing?**

_____ 32. Brand recognition can be built using:

a. public relations
b. the Internet to increase customer interaction
c. product giveaways
d. all of these answers are correct

_____ 33. Tailoring mass-market goods and services to the unique needs of the individual is known as:

a. technology-based manufacturing
b. computer-assisted automation
c. mass customization
d. computer-assisted design

TRUE/FALSE

Directions: Place a T or an F in the space provided to the left of each question to indicate whether it is True or False.

>lg 1   **What is a product and how is it classified?**

_____ 1. The term product is used exclusively to define any good along with its perceived attributes and benefits that create value for the customer.

_____ 2. Because most things sold are a blend of goods and services, the term product can be used to refer to both.

_____ 3. Consumer nondurables are those consumer products that last for a long time and are indestructible.

_____ 4. Capital products are typically large, durable, and expensive items with a long life span.

_____ 5. Large, expensive capital items that determine the nature, scope, and efficiency of a company are know as installations.

>lg 2   **How does branding distinguish a product from its competitors?**

_____ 6. Brand equity is the legally exclusive design, name, or other identifying mark associated with a company's brand.

_____ 7. A brand that has high awareness, perceived quality, and brand loyalty is considered a master brand.

_____ 8. By building brand loyalty, a firm can protect its share of a market, discourage new competitors, and thus prolong the brand's life.

_____ 9. Manufacturers' brands are owned by national or regional manufacturers and are widely distributed, while dealer brands carry the name of the wholesaler or retailer rather than that of the manufacturer.

>lg 3 **What are the functions of packaging?**

_____ **10.** Implied warranties can guarantee the makeup of the content of an item as well as indicate the degree of performance to be expected by the consumer.

_____ **11.** An implied warranty is an unwritten guarantee that the product is fit for the purpose for which it was sold.

_____ **12.** An implied warranty does not exist under the Uniform Commercial Code.

>lg 4 **How do organizations create new products?**

_____ **13.** When a firm introduces a product that has a new brand name and is in a product category that is new to the organization, it is practicing line extension.

_____ **14.** The goal of focus group research is to learn and understand what people have to say about a product or service and why they say it.

_____ **15.** Brainstorming is involved with the evaluation of new product ideas that have been generated by groups within the firm.

_____ **16.** Prior to the development of product prototypes, a promotional strategy is developed to communicate the nature of the new product to potential customers.

_____ **17.** A product manager develops and implements a complete strategy and marketing program for a specific brand or product.

>lg 5 **What are the stages of the product life cycle?**

_____ **18.** In the growth stage of the product life cycle, the product will undergo frequent modifications, limited distribution, and heavy promotion.

_____ **19.** In the growth stage of the product life cycle, sales grow at an increasing rate, profits are healthy, and many competitors enter the market.

_____ **20.** The rate of decline for a product is governed by two factors: the rate of change in consumer tastes and the rate at which new products enter the market.

_____ **21.** At the maturity stage of the product life cycle, sales continue to grow at an increasing rate, as do profits.

>lg 6 **What is the role of pricing in marketing?**

_____ **22.** The price you pay for a product is based on the expected satisfaction you will receive and not necessarily from the actual satisfaction you will receive.

_____ **23.** Price depends upon the actual value of a product to customers and not on the perceived value to customers.

_____ **24.** Three common pricing objectives are, maximizing profits, achieving a target return on the investment, and offering a good value at a fair price.

_____ **25.** A net profit of $350,000 on costs of $1,000,000 to develop, launch, and market a new product, yields a return on investment of 35 percent.

_____ **26.** Value pricing means that a product is of high quality but sells at a high price.

>lg 7 **How are product prices determined?**

_____ **27.** Setting the retail price at _cost plus markup_ is known as markup pricing.

_____ **28.** The breakeven point for a product is attained when cost plus markup equals selling price.

_____ 29. The point at which all costs are covered and additional sales result in a profit is known as the breakeven point.

>lg 8   **What strategies are used for pricing new products?**

_____ 30. Penetration pricing involves pricing a new product with a high price and lowering the price over time.

_____ 31. When pursuing a strategy of penetration pricing, a company offers new products at a low price in the hope of achieving a large sales volume.

_____ 32. Items that are not well known are usually leader priced in order to appeal to many customers.

_____ 33. A bundling strategy can be used to reach a segment of the market that the products, if sold separately, would not reach as effectively.

_____ 34. Psychological pricing is a strategy of raising the price of a product so consumers will perceive it as being of higher quality.

_____ 35. Prestige pricing is common where high prices indicate high status.

>lg 9   **What trends are occurring in products and pricing?**

_____ 36. The use of public relations is not a recommended strategy to build brand recognition.

_____ 37. Giveaways are costly and cannot be used effectively to build brand loyalty.

_____ 38. Mass customization involves tailoring mass-market goods and services to the unique needs of the individuals who buy them.

ENHANCE YOUR VOCABULARY

Aficionados	Devotee
Connotation	Something suggested by a word or thing; implication
Contraption	A mechanical device, gadget
Cutting-edge technology	State-of-the-art application of science
Dialogue	A composition in which two or more characters are represented as conversing
Disgruntled	To make ill-humored or discontented
Fanatically	Marked by excessive enthusiasm and often intense uncritical devotion
Fetched	To go or come after and bring or take back
Prolong	To lengthen in time, continue
Surpassing	Greatly exceeding others

Directions: Select the definition in Column B that best defines the word in Column A.

	Column A		Column B
_____	1. Dialogue	a.	Implication
_____	2. Cutting-edge technology	b.	A conversation with two or more characters
_____	3. Aficionados	c.	To go after and bring back
_____	4. Prolong	d.	A devotee
_____	5. Contraption	e.	Greatly exceeding others
_____	6. Disgruntled	f.	Excessive enthusiasm
_____	7. Connotation	g.	State-of-the art application of science

_____	**8.** Surpassing	**h.**	A mechanical device, gadget
_____	**9.** Fanatically	**i.**	To make ill-humored or discontented
_____	**10.** Fetched	**j.**	To lengthen in time

REVIEW YOUR KEY TERMS

Directions: Select the definition in Column B that best defines the word in Column A.

Column A

_____ 1. Product

_____ 2. Capital products

_____ 3. Trademark

_____ 4. Warranty

_____ 5. Test-marketing

_____ 6. Line extension

_____ 7. Unsought products

_____ 8. Full warranty

_____ 9. Shopping products

_____ 10. Manufacturer brands

_____ 11. Product manager

_____ 12. Brand

_____ 13. Brand loyalty

_____ 14. Dealer brands

_____ 15. Product life cycle

_____ 16. Brainstorming

Column B

a. A brand so dominant that consumers think of it immediately when a product category, use, attribute, or customer benefit is mentioned.

b. Items that are bought after considerable planning including brand-to-brand and store-to-store comparisons of price, suitability, and style.

c. Large, expensive items with a long life span that are purchased by businesses for use in making other products or providing a service.

d. A guarantee that the manufacturer will meet certain minimum standards, including repairing any defects "within a reasonable time and without charge" or replacing the merchandise or providing a full refund if the product does not work "after a reasonable number of attempts" at repair.

e. In marketing, any good or service, along with its perceived attributes and benefits, that creates value for the customer.

f. Brands that are owned by national or regional manufacturers and widely distributed; also called national brands.

g. A company's product identifier that distinguishes the company's products from those of its competitors.

h. Brands that carry the name of the wholesaler or retailer rather than the name of the manufacturer.

i. A consumer's preference for a particular brand.

j. The process of testing a new product among potential users.

k. Products that either are unknown to the potential buyer or are known but the buyer does not actively seek them.

l. A written guarantee about a product such as that it contains certain materials, will perform a certain way, or is otherwise fit for the purpose for which it was sold.

m. Relatively inexpensive items that require little shopping effort and are purchased routinely without planning.

n. A method of generating ideas in which group members suggest as many possibilities as they can without criticizing or evaluating any of the suggestions; used to generate ideas for new products.

o. Products that carry no brand name, come in plain containers, and sell for much less than brand-name products.

p. A new flavor, size, or model using an existing brand in an existing category.

_____ **17.** Generic products

q. The person who develops and implements a complete strategy and marketing program for a specific product or brand.

_____ **18.** Convenience products

r. Items for which consumers search long and hard and for which they refuse to accept substitutes.

_____ **19.** Expense items

s. The value of company and brand names.

_____ **20.** Implied warranty

t. The pattern of sales and profits over time for a product or product category; consists of introductory, growth, maturity, and decline stages.

_____ **21.** Total profit

u. A flexible manufacturing technique in which mass-market goods and services are tailored to the unique needs of the individuals who buy them.

_____ **22.** Express warranty

v. A guarantee of the quality of a good or service.

_____ **23.** Brand equity

w. An unwritten guarantee that a product is fit for the purpose for which it is sold.

_____ **24.** Master brand

x. Items, purchased by businesses, that are smaller and less expensive than capital products and usually have a life span of less than one year.

_____ **25.** Specialty products

y. The legally exclusive design, name, or other identifying mark associated with a company's brand.

_____ **26.** Profit maximization

z. The sum of the fixed costs and the variable costs.

_____ **27.** Total cost

aa. A pricing objective that entails getting the largest possible profit from a product by producing the product as long as the revenue from selling it exceeds the cost of producing it.

_____ **28.** Mass customization

bb. The selling price per unit (revenue) minus the variable costs per unit.

_____ **29.** Price skimming

cc. A pricing objective where the price of a product is set so as to give the company the desired profitability in terms of return on its money.

_____ **30.** Breakeven point

dd. The selling price per unit times the number of units sold.

_____ **31.** Target return on investment

ee. Costs that change with different levels of output; for example, wages and costs of raw materials.

_____ **32.** Loss leader

ff. Total revenue minus total cost.

_____ **33.** Total revenue

gg. The strategy of increasing the price of a product so that consumers will perceive it as being of higher quality, status, or value.

_____ **34.** Fixed-cost contribution

hh. A pricing strategy in which the target market is offered a high-quality product at a fair price and with good service.

_____ **35.** Penetration pricing

ii. The strategy of setting a price at an odd number to connote a bargain and an even number to suggest quality.

_____ **36.** Value pricing

jj. Costs that do not vary with different levels of output; for example, rent.

_____ **37.** Variable costs

kk. A method of pricing in which a certain percentage (the markup) is added to the product's cost to arrive at the price.

_____ **38.** Prestige pricing

ll. The strategy of introducing a product with a high initial price and lowering the price over time as the product moves through its life cycle.

_____ **39.** Markup pricing

mm. The price at which a product's costs are covered, so additional sales result in profit.

_____ **40.** Leader pricing

nn. A product priced below cost as part of a pricing strategy.

_____ **41.** Fixed costs

oo. The strategy of grouping two or more related products together and pricing them as a single product.

_____ **42.** Odd-even (psychological) pricing

pp. The strategy of selling new products at low prices in the hope of achieving a large sales volume.

_____ **43.** Bundling

qq. The strategy of pricing products below the normal markup or even below cost to attract customers to a store where they would not otherwise shop.

CRITICAL THINKING EXERCISES

1. P.O.V. (Point of View)

Directions: In this exercise you will be asked to provide your personal opinion regarding some of the topics discussed in the chapter. At the completion of this exercise, your instructor may wish to poll the entire class regarding their responses.

    a. Price skimming is unfair to consumers because those who purchase the product or service when it is first offered for sale pay an unreasonably high price, even though the item is clearly not worth the price being charged. Marketers should not be 'playing games' with consumers in an effort to take away their hard-earned money.

    Agree _____   Disagree _____

    Explain:

_____

_____

_____

_____

    b. Marketing strategies, such as new packaging and warranties, serve to distinguish a product from others and are said to increase their value to customers. However, these strategies often add to the cost of the item. It would be better if customers were given a choice of low-cost packaging and the right to refuse warranties, so that the goods could be purchased at lower prices.

    Agree _____   Disagree _____

    Explain:

_____

_____

_____

_____

2. Using the Internet

Directions: It is widely held that the use of brand names helps consumers to identify and differentiate products. Click on **http://www.corebrand.com** and then proceed to the next page by clicking on the arrow in the lower left-hand corner of the Corporate Branding home page.

    a. Describe the services that Corporate Branding provides.

    b. Click on About Brands and summarize the company's view of branding as a business tool.

    c. Click on Our Services and summarize the four services shown – intelligence, strategy, communications, and management.

    d. Do you agree that the view of branding held by Corporate Branding is essential for the success of a business? Why?

3. Writing Skills

Directions: The head of your division asks you to write a report on the various strategies used for pricing the new product they are considering marketing – Skippy Scooters. Outline your report first, and don't forget to use headings and subheadings where appropriate.

Chapter 15

Distributing Products in a Timely and Efficient Manner

OUTLINE

MULTIPLE CHOICE

Directions: Place the letter of the response that best completes the questions that follow in the blank space at the left.

>lg 1   **What are physical distribution (logistics) and logistics management?**

_____   1. Physical distribution is:
  a. usually the responsibility of the production department
  b. not an activity included in the supply chain
  c. the movement of products from the producer or manufacturer to industrial users and consumers
  d. not concerned with logistics

_____   2. Supply chain management:
  a. minimizes inventory and moves goods efficiently from producers to ultimate users
  b. involves the movement of materials and products within plants and warehouses
  c. oversees the movement of raw materials between plants
  d. concerns the movement of finished goods within plants

_____   3. Industrial distributors:
  a. sell finished goods to retailers, manufacturers, and institutions
  b. sell goods to industries and consumers for their own consumption
  c. buy products for internal use or for producing other products
  d. are independent wholesalers that buy related product lines from many manufacturers and sell them to industrial users

>lg 2   **What are distribution channels and their functions?**

_____   4. Allocating consists of:
  a. storing goods in safe places
  b. bringing dissimilar products together
  c. setting up assortments of goods
  d. breaking similar products into smaller and smaller lots

_____   5. Bringing similar stocks together into a larger quantity is called:
  a. sorting out   **c.** allocating
  b. accumulating   **d.** breaking bulk

_____   6. A useful rule to remember regarding channel members is:
  a. go-betweens create higher prices
  b. as channel members increase, so does the complexity of the product or service
  c. although channel members can be eliminated, their functions cannot
  d. use of channel members decreases profit for manufacturers

>lg 3   **How can channels be organized?**

_____   7. In a corporate distribution system:
  a. a manufacturer acquires a marketing intermediary closer to wholesalers or retailers
  b. one firm owns the entire channel of distribution
  c. firms are aligned in a hierarchy
  d. a strong organization takes over and sets channel policies

      8. When forward integration occurs:
          a. a manufacturer acquires a marketing intermediary closer to wholesalers or retailers
          b. one firm owns the entire channel of distribution
          c. firms are aligned in a hierarchy
          d. a strong organization takes over and sets channel policies

      9. In a vertical marketing system:
          a. a manufacturer acquires a marketing intermediary closer to wholesalers or retailers
          b. one firm owns the entire channel of distribution
          c. firms are aligned in a hierarchy
          d. a strong organization takes over and sets channel policies

>lg 4   **When would a marketer use exclusive, selective, or intensive distribution?**

      10. In exclusive distribution:
          a. only items that are in strong demand can be distributed
          b. a limited number of dealers (more than one or two) in an area handle a product
          c. a manufacturer wants to sell its products everywhere there are potential customers
          d. none of these answers is correct

      11. In selective distribution:
          a. only items that are in strong demand can be distributed
          b. a limited number of dealers (more than one or two) in an area handle a product
          c a manufacturer wants to sell its products everywhere there are potential customers
          d. none of these answers is correct

      12. In intensive distribution:
          a. only items that are in strong demand can be distributed
          b. a limited number of dealers (more than one or two) in an area handle a product
          c. a manufacturer wants to sell its products everywhere there are potential customers
          d. none of these answers is correct

>lg 5   **What is wholesaling, and what are the types of wholesalers?**

      13. A manufacturer's representative:
          a. buys goods from manufacturers and resells them to business, government agencies, other wholesalers, or retailers
          b. performs only a few of the full-service merchant wholesaler's activities
          c. performs all functions required by a manufacturer
          d. is an independent agent who represents noncompeting manufacturers

      14. A full-service wholesaler:
          a. buys goods from manufacturers and resells them to business, government agencies, other wholesalers, or retailers
          b. performs only a few of the full-service merchant wholesaler's activities
          c. performs all functions required by a manufacturer
          d. is an independent agent who represents noncompeting manufacturers

_____ **15.** A limited-service merchant wholesaler:
  a. buys goods from manufacturers and resells them to business, government agencies, other wholesalers, or retailers
  b. performs only a few of the full-service merchant wholesaler's activities
  c. performs all functions required by a manufacturer
  d. is an independent agent who represents noncompeting manufacturers

_____ **16.** A merchant wholesaler:
  a. buys goods from manufacturers and resells them to business, government agencies, other wholesalers, or retailers
  b. performs only a few of the full-service merchant wholesaler's activities
  c. performs all functions required by a manufacturer
  d. is an independent agent who represents noncompeting manufacturers

>lg 6

What are the different kinds of retail operations?

_____ **17.** A major category of retail operation is:
  a. direct selling   **c.** nonstore retailing
  b. vending   **d.** home shopping networks

_____ **18.** A major category of retail operation is:
  a. face-to-face contact   **c.** direct sales
  b. vending machine selling **d.** in-store retailing

>lg 7

What are the components of a successful retailing strategy?

_____ **19.** The first and foremost task in developing a retail strategy is:
  a. the product offering
  b. to define the target market
  c. bundling the product assortment
  d. the product mix

_____ **20.** Efficient consumer response:
  a. is the computer-to-computer exchange of information regarding such things as shipping notifications, inventory data, and forecasts
  b. involves the quick response to requests for manufacturers' rebates by consumers
  c. allows the retailer to retrieve merchandise for customers from inventory
  d. provides large discounts to consumers who respond to requests to purchase merchandise quickly

_____ **21.** The second element in determining a retail strategy is:
  a. the product offering   **c.** bundling the product
  b. to define the target market **d.** the retail base

_____ **22.** Choosing a location for a retail operation should be based on the:
  a. political climate   **c.** local economy
  b. nature of competition   **d.** all of these answers are correct

>lg 8

What are functions of physical distribution?

_____ **23.** The decision of where to put a warehouse is:
  a. determined by those firms that specialize in warehousing
  b. not significant in terms of the overall retail strategy
  c. mostly a matter of deciding which markets will be served and where production facilities will be located
  d. none of these answers is correct

_____ **24.** A special form of warehouse which specializes in changing the size of shipments rather than storing goods is known as a:
   a. transport center   **c.** distribution center
   b. accessibility warehouse   **d.** reliability junction center

>lg 9   **What are the trends in distribution?**

_____ **25.** The practice of buying all of a competitor's merchandise from the shelves of a retailer and replacing them with those that you manufacture is known as a:
   a. buyout   **c.** wipeout
   b. stocklift   **d.** shakedown

_____ **26.** Service distribution focuses on:
   a. managing service capacity
   b. minimizing wait times
   c. improving delivery through new distribution channels
   d. all of the answers are correct

TRUE/FALSE

Directions: Place a T or an F in the space provided to the left of each question to indicate whether it is True or False.

>lg 1   **What are physical distribution (logistics) and logistics management?**

_____ **1.** Physical distribution activities are usually the responsibility of the production department and are part of the large series of activities included in the supply chain.

_____ **2.** Logistics is the movement of products from the producer or manufacturer to industrial users and consumers.

_____ **3.** Industrial distributors are firms that sell finished goods to retailers, manufacturers, and institutions.

_____ **4.** Wholesalers are independent distributors that buy related product lines from many manufacturers and sell them to industrial users.

>lg 2   **What are distribution channels and their functions?**

_____ **5.** Channels make distribution more complex by increasing the number of transactions required to get a product from the manufacturer to the consumer.

_____ **6.** Marketing intermediaries are organizations that assist in moving goods and services from producers to end users and consumers.

_____ **7.** Agents are entities that bring buyers and sellers together, and brokers are sales representatives of manufacturers and wholesalers.

_____ **8.** The sorting function as practiced in a distribution channel includes accumulating, allocating, and sorting out.

_____ **9.** A useful rule that relates to the existence of distribution channels is that, although channel members can be eliminated, their functions cannot.

>lg 3   **How can channels be organized?**

_____ **10.** In a corporate distribution system, a manufacturer acquires a marketing intermediary closer to the customer.

_____ **11.** Backward integration occurs when a wholesaler or retailer gains control over the production process.

_____ **12.** A contractual distribution system is a network of independent firms at different levels that coordinate their distribution activities through a written contract.

>lg 4   When would a marketer use exclusive, selective, or intensive distribution?

_____ **13.** Exclusive distribution, where one or two dealers in an area market a product, can be successful only for items that are in strong demand.

_____ **14.** Selective distribution involves selling a product everywhere there are potential customers.

_____ **15.** Intensive distribution occurs when a manufacturer chooses a limited number of dealers (but more than one or two) in an area to sell its products.

>lg 5   What is wholesaling, and what are the types of wholesalers?

_____ **16.** Channel members that buy finished products from manufacturers and sell them to retailers are known as wholesalers.

_____ **17.** A merchant wholesaler is an independent agent that represents competing manufacturers when selling goods to retailers.

_____ **18.** A cash and carry wholesaler is a limited-service merchant wholesaler who does not offer credit to customers.

>lg 6   What are the different kinds of retail operations?

_____ **19.** Vending, direct selling, direct-response marketing, home shopping networks, and Internet retailing are all forms of nonstore selling.

_____ **20.** Direct selling involves face-to-face contact between the buyer and seller in a retail store.

_____ **21.** Direct-response marketing is carried out through media such as catalogs, television, newspapers, and radio.

>lg 7   What are the components of a successful retailing strategy?

_____ **22.** When defining a target market, a retailer should be concerned initially with market segmentation.

_____ **23.** Target markets in retailing are usually defined by psychographics.

_____ **24.** Retailers decide what to sell on the basis of what goods producers and wholesalers seek to supply them with.

_____ **25.** Electronic data interchange is at the heart of ECR, which involves the use of new methods of managing inventory and streamlining the way products are moved from supplier to distributor to retailer.

>lg 8   What are the functions of physical distribution?

_____ **26.** A typical storage warehouse specializes in changing shipment sizes and holding them for delivery later on.

_____ **27.** Distribution centers are the wave of the future because they specialize in quickly sorting merchandise and delivering it to retail stores.

_____ **28.** Air, as a mode of transportation for goods, provides the lowest transit time at the highest relative cost.

>lg 9 **What are the trends in distribution?**

_____ **29.** A stocklift involves one manufacturer purchasing all of another manufacturer's products from a retailer, and then restocking the emptied shelves with their own goods.

_____ **30.** It is extremely difficult to transfer the skills, techniques, and strategies used to manage goods inventories to the management of service sector inventories.

ENHANCE YOUR VOCABULARY

Configure	The arrangement of the parts or elements of something
Constraints	The state of being checked, restricted, or compelled to avoid or perform some action
Density	The amount of something per unit measure; impenetrability; stupidity
Detract	To diminish the importance, value or effectiveness of something
Entities	Something that exists independently or self-contained existence
Implemented	Carried out, accomplished
Queries	Question, inquiry, a question in the mind; doubt; reservation
Strategy	A careful plan or method
Vendor	One who sells; seller
Versions	An account or description from a particular point of view, especially as contrasted with another account

Directions: Select the definition in Column B that best defines the word in column A

	Column A		Column B
_____	1. Detract	a.	The arrangement of the parts of something
_____	2. Strategy	b.	One who sells; seller
_____	3. Versions	c.	To diminish the importance of
_____	4. Density	d.	Restrictions
_____	5. Queries	e.	Carried out, accomplished
_____	6. Entities	f.	A careful plan
_____	7. Configure	g.	The amount of something per unit
_____	8. Vendor	h.	A description from a particular point of view
_____	9. Constraints	i.	Self-contained existence
_____	10. Implemented	j.	Question; inquiry; reservation

REVIEW YOUR KEY TERMS

Directions: Select the definition in Column B that best defines the word in Column A.

	Column A		Column B
_____	1. Supply chain management	a.	Firms that sell finished goods to retailers, manufacturers, and institutions.
_____	2. Marketing intermediaries	b.	Go-betweens that bring buyers and sellers together.

_____ 3. Distribution channel

c. The movement of products from the producer to industrial users and consumers.

_____ 4. Brokers

d. Independent wholesalers that buy related product lines from many manufacturers and sell them to industrial users.

_____ 5. Vertical marketing system

e. A producer; an organization that converts raw materials to finished products.

_____ 6. Merchant wholesaler

f. A vertical marketing system in which one firm owns the entire distribution channel.

_____ 7. Contractual distribution system

g. A vertical marketing system in which a strong organization takes over as leader and sets policies for the distribution channel.

_____ 8. Wholesalers

h. The management of the activities in a supply chain to minimize inventory and move goods efficiently from producers to the ultimate user.

_____ 9. Intensive distribution

i. A vertical marketing system in which a network of independent firms at different levels (manufacturer, wholesaler, retailer) coordinate their distribution activities through a written contract.

_____ 10. Corporate distribution system

j. An institution that buys goods from manufacturers and resells them to businesses, government agencies, other wholesalers, or retailers.

_____ 11. Stocklift (buyback)

k. An organized, formal distribution channel in which firms are aligned in a hierarchy from manufacturer to wholesaler to retailer.

_____ 12. Full-service merchant wholesalers

l. The management of the physical distribution process; involves managing the movement of raw materials, the movement of materials and products within plants and warehouses, and the movement of finished goods to intermediaries and buyers.

_____ 13. Manufacturers' representatives (manufacturers' agents)

m. Computer-to-computer exchange of information, including automatic shipping notifications, invoices, inventory data, and forecasts; used in efficient consumer response systems.

_____ 14. Forward integration

n. A distribution system in which a manufacturer tries to sell its products wherever there are potential customers.

_____ 15. Limited-service merchant

o. Wholesalers that provide many services for their clients, such as providing credit, offering promotional and technical advice, storing and delivering merchandise, or providing installation and repairs.

_____ 16. Physical distribution (logistics)

p. The process of breaking large shipments of similar products into smaller, more usable lots that can be sold to retailers at the wholesale level.

_____ 17. Retailers

q. A system of managing inventory in which the supplier manages the distributor's inventory, thereby reversing the traditional arrangement; helps the supplier focus its manufacturing efforts to ensure that the right products will be delivered to the right places at the right time and thus helps the distributor improve sales.

_____ 18. Backward integration

r. A distribution system in which a manufacturer selects a limited number of dealers in an area (but more than one or two) to market its products.

_____ 19. Exclusive distribution

s. The acquisition by a manufacturer of a marketing intermediary closer to the customer, such as a wholesaler or retailer.

_____ **20.** Logistics management

t. The series of marketing entities through which goods and services pass on their way from producers to end users and consumers.

_____ **21.** Agents

u. Firms that sell goods to consumers and to industrial users for their own consumption.

_____ **22.** Cash and carry wholesaler

v. Wholesalers that typically carry a limited line of fast-moving merchandise and do not offer many services to their clients.

_____ **23.** Distribution centers

w. Organizations that assist in moving goods and services from producers to end users and consumers.

_____ **24.** Efficient consumer response (ECR)

x. A distribution system in which a manufacturer selects only one or two dealers in an area to market its products.

_____ **25.** Administrative distribution system

y. The acquisition of the production process by a wholesaler or retailer.

_____ **26.** Vendor-managed inventory

z. The practice in which a company purchases all of a competitor's products from retailers and replaces the merchandise with its own products.

_____ **27.** Electronic data interchange (EDI)

aa. A limited-service merchant wholesaler that does not offer credit or delivery services.

_____ **28.** Manufacturer

bb. Warehouses that specialize in changing shipment sizes, rather than in storing goods.

_____ **29.** Breaking bulk

cc. Sales representatives of manufacturers and wholesalers.

_____ **30.** Industrial distributors

dd. Salespeople who represent noncompeting manufacturers; function as independent agents rather than as salaried employees of the manufacturers.

_____ **31.** Selective distribution

ee. A method of managing inventory and streamlining the movement of products from supplier to distributor to retailer; relies on electronic data interchange to communicate information such as automatic shipping notifications, invoices, inventory data, and forecasts.

CRITICAL THINKING EXERCISES

1. P.O.V. (Point of View)

Directions: In this exercise you will be asked to provide your personal opinion regarding some of the topics discussed in the chapter. At the completion of this exercise, your instructor may wish to poll the entire class regarding their responses.

a. Rather than conducting extensive market research and attempting to define and focus on a specific target market, retailers should attempt to utilize a 'shotgun strategy' – that is try to target all customers first, then determine whom their appropriate target market is.

Agree _____   Disagree _____

Explain:

_____

_____

_____

_____

b. A retailer that permits 'stocklifting, or 'buybacks' is engaged in an unethical business practice. This tactic, which occurs when a manufacturer purchases all the inventory of a competing firm's products from a retailer's shelves and replaces them with its own, should be made illegal because it represents a practice that is a restraint of trade.

Agree _____   Disagree _____

Explain:

_____

_____

_____

_____

2. Using the Internet

Directions: Go to **http://www.costco.com** and click on membership and then click on Why Become a Costco Member.

a. What image and promotional strategy has Costco used to achieve market penetration?
b. What market segmentation strategy has Costco adopted and how has its target market changed over the years?
c. Discuss the career opportunities that are available to those who seek employment at Costco.

3. Writing Skills

Directions: You work in your firm's human resources department hiring salespeople to sell your firm's goods. They are salaried, full-time employees, receiving expensive benefits packages. Write a memo to the Vice-President of Human Resources suggesting that we consider hiring sales people who represent manufacturers and function as independent sales agents for us, rather than our salaried employees. In this memo discuss the advantages and disadvantages of using manufacturers' representatives.

Chapter 16

Using Integrated Marketing Communications to Promote Products

OUTLINE

MULTIPLE CHOICE

Directions: Place the letter of the response that best completes the questions that follow in the blank space at the left.

>lg 1

What are the goals of promotional strategy?

_____   1. A set of unique features that the target market perceives as important and better than the competition's is called a(an):
   a. promotional advantage   **c.** absolute advantage
   b. advertising advantage   **d.** differential advantage

_____   2. An attempt by marketers to inform, persuade, or remind consumers and industrial users to engage in the exchange process is called:
   a. public relations   **c.** an advantage
   b. promotion   **d.** the mix

>lg 2

What is the promotional mix and what are its elements?

_____   3. Advertising is:
   a. the linking of organizational goals with key aspects of the public interest and the development of programs designed to earn public access and acceptance
   b. face-to-face presentation to a prospective buyer
   c. any paid form of nonpersonal promotion by an identified sponsor
   d. an activity designed to stimulate consumer buying that might include the use of coupons and samples, displays, shows and exhibitions, demonstrations, and other types of selling

_____   4. Public relations is:
   a. the linking of organizational goals with key aspects of the public interest and the development of programs designed to earn public access and acceptance
   b. face-to-face presentation to a prospective buyer
   c. any paid form of nonpersonal promotion by an identified sponsor
   d. an activity designed to stimulate consumer buying that might include the use of coupons and samples, displays, shows and exhibitions, demonstrations, and other types of selling

_____   5. Sales promotion is:
   a. the linking of organizational goals with key aspects of the public interest and the development of programs designed to earn public access and acceptance
   b. face-to-face presentation to a prospective buyer
   c. any paid form of nonpersonal promotion by an identified sponsor
   d. an activity designed to stimulate consumer buying that might include the use of coupons and samples, displays, shows and exhibitions, demonstrations, and other types of selling

_____   6. Personal selling is:
   a. the linking of organizational goals with key aspects of the public interest and the development of programs designed to earn public access and acceptance
   b. face-to-face presentation to a prospective buyer
   c. any paid form of nonpersonal promotion by an identified sponsor
   d. an activity designed to stimulate consumer buying that might include the use of coupons and samples, displays, shows and exhibitions, demonstrations, and other types of selling

>lg 3   **What are the types of advertising?**

_____ **7.** Product advertising:
   a. features a specific good or service
   b. compares a company's product with competing, named products
   c. is used to keep the product's name in the public's mind
   d. creates a positive image for a company and its ideals, services, and roles in the community

_____ **8.** Institutional advertising:
   a. features a specific good or service
   b. compares a company's product with competing, named products
   c. is used to keep the product's name in the public's mind
   d. creates a positive picture for a company and its ideals, services, and roles in the community

_____ **9.** Reminder advertising:
   a. features a specific good or service
   b. compares a company's product with competing, named products
   c. is used to keep the product's name in the public's mind
   d. creates a positive picture for a company and its ideals, services, and roles in the community

_____ **10.** Advertising that takes a stand on a social or economic issue is called:
   a. comparative advertising   **c.** advocacy advertising
   b. institutional advertising   **d.** corrective advertising

>lg 4   **What are the advertising media and how are they selected?**

_____ **11.** The channels through which advertising is carried to prospective customers are the:
   a. frequencies   **c.** advertising agencies
   b. audience selection processes   **d.** advertising media

_____ **12.** Reach is:
   a. the number of times an individual is exposed to a message
   b. the number of different target customers who are exposed to a commercial at least once during a specific period
   c. a medium's ability to get to a precisely defined market
   d. the ability of an advertising agency to add an account to its list of clients

_____ **13.** Frequency is:
   a. the number of times an individual is exposed to a message
   b. the number of different target customers who are exposed to a commercial at least once during a specific period
   c. a medium's ability to get to a precisely defined market
   d. the ability of an advertising agency to add an account to its list of clients

_____ **14.** Audience selectivity is:
   a. the number of times an individual is exposed to a message
   b. the number of different target customers who are exposed to a commercial at least once during a specific period
   c. a medium's ability to get to a precisely defined market
   d. the ability of an advertising agency to add an account to its list of clients

_____ **15.** An agency that will step in when self-regulation of advertising fails, is the:
  a. National Advertising Division (NAD) of the Council of Better Business Bureaus
  b. Federal Trade Commission (FTC)
  c. National Advertising Review Board (NARB)
  d. Corrective Advertising Association (CAA)

>lg 5

What is the selling process?

_____ **16.** The initial step in the selling process that consists of looking for companies and people who are most likely to buy a seller's products is called:
  a. approaching   **c.** handling objections
  b. presenting   **d.** prospecting

_____ **17.** Qualifying involves:
  a. separating prospects from those who do not have the potential to make a purchase
  b. explaining the reason for a sales call to a potential customer
  c. demonstrating the ability of the product to perform up to a customer's expectations
  d. visiting the customer after a purchase is made to see if the customer is satisfied with the product

_____ **18.** Following up on a sale involves:
  a. separating prospects from those who do not have the potential to make a purchase
  b. explaining the reason for a sales call to a potential customer
  c. demonstrating the ability of the product to perform up to a customer's expectations
  d. visiting the customer after a purchase is made to see if the customer is satisfied with the product

>lg 6

What are the goals of sales promotion and what are several types of sales promotion?

_____ **19.** Marketing events or sales efforts—not including advertising, personal selling, and public relations—that stimulate consumer buying are called:
  a. loyalty marketing programs   **c.** promotions
  b. sweepstakes   **d.** trade deals

_____ **20.** A "dangler" is a:
  a. sign hanging down from a shelf that sways when shoppers pass
  b. jiggling sign
  c. coupon hanging on a bottle neck
  d. small plastic "stage" that elevates one product above the rest

_____ **21.** A "glorifier" is a:
  a. sign hanging down from a shelf that sways when shoppers pass
  b. jiggling sign
  c. coupon hanging on a bottle neck
  d. small plastic "stage" that elevates one product above the rest

_____ **22.** A "wobbler" is a:
  a. sign hanging down from a shelf that sways when shoppers pass
  b. jiggling sign
  c. coupon hanging on a bottle neck
  d. small plastic "stage" that elevates one product above the rest

>lg 7

How does public relations fit into the promotional mix?

_____ 23. Public relations is:
   a. advertising that takes a stand on a social or economic issue
   b. any communication or activity designed to win goodwill or prestige for a company or a person
   c. marketing events or sales efforts-not including advertising, personal selling, and public relations-that stimulate consumer buying
   d. the channels through which advertising is carried to prospective customers

_____ 24. The main form of public relations is:
   a. advertising   c. frequency of reach
   b. promotion   d. publicity

_____ 25. The functions of a public relations department include:
   a. reach   c. crisis management
   b. advertising   d. none of these answers are correct

>lg 8

What factors affect the promotional mix?

_____ 26. Salespeople who are hired to physically deliver and stock merchandise perform a function called:
   a. lobbying   c. unloading
   b. detailing   d. piling

_____ 27. When a manufacturer utilizes promotional efforts focused on end consumers to create demand for its products, it is practicing a:
   a. pull strategy   c. flanking strategy
   b. yanking strategy   d. push strategy

_____ 28. When a manufacturer utilizes aggressive personal selling and trade advertising to convince a wholesaler or retailer to carry and sell its merchandise, it is practicing a:
   a. pull strategy   c. flanking strategy
   b. yanking strategy   d. push strategy

>lg 9

What are three important trends in promotion?

_____ 29. When a company adopts a program of integrated marketing communications, it:
   a. builds a buzz for its products by investing heavily in on-line web advertising to knock out competing products
   b. merges the emotional sell of a traditional brand with a concrete service that can only be offered online
   c. carefully coordinates all promotional activities to produce a consistent, unified message that is customer focused
   d. attempts to attract consumer interest by introducing a disjointed approach when delivering its message

_____ 30. The marriage of the emotional sell of traditional brand marketing with a concrete service that is offered only online is called:
   a. national branding   c. rational branding
   b. store branding   d. cross-branding

TRUE/FALSE

Directions: Place a T or an F in the space provided to the left of each question to indicate whether it is True or False.

>lg 1   **What are the goals of promotional strategy?**

_____ 1. The set of unique features that the target market perceives as important and better than the competition is called promotion.

_____ 2. The features of a differential advantage might include high quality, fast delivery, low price, and good service.

_____ 3. Creating awareness, getting customers to try new products, providing information, retaining loyal customers, increasing the quantity and frequency of use, and identifying target customers are all promotional goals.

>lg 2   **What is the promotional mix, and what are its elements?**

_____ 4. Sales promotion is any face-to-face presentation to a prospective buyer.

_____ 5. Advertising is any form of paid nonpersonal promotion by an identified sponsor.

_____ 6. The promotional mix consists of marketing activities (other than personal selling) that stimulate consumer buying, including coupons and samples, displays, shows and exhibitions, demonstrations, and other types of selling efforts.

_____ 7. Public relations links the organization's goals with key aspects of the public interest and the development of programs designed to earn public understanding and acceptance.

>lg 3   **What are the types of advertising?**

_____ 8. Reminder advertising is a form of product advertising in which a company's product is compared with competing, named products.

_____ 9. Institutional advertising is used to keep a product name in the public mind.

_____ 10. Advocacy advertising is synonymous with grassroots lobbying.

_____ 11. Comparative advertising is a form of product advertising in which a firm seeks to keep the product name in the public's mind.

>lg 4   **What are the advertising media, and how are they related?**

_____ 12. The channels through which advertising is carried to prospective customers are the advertising media that are determined by the cost of the medium and the audience reached by it.

_____ 13. When advertising costs are expressed in terms of CPM, they are being quoted in terms of a cost per thousand contacts basis.

_____ 14. Reach is the number of times an individual is exposed to a commercial message.

_____ 15. Frequency is the number of different target customers who are exposed to a commercial at least once during a specific period of time.

_____ 16. Matching an advertising medium with a product's target market and the ability of the medium to reach a precisely defined market refers to audience selectivity.

_____ 17. The FTC can require businesses to run corrective advertising so that false impressions left by previous ads can be corrected.

_____ 18. Both the NAD and the NARB issue cease-and-desist orders as a remedy for deceptive advertising.

>lg 5 **What is the selling process?**

_____ 19. Of the approximately 6.5 million people engaged in personal selling in the United States, slightly over 45 percent are women.

_____ 20. The greatest weakness of personal selling is that it is less effective than other forms of promotion in obtaining a sale and gaining a satisfied customer.

_____ 21. Prospecting and qualifying involves seeking those companies and people that are most likely to buy the seller's offerings.

_____ 22. Customers ask qualifying questions when they seek information concerning a product or service.

>lg 6 **What are the goals of sales promotion, and what are several types of sales promotion?**

_____ 23. Sales promotions are marketing efforts, including advertising, personal selling, and public relations that stimulate consumer buying.

_____ 24. A "lipstick board" is a plastic surface on which promotional messages are written with crayons.

_____ 25. Cents-off coupons and free samples are effective promotional tools to strengthen brand loyalty.

>lg 7 **How does public relations fit into the promotional mix?**

_____ 26. Publicity is the main form of public relations where information about a company or product is presented in the news media and is not directly paid for by the company.

_____ 27. Lobbying is a public relations activity that is used to build and maintain national or local community relations.

_____ 28. During the introductory period, an especially new product can benefit from press releases designed to generate news about it.

>lg 8 **What factors affect the promotional mix?**

_____ 29. The use of promotional mixes has become standardized for most products since the roles of sales promotion, personal selling, and public relations have diminished.

_____ 30. Personal selling is especially important in marketing consumer nondurables.

_____ 31. Detailing occurs when salespeople are also required to physically stock the merchandise that they deliver to a retail outlet.

_____ 32. The use of aggressive personal selling and trade advertising to convince a wholesaler or retailer to carry their merchandise is consistent with a push strategy.

_____ 33. Rather than trying to sell to the end consumer, a manufacturer may use a pull strategy and focus on selling to the wholesaler.

>lg 9   What are three important trends in promotion?

_____ **34.** Integrated marketing communications involves carefully coordinating all promotional activities to produce a consistent, unified message that is customer focused.

_____ **35.** Advertising tactics that have been practiced on the Web have been highly successful.

_____ **36.** On the Internet, companies are attempting to attract consumers by using rational branding—marrying the emotional sell of traditional brand marketing with a concrete service that is offered only online.

ENHANCE YOUR VOCABULARY

Catapult	A military device for hurling missiles; to spring up abruptly
Clutter	A crowded or confused mass; to fill with disordered things that impede movement
Copywriter	A writer of advertising or publicity copy
Diversified	Give variety to; balanced (as an investment portfolio) by dividing funds among securities of different industries
Gratuitous	Given unearned or without recompense; not involving a return benefit, compensation or consideration; free
Perceptive	Responsive to sensory stimuli; discerning; capable of or exhibiting keen perception; observant
Reinforce	To strengthen by additional material or support; make stronger
Repository	A place, room, or container where something is stored
Skepticism	An attitude of doubt or a disposition to incredulity; uncertainty
Skeet shooting	A form of trapshooting in which clay targets are used to simulate birds in flight

Directions: Select the definition in Column B that best defines the word in Column A.

	Column A		Column B
_____ 1.	Repository	a.	A crowded or confused mass
_____ 2.	Diversified	b.	A military device for hurling missiles
_____ 3.	Perceptive	c.	A form of trapshooting in which clay targets are used to simulate birds in flight
_____ 4.	Catapults	d.	Discerning; observant
_____ 5.	Skeet shooting	e.	Balanced
_____ 6.	Clutter	f.	A place, room, or container where something is stored
_____ 7.	Gratuitous	g.	To make stronger
_____ 8.	Copywriter	h.	Not involving a return benefit; free
_____ 9.	Reinforce	i.	An attitude of doubt; uncertainty
_____ 10.	Skepticism	j.	A writer of advertising or publicity copy

REVIEW YOUR KEY TERMS

Directions: Select the definition in Column B that best defines the word in Column A.

Column A

_____ **1.** Promotion

_____ **2.** Comparative advertising

_____ **3.** Reach

_____ **4.** Advertising

_____ **5.** Corrective advertising

_____ **6.** Advertising media

_____ **7.** National Advertising Review Board (NARB)

_____ **8.** Advertising agencies

_____ **9.** Federal Trade Commission

_____ **10.** Audience selectivity

_____ **11.** Differential advantage

_____ **12.** Prospecting

_____ **13.** Pull strategy

_____ **14.** Reminder advertising

_____ **15.** Promotional mix

_____ **16.** CPM

_____ **17.** Advocacy advertising

_____ **18.** Frequency

Column B

a. Advertising that creates a positive picture of a company and its ideals, services, and roles in the community; aimed at building goodwill for the company rather than selling a specific product.

b. The channels through which advertising is carried to prospective customers; includes newspapers, magazines, radio, television, outdoor advertising, direct mail and the Internet.

c. An appeals board that may be used if the NAD is deadlocked on an issue or if the losing party wishes to appeal.

d. Companies that help create ads and place them in the proper media.

e. Marketing events or sales efforts—not including advertising, personal selling, and public relations—that stimulate consumer buying.

f. The attempt by marketers to inform, persuade, or remind consumers and industrial users to engage in the exchange process.

g. Advertising that compares the company's product with competing, named products.

h. An agency of the U.S. government that works to prevent deception and misrepresentation in advertising; generally issues a cease-and-desist order if advertising is found to be deceptive, but may also require a corrective message.

i. The number of different target consumers who are exposed to a commercial at least once during a specific period, usually four weeks.

j. A subdivision of the Council of Better Business Bureaus that investigates complaints about advertising from consumers and other advertisers.

k. Advertising that takes a stand on a social or economic issue; also called grass-roots lobbying.

l. The combination of advertising, personal selling, sales promotion, and public relations used to promote a product.

m. A set of unique features of a product that the target market perceives as important and better than the competition's features.

n. Information about a company or product that appears in the news media and is not directly paid for by the company.

o. Any paid form of nonpersonal presentation by an identified sponsor.

p. The number of times an individual is exposed to an advertising message.

q. Advertising that features a specific good or service.

r. An advertisement run to correct false impressions left by previous ads; can be required by the Federal Trade Commission.

_____ **19.** National Advertising Division (NAD)

s. A term used in expressing advertising costs; refers to the cost of reaching 1,000 members of the target market.

_____ **20.** Product advertising

t. Advertising that is used to keep a product's name in the public's mind; often used during the maturity stage of the product life cycle.

_____ **21.** Institutional advertising

u. An advertising medium's ability to reach a precisely defined market.

_____ **22.** Personal selling

v. The companies and people who are most likely to buy a seller's offerings.

_____ **23.** Qualifying questions

w. A face-to-face sales presentation to a prospective customer.

_____ **24.** Sales prospects

x. The process of looking for sales prospects.

_____ **25.** Sales promotions

y. A tactic for advertising on the Internet that combines the emotional aspect of traditional brand marketing with a concrete service that is offered only online.

_____ **26.** Rational branding

z. The careful coordination of all promotional activities—media advertising, sales promotion, personal selling, and public relations, as well as direct marketing, packaging, and other forms of promotion—to produce a consistent, unified message that is customer focused.

_____ **27.** Detailing

aa. A promotional strategy in which a manufacturer focuses on stimulating consumer demand for its product, rather than on trying to persuade wholesalers to carry the product.

_____ **28.** Integrated marketing

bb. Inquiries used by salespeople to separate prospects from those who do not have the potential to buy.

_____ **29.** Publicity

cc. A strategy in which a manufacturer uses aggressive personal selling and trade advertising to convince a wholesaler or retailer to carry and sell its merchandise.

_____ **30.** Push strategy

dd. Any communication or activity designed to win goodwill or prestige for a company or person.

_____ **31.** Public relations

ee. The physical stocking of merchandise at a retailer by the salesperson who delivers the merchandise.

CRITICAL THINKING EXERCISES

1. P.O.V. (Point of View)

Directions: In this exercise you will be asked to provide your personal opinion regarding some of the topics discussed in the chapter. At the completion of this exercise, your instructor may wish to poll the entire class regarding their responses.

    a. Advertising and promotion have crept into all aspects of our lives. We all have seen people who proudly wear clothing with corporate logos on them and heard of the introduction of advertising into elementary and high school classrooms. In addition, corporate promotion has been introduced on public television as a means of acknowledging corporate charity. Is nothing to be spared from the intrusion of advertising and promotion? This type of advertising should be eliminated.

Agree _____   Disagree _____

Explain

_____

_____

_____

_____

b. It has been suggested that the cost of college textbooks has become so prohibitive that advertising and promotional materials should be placed within them in order to cover some of their production costs and thereby lower their price. Others have argued that this would herald the dawn of an era when advertisers who choose specific textbooks in which to place their advertising would dictate which books would be published.

Agree _____   Disagree _____

Explain:

_____

_____

_____

_____

2. Using the Internet

Directions: The movement to block advertisers from reaching consumers has gained popularity. Go to **http://www.junkbusters.com**.

    a. What is the primary mission of this organization?
    b. Click on Fed up with having your personal data exploited? Ready to join the fight for privacy rights? What action is being suggested?
    c. What do 'Guidescope' and 'Junkbuster' provide users?
    d. Is it fair to advertisers for this web site to offer software over the Internet at no cost to users?

3. Writing Skills

Directions: You are the product manager for a new unisex perfume called Uniscent. Provide a detailed description of the promotional mix that is required in order to market this product.

NOTES ON CHAPTER 16

Chapter 17

Using Technology to Manage Information

OUTLINE

MULTIPLE CHOICE

Directions: Place the letter of the response that best completes the questions that follow in the blank space at the left.

>lg 1

How does information play a role in decision making?

_C_ 1. To be useful, information must be:
    a. timely   c. relevant
    b. accurate   d. all of these answers are correct

_C_ 2. An information system is:
    a. all of the facts that describe the company's status
    b. a meaningful and useful summary of data
    c. all methods and equipment that provide information about all aspects of a firm's operations
    d. a piece of hardware that is responsible for managing information resources

_b_ 3. Information is:
    a. a means to collecting data
    b. a meaningful and useful summary of data
    c. all methods and equipment that provide information about all aspects of a firm's operations
    d. a piece of hardware that is responsible for managing information resources

_C_ 4. When a manager reviews data, he/she is looking at:
    a. many facts that describe the company's status
    b. a meaningful and useful summary of data
    c. all methods and equipment that provide information about all aspects of a firm's operations
    d. pieces of hardware that are responsible for managing information resources

>lg 2

What are the components of a computer, and how are computers categorized by size?

_a_ 5. A machine that stores and manipulates symbols based upon a set of instructions is called a:
    a. computer   c. storage system
    b. hardware   d. CPU

_C_ 6. The brain of a computer system that performs all calculations, interprets program instructions, remembers information, and tells other parts of the computer what to do is a:
    a. secondary storage system c. CPU
    b. hardware   d. RAM

_d_ 7. Computers need a secondary storage system because:
    a. other parts of the computer have to be told what to do
    b. it provides primary memory for the RAM system
    c. temporary storage is needed as part of the overall system
    d. long-term storage of programs is essential for information retrieval

_b_ 8. Microcomputers are also called:
    a. GIGOs   c. CPUs
    b. PCs   d. RAMs

d **9.** Medium-sized computers that are often housed in one or two cabinets about the size of a file cabinet are called:
- **a.** mainframe computers
- **b.** microcomputers
- **c.** supercomputers
- **d.** minicomputers

C **10.** Computers used to simulate or predict solutions to difficult problems are known as:
- **a.** mainframe computers
- **b.** microcomputers
- **c.** supercomputers
- **d.** minicomputers

>lg 3   **How does software make a computer useful?**

a **11.** The set of instructions that controls computers and provides program routines that enable applications programs to run on a particular computer is known as:
- **a.** systems software
- **b.** applications software
- **c.** an operating system
- **d.** spreadsheet software

b **12.** Applications software:
- **a.** controls the computer and provides program routines that enable applications software to run properly
- **b.** is used to perform a specific task or to solve a particular problem
- **c.** manages the computer's system activities
- **d.** is also known as an operating system

d **13.** Database software is used to:
- **a.** write, edit, and format letters to individuals and reports for managers
- **b.** perform complex spreadsheet operations
- **c.** create charts and graphs
- **d.** record, update, and store information for possible retrieval later on

a **14.** The transmission of data between computer systems via telephone links is performed using:
- **a.** desktop publishing software
- **b.** spreadsheets
- **c.** a modem and appropriate software
- **d.** graphics

>lg 4   **Why are computer networks an important part of today's business information systems?**

b **15.** A computer network is a:
- **a.** large program with integrated modules
- **b.** group of two or more computer systems linked together by communications channels to share data and information
- **c.** series of computers that work on enterprise resource planning
- **d.** group of microcomputers that work independently of one another

a **16.** A wide area network (WAN):
- **a.** connects computers at different sites via telecommunications media such as phone lines, satellites, and microwaves
- **b.** lets people at one site exchange data and share the use of hardware and software from a variety of computer manufacturers
- **c.** is a private corporate computer network
- **d.** is a tool that is used to obtain sensitive corporate information from competitors

17. An intranet:
    a. connects computers at different sites via telecommunications media such as phone lines, satellites, and microwaves
    b. lets people at one site exchange data and share the use of hardware and software from a variety of computer manufacturers
    c. is a private corporate computer network
    d. is a tool that is used to obtain sensitive corporate information from competitors

18. A local area network (LAN):
    a. connects computers at different sites via telecommunications media such as phone lines, satellites, and microwaves
    b. lets people at one site exchange data and share the use of hardware and software from a variety of computer manufacturers
    c. is a private corporate computer network
    d. is a tool that is used to obtain sensitive corporate information from competitors

>lg 5   **What is the structure of a typical information system?**

19. When data are collected over some time period and are processed together, a firm is updating its database using a(n):
    a. on-line processing system   **c.** off-line processing system
    b. real-time processing system   **d.** batch processing system

20. The role of the management support system (MSS) is to:
    a. process data as they become available
    b. prepare data for storage in a database
    c. provide data for improved decision making
    d. process data that has been collected over some period of time

21. An executive information system (EIS):
    a. utilizes computer models that describe real world conditions in order to help managers to make decisions
    b. is a decision support system (DSS) that has been customized for an individual executive
    c. uses artificial intelligence to provide managers with advice that is similar to what they would get from a human consultant
    d. makes use of computer networks in many companies to improve communications

22. An expert system:
    a. utilizes computer models that describe real world conditions in order to help managers to make decisions
    b. is a decision support system (DSS) that has been customized for an individual executive
    c. uses artificial intelligence to provide managers with advice that is similar to what they would get from a human consultant
    d. makes use of computer networks in many companies to improve communications

>lg 6   How can companies manage information technology to their advantage?

23. The first step in technology planning is:
    a. ranking of projects   **c.** selecting new software
    b. choosing hardware   **d.** a general needs assessment

___b___ **24.** An important data security issue faced by firms that employ the latest technological advances is:
  a. software piracy
  b. unauthorized access and use of computer systems
  c. computer viruses
  d. all of these answers are correct

>lg 7

What are the leading trends in information technology?

___a___ **25.** Collecting, processing, and condensing information is known as:

a. information management	**c.** information analysis
b. knowledge management	**d.** workplace assessment

___b___ **26.** Gathering and sharing an organization's collective knowledge to improve productivity and foster innovation is known as:

a. information management	**c.** information analysis
b. knowledge management	**d.** workplace assessment

TRUE/FALSE

Directions: Place a T or an F in the space provided to the left of each question to indicate whether it is True or False.

>lg 1

How does information play a role in decision making?

___T___ **1.** The equipment and techniques that manage and process information are known as information technology (IT), and include computers, telecommunications, and Internet related products.

___F___ **2.** The advent of information technology has all but made the need for management systems obsolete.

___T___ **3.** Information must be turned into data that is a meaningful and useful summary of information.

>lg 2

What are the components of a computer, and how are computers categorized by size?

___T___ **4.** The input system, the central processing unit with primary storage, secondary storage, and the output system are the main categories of computer hardware.

___F___ **5.** The random access memory of a computer performs all calculations, interprets program instructions, remembers information, and tells other parts of the computer what to do.

___F___ **6.** Secondary storage usually consists of the active, short-term memory that stores data and instructions to manipulate output.

___T___ **7.** Microcomputers, often called PCs or desktop computers, are the most widely used type of computer.

___F___ **8.** Minicomputers, often called laptops or notebooks, are portable units that rival desktops in computing power.

___T___ **9.** Mainframe computers have much greater storage capacity than PCs or minicomputers and can serve many users at the same time.

_____ F   10.   Supercomputers, once only used for highly complex problems, are now being used to solve government and business problems. It is predicted that by the year 2004 they will have processing speeds close to 100 teraflops.

>lg 3   **How does software make a computer useful?**

_____ T   11.   Systems software controls the computer and provides program routines that enable applications programs to run on a particular computer. These program routines are part of an operating system.

_____ F   12.   Applications software is used to write, edit, and format letters.

_____ T   13.   Spreadsheet software is used to prepare sales and expense reports, price estimates and bids, as well as other materials involving rows and columns of numbers.

_____ F   14.   Database software is used to design and produce such items as sales brochures, catalogs, advertisements, and newsletters.

_____ T   15.   Database software provides businesspeople with the ability to search through customer information in order to sort and organize the records in a database.

_____ F   16.   An integrated software package or software suite combines several types of programs that perform numerous tasks. The component programs are designed to work together and allow for information to be imported and exported between them.

>lg 4   **Why are computer networks an important part of today's business information systems?**

_____ T   17.   A computer network is a group of two or more computer systems linked together by communications channels to share data and information.

_____ F   18.   A local area network (LAN) connects computers at different sites via telecommunications media such as phone lines, satellites, and microwaves.

_____ F   19.   Wide area networks (WAN) let people at one site exchange data and share the use of hardware and software from a variety of computer manufacturers.

_____ T   20.   Intranets are like LANs in that they are private corporate networks. But they are like WANs because they link employees in many locations and with different types of computers.

>lg 5   **What is the structure of a typical information system?**

_____ F   21.   A management support, or an analytic system, handles the daily business operations of the firm. It is used to capture and organize raw data and covert these data into information.

_____ F   22.   A batch processing system is used to process data as they become available.

_____ T   23.   On-line, or real-time processing, is typically used by a business such as an airline, where flight information is entered into the computer system and is quickly confirmed.

_____ T   24.   A database management tracking system tracks data and allows users to query the database for the information that is needed.

_____ T   25.   A data warehouse combines many databases across the whole company into one central database that supports management decision making.

T

26. An executive information system gives managers advice such as they would get from a human consultant through the use of artificial intelligence, which enables computers to reason and learn to solve problems.

F

27. An expert system would include cellular phones, E-mail systems, pagers, voice mail systems, and facsimile machines.

>lg 6

How can companies manage information technology to their advantage?

T

28. The first step in technology planning is a general needs assessment, followed by a ranking of projects and the specific choices of hardware and software.

F

29. In order to protect information, most businesses rely on fault-tolerance software that is built into most computer systems when they are purchased.

T

30. Computer data security issues include the unauthorized access and use of systems and information, software piracy, deliberate damage to information, and computer viruses.

F

31. It is widely accepted that the existence of huge electronic files of personal information does not represent a threat to our personal privacy because these records are stored in separate computer systems.

>lg 7

What are the leading trends in information technology?

T

32. Information management involves gathering and sharing an organization's collective knowledge to improve productivity and foster innovation.

T

33. Knowledge management focuses on collecting, processing, and condensing information.

T

34. "Information appliances" may soon replace the PC.

ENHANCE YOUR VOCABULARY

Advocate	To plead in favor of; support
Auditing	Formally examining or verifying financial records
Consolidating	Joining together into one whole; uniting
Convert	To bring over from one belief, view, or party to another
Laurels	A shrub or tree; used by the ancient Greeks to crown victors in the Pythian games; to deck or crown with laurel—thus the phrase to "rest on your laurels"
Outages	A failure or interruption in use or functioning especially of electric current
Prescreening	Viewing a motion picture before it is released for public showing
Query	Question, inquiry
Sites	The place, scene, or location
Synergies	Combined action or operation

Directions: Select the definition in Column B that best defines the word in Column A.

	Column A		Column B
h	**1.** Convert	a.	To plead in favor of; support
a	**2.** Advocate	b.	The place, scene, or location
s	**3.** Laurels	c.	A failure or interruption in use
e	**4.** Synergies	d.	An examination of financial records

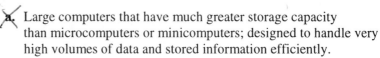

_d_ **5.** Auditing	_e._ Combined action or operation
_g_ **6.** Consolidating	_f._ Question, inquiry
_c_ **7.** Outages	_g._ Joining together into one whole; unite
_i_ **8.** Prescreening	_h._ To bring over from one view to another
_b_ **9.** Sites	_i._ Viewing a motion picture before it is released
_f_ **10.** Query	_j._ A shrub or tree

REVIEW YOUR KEY TERMS

Directions: Select the definition in Column B that best defines the word in Column A

Column A

 1. Information technology (IT)

 2. Central processing unit (CPU)

 3. Mainframe computers

 4. Database software

 5. Software

 6. Computer network

 7. Supercomputers

 8. Transaction processing system (TPS)

 9. Executive information system (EIS)

 10. Management support system (MSS)

 11. Computer virus

 12. Chief information officer

Column B

 a. Large computers that have much greater storage capacity than microcomputers or minicomputers; designed to handle very high volumes of data and stored information efficiently.

b. An executive with responsibility for managing all information resources in an organization.

 c. An internal corporate-wide area network that uses Internet technology to link employees in many locations and with different types of computers.

d. The part of a computer that provides long-term storage for programs and data; typically uses a combination of hard disk drives and other devices such as floppy disk drives, CD-ROM drives, tape drives, and Zip drives.

 e. Software that is used to prepare and analyze numerical data such as for financial statements, sales forecasts, and budgets.

 f. The equipment and techniques used to manage and process information.

g. The part of a computer system that translates data into a form that can be transmitted.

h. A method of updating a database in which data are processed as they become available.

 i. An information system that handles the daily business operations of a firm. The system captures and organizes raw data from internal and external sources for storage in a database.

 j. A management support system that helps managers make decisions using computer models that describe real-world processes.

 k. An information technology that combines many databases across an entire company into one central database that supports management decision making.

 l. A dynamic information system that helps managers make decisions by allowing them to analyze data, identify business trends, make forecasts, and model business strategies; may include an information reporting system, decision support system, executive information system, and expert system.

_g_ **13.** Modem

_c_ **14.** Intranet

_e_ **15.** Spreadsheet software

_o_ **16.** Information system

_d_ **17.** Secondary storage

_n_ **18.** Applications software

_hh_ **19.** Minicomputers

_u_ **20.** Systems software

_X_ **21.** Desktop publishing software

_aa_ **22.** Operating system

_s_ **23.** Information

_LL_ **24.** Office automation system

_J_ **25.** Decision support system (DSS)

_gg_ **26.** Random access memory (RAM)

_bb_ **27.** Word processing software

_V_ **28.** Wide area network (WAN)

_t_ **29.** Local area network (LAN)

_ee_ **30.** Data

_W_ **31.** Microcomputers

m. The most powerful computers. Only slightly larger than the typical microcomputer, they can perform many interrelated calculations quickly and are used to do complex computations to simulate or predict difficult problems.

n. Software that is applied to a real-world task; used to perform a specific particular task or to solve a particular problem.

o. The methods and equipment that provide information about all aspects of a firm's operations.

p. The equipment associated with a computer system; includes the input system, the central processing unit with primary storage, secondary storage, and the output system.

q. The central part of a computer system that performs all calculations, interprets program instructions, remembers information, and tells other parts of the computer what to do. It is made up of microprocessor chips.

r. The set of instructions that directs a computer's activities.

s. A meaningful and useful summary of data.

t. A network that connects computers at one site, enabling the computer users to exchange data and share the use of hardware and software from a variety of computer manufacturers.

u. Software that controls the computer and provides program routines that enable applications programs to run on a particular computer.

v. A network that connects computers at different sites via telecommunications media such as phone lines, satellites, or microwaves.

w. Small computers that can fit on a desktop; also called personal computers or desktop computers.

x. Software that combines word processing, graphics, and page layout software and is used to create documents such as sales brochures, newsletters, and catalogs.

y. A method of updating a database in which data are collected over some time period and processed together.

z. A machine that stores and manipulates symbols based on a set of instructions.

aa. A collection of programs that manage a computer system's activities and run applications software.

bb. Software that is used to write, edit, and format letters and other documents.

cc. Software that records, updates, and stores information.

dd. A group of two or more computer systems linked together by communications channels to share data and information.

ee. The many facts that together describe a company's status.

_____ **32.** Batch processing

ff. The first level of a management support system; uses summary data collected by the transaction processing system to produce reports with statistics that managers can use to make decisions.

_____ **33.** Expert system

gg. The primary type of memory in a computer's central processing unit; an active, short-term memory that stores data and instructions for manipulating the data.

_____ **34.** Information reporting system

hh. Medium-sized computers that are too large for a desktop but small enough to fit in an office. They offer greater processing speed than microcomputers and are often linked in a computer network.

_____ **35.** Hardware

ii. A management support system that is customized for an individual executive; provides specific information for strategic decisions.

_____ **36.** Computer

jj. A management support system that uses artificial intelligence to enable computers to reason and learn to solve problems in much the way that humans do.

_____ **37.** Online (real-time) processing

kk. A computer program that copies itself into other software and can spread to other computer systems.

_____ **38.** Data warehouse

ll. An information system that uses information technology tools such as e-mail systems, word processing systems, fax machines, cellular phones, and pagers to improve communications throughout an organization.

CRITICAL THINKING EXERCISES

1. P.O.V. (Point of View)

Directions: In this exercise you will be asked to provide your personal opinion regarding some of the topics discussed in the chapter. At the completion of this exercise, your instructor may wish to poll the entire class regarding their responses.

a. It has been suggested that a 'Universal Data Bank' be established which would pool all information about individuals in one database and would be controlled by the government. Proponents say that keeping all information in one place would eliminate all of the confusion that occurs when different databases hold different types of personal information about people and that the government would then have the ability to follow-up on individual medical, tax, and personal records.

Agree _✓_   Disagree _____

Explain:

Database of personal information about people should be kept all in one place so that confidentiality of the identity of people would be kept personal and safe.

_____

b. Computerization and information processing has improved record keeping along with the management of information and data at the expense of personalized service. Purchasing is often made more difficult because of the lack of sales assistance when buying things over the Internet. Also, individuals intent upon committing fraud can steal the identity of other people who transmit such information over the Internet. The best approach would be to limit the use of computers for processing information.

Agree _____ Disagree ✓_____

Explain:

Find a better programming device for computers that limit the identity theft and fraud and track down these criminals and have them pay for their crime.

2. Using the Internet

Directions: Go to **http://www.Dell.com** and under the heading Business, click on Medium and Large Business.

http://ecomm.dell.com/deilstore/basket.aspx?c=us&1=en&cs=555&itemtype=SNACFG 3/22/04

a. Surf the site clicking on various headings to familiarize yourself with the computers and systems that are being sold to businesses.

b. Prepare an estimate of the cost to purchase 100 computer workstations, laptops, and printers for your entire staff of employees. Include two large fileservers to handle your workload needs. Your estimate should include three systems - low-end, medium-level, and high-end. _2x 1440 VA Dell smart-UPS by APC $1,119_

3. Writing Skills _100x Personal All-in-One Printer A960 with 1yr Advanced exchange serv._

Directions: Outline an informal talk you are presenting to your employees on the appropriate and inappropriate uses of E-mail. _$17,900_

100x Latitude D800 $249,200.00

100x Dell Precision Workstation 650
_$208,500.00_

total $476,719.00

Appropriate use of E-mail   _Inappropriate use of E-mail_

NOTES ON CHAPTER 17

Chapter 18

Using the Internet for Business

OUTLINE

MULTIPLE CHOICE

Directions: Place the letter of the response that best completes the questions that follow in the blank space at the left.

>lg 1   What is the Internet, and how does it work?

_____   **1.** A communications technology that allows different computer platforms to communicate with each other and transfer data is known as:
  a. the World Wide Web   **c.** hypertext
  b. a browser   **d.** transmission control protocol/Internet protocol

_____   **2.** A subsystem of the Internet that is an information retrieval system is called the:
  a. the World Wide Web   **c.** hypertext
  b. host computer   **d.** transmission control protocol/Internet protocol

_____   **3.** Software that allows users to access the Web with a graphical point and click interface is known as a:
  a. Web site   **c.** host computer
  b. browser   **d.** hypertext

_____   **4.** A host computer:
  a. allows users to access the Web with a graphical point and click interface
  b. stores services and data used by other computers on a network
  c. is the first document that computer users see when they enter a Web site
  d. none of these answers are correct

_____   **5.** Servers are:
  a. the first documents that computer users see when they enter a Web site
  b. identical to the World Wide Web and the Internet
  c. computers that store data and "serve" information to other computers called clients, upon request
  d. able to replace hypertext as links to documents at the same or other Web sites

>lg 2   Who uses the Internet, and for what?

_____   **6.** As of September 2000, the number of people that were on line to the World Wide Web was approximately:
  a. 17 million   **c.** 117 million
  b. 70 million   **d.** 378 million

_____   **7.** The percent of male/female computer users is approximately:
  a. 20%/80%   **c.** 50%/50%
  b. 42%/58%   **d.** 80%/20%

_____   **8.** The *least* popular reason for people to use the Internet is:
  a. visit financial sites   **c.** use search engines
  b. send e-mail   **d.** research product purchases

_____   **9.** Of the businesses and corporations that are active Web participants, the percentage that allowed customers to make purchases on line is approximately:
  a. 17%   **c.** 37%
  b. 25%   **d.** 56%

>lg 3   **How has the Internet economy changed the business environment?**

_____ **10.** New Internet businesses:
- **a.** incur substantial costs for physical distribution
- **b.** have the same cost for acquiring a new customer regardless of their geographic location
- **c.** find it more difficult to enter new markets
- **d.** must operate during standard business hours to be successful

_____ **11.** As a result of conducting business on the Internet, companies:
- **a.** must rely more heavily on intermediaries to connect with participants in the supply chain
- **b.** have been able to maintain the same relationships among channel members
- **c.** can bypass traditional channels of distribution to deal with other participants in the supply chain
- **d.** none of these answers are correct

_____ **12.** A Web site at which many resources are gathered into one convenient gateway to the Web is called a:
- **a.** intelligent site
- **b.** hot link
- **c.** portal
- **d.** net site

>lg 4   **How can companies incorporate e-commerce into their overall business strategies?**

_____ **13.** The entire process of selling a product or service via the Internet is called:
- **a.** e-tailing
- **b.** on-line shopping
- **c.** d-tailing
- **d.** e-commerce

_____ **14.** E-tailing involves:
- **a.** transactions between companies for raw materials
- **b.** transactions between businesses and end users of goods and services
- **c.** retail sales via catalogues
- **d.** developing detailed data bases for all types of business activities

_____ **15.** New types of business models that are emerging on the Internet include:
- **a.** consumer infomediaries and portal sites
- **b.** providing entertainment or information for a fee-for-service or subscription basis
- **c.** selling merchandise or services
- **d.** providing advertising or referral-supported entertainment or information sites for free

_____ **16.** Internet consumer infomediaries and portal sites:
- **a.** are an e-service that consists of business consultants and technology outsourcing companies
- **b.** make recommendations for site development enhancements
- **c.** provide auction sites for Web firms
- **d.** simplify the online experience by bringing together a combination of information, goods, and services from many individual companies

_____ **17.** An extranet is a:
- **a.** public network that is accessible to anyone within a region
- **b.** consumer infomediary and portal site
- **c.** private network that uses Internet technology and a browser interface, and is accessible only to authorized individuals
- **d.** form of e-commerce

_____ **18.** E-tailers are finding it difficult to make a profit from their activities because:
  a. price comparisons by consumers is relatively simple and price wars cut into profit margins
  b. cannibalization often takes place
  c. aggressive growth can lead to high investment costs
  d. all of these answers are correct

>lg 5

What benefits do businesses achieve through e-commerce?

_____ **19.** Companies that use the Internet gain an advantage over other firms by having access to customer and product sales data, because the Internet:
  a. allows companies to develop customer lists and learn about buying characteristics as well as which products are selling best
  b. provides extensive product information to customers around the world on a 24/7 basis
  c. lets purchasing agents and individuals find numerous vendors and retailers for almost any product
  d. leads to competition and lower prices

_____ **20.** Companies that use the Internet can benefit from a greater selection of products and vendors, because the Internet:
  a. allows companies to develop customer lists and learn about buying characteristics as well as which products are selling best
  b. provides extensive product information to customers around the world on a 24/7 basis
  c. lets purchasing agents and individuals find numerous vendors and retailers for almost any product
  d. leads to competition and lower prices

_____ **21.** A barrier to e-commerce that has developed despite the widespread acceptance of the use of the Internet is:
  a. disruption in channel relationships
  b. poor customer service
  c. payment problems
  d. all of these answers are correct

>lg 6

What steps are involved in launching an e-commerce venture?

_____ **22.** A key merchandising issue that must be dealt with when developing an e-commerce strategy is:
  a. complete and accurate product descriptions
  b. the quality of content at the Web site
  c. reward programs
  d. easy-to-use order forms

_____ **23.** A key Web site issue that must be dealt with when developing an e-commerce strategy is:
  a. complete and accurate product descriptions
  b. the quality of content at the Web site
  c. reward programs
  d. easy-to-use order forms

_____ 24. A key marketing issue that must be dealt with when developing an e-commerce strategy is:
a. complete and accurate product descriptions
b. the quality of content at the Web site
c. reward programs
d. easy-to-use order forms

>lg 7   **What lies ahead for the Information Superhighway?**

_____ 25. With the Internet, companies can:
a. meet face-to-face with customers
b. guarantee a secure transfer of information
c. guarantee a secure transfer of funds
d. collect, track, and analyze customer data to identify consumer behavior and buying patterns

TRUE/FALSE

Directions: Place a T or an F in the space provided to the left of each question to indicate whether it is True or False.

>lg 1   **What is the Internet, and how does it work?**

_____ 1. The information technology industry is growing at twice the rate of the economy in general.

_____ 2. Internet technology has been available for the past twenty-five years and it has taken longer for it to become part of the daily environment than any other technological advance.

_____ 3. TCP/IP is a communications technology that allows different computer platforms to communicate with each other to transfer data.

_____ 4. The Internet, as we know it, is a subsystem of the World Wide Web.

_____ 5. Browsers are Internet shoppers who visit Web sites but never make a purchase.

_____ 6. A host computer stores services and data used by other computers on a network.

_____ 7. A server is an automated computer robot that physically brings hardware and software from storage to a user.

>lg 2   **Who uses the Internet, and for what?**

_____ 8. Although the Internet was dominated for many years by women, males now represent the one of the fastest growing groups of users.

_____ 9. An Internet site that helps women find solutions to their problems is iVillage.

_____ 10. 37 percent of businesses that allow visitors to their Web sites also allow them to make purchases.

>lg 3   **How has the Internet economy changed the business environment?**

_____ 11. The originators of the Internet were able to anticipate the numerous uses to which it has been put. However, they thought that it would take much more time for it to gain widespread acceptance.

_____ 12. The Internet represents the application of existing business models utilizing a new form of technology.

_____ 13. Many established companies, confident that their size would allow them to push small Internet firms out of business, were surprised to find that they were left in the dust by these new companies.

_____ 14. The Internet is blurring the traditional barriers of geography and time while businesses are finding that they encounter fewer barriers than traditional businesses when entering new markets.

_____ 15. Although the Internet is changing many elements of the business environment, it has not changed the relationships among channel members.

_____ 16. *Intelligent agents* are infomediaries who scour the Web's many databases to compare prices for consumers.

>lg 4   How can companies incorporate e-commerce into their overall business strategies?

_____ 17. E-commerce is able to provide benefits to customers such as convenience, increased efficiency, and better service.

_____ 18. E-tailing involves business-to-business e-commerce.

_____ 19. Consumer infomediaries and portal sites bring such diverse groups as consultants and technology outsourcing companies together.

_____ 20. The Internet allows industry exchanges and other information gatherers to serve as infomediaries bringing together multiple buyers and sellers within one industry.

_____ 21. The Extranet is a public network that provides information in addition to that which is gathered over the Internet.

_____ 22. Price comparisons, cannibalization, unexpected costs, and the need for aggressive growth are factors that make profitability difficult for e-tailers.

>lg 5   What benefits do businesses achieve through e-commerce?

_____ 23. A major drawback of e-commerce is the inability of purchasing agents to find a variety of vendors and retailers who will serve their needs.

_____ 24. Among the advantages of lower costs that ensue from engaging in e-commerce, firms find that they benefit from distribution savings, staff reductions, and lower costs of purchasing supplies.

_____ 25. E-commerce may jeopardize the relationships between a manufacturer and a distributor when the manufacturer sells directly to customers.

_____ 26. The three main reasons for dissatisfaction with Internet shopping are: product availability problems, high shipping and handling costs, and slow Web site performance.

>lg 6   What steps are involved in launching an e-commerce venture?

_____ 27. Positive returns on an Internet investment must be realized by a firm at the Basic Presence Stage (Level 1), of the Four Stages of E-Commerce, in order achieve ultimate success with a Web site.

_____ 28. Many companies underestimate the effort required to effectively merchandise products on the Internet. This includes failure to sell the appropriate products and to price them correctly.

_____ 29. Simplicity, ease of navigation, visual appeal, download speed, and good product information are important design considerations for business Web sites.

_____ 30. Building brand equity is not an important issue in e-commerce marketing.

_____ 31. Studies show that Web site e-businesses have been able to convert e-shoppers into e-buyers.

_____ 32. Page impressions, reach, total number of site visits, time online, and click-throughs on linked ads are all common measurements for analyzing Web traffic.

>lg 7   What lies ahead for the Information Superhighway?

_____ 33. The implementation of customized Web services is reported to lead to customer and sales growth.

_____ 34. The Federal Trade Commission has ruled that a firm doing business on the Web cannot collect personal information.

_____ 35. A trend among retail firms doing business on the Internet is the development of strategic alliances, which attempt to ward off encroachment by newcomers into their industry.

ENHANCE YOUR VOCABULARY

Affiliate	To associate with; to bring or receive into close connection as a member or branch.
Breadth	Distance from side to side: width; comprehensive quality: scope
Dismay	Sudden disappointment; sudden loss of courage from alarm or fear
Dispense	To prepare and distribute (medication); to deal out in portions
Encroachment	To advance beyond the usual or proper limits
Encrypt	Encode; to convert (a message) into code
Envisioned	Pictured to oneself; think
Niche	A recess in a wall; a place, employment, status, or activity for which a person or thing is best fitted
Nimble	Quick and light in motion: agile
Turnkey	Built, supplied, or installed complete and ready to operate

Directions: Select the definition in Column B that best defines the word in Column A.

	Column A		Column B
_____	1. Envisioned	a.	Built, supplied, or installed complete and ready to operate
_____	2. Encroachment	b.	Pictured to oneself
_____	3. Affiliate	c.	To deal out in portions
_____	4. Dismay	d.	Quick and light in motion: agile
_____	5. Breadth	e.	To associate with
_____	6. Turnkey	f.	Sudden disappointment
_____	7. Niche	g.	Distance from side to side; scope
_____	8. Dispense	h.	To advance beyond the proper limits
_____	9. Nimble	i.	To convert (a message) into code
_____	10. Encrypt	j.	A place for which a person or thing is best fitted

REVIEW YOUR KEY TERMS

Directions: Select the definition in Column B that best defines the word in Column A.

Column A

_____ 1. Internet

_____ 2. Browser

_____ 3. Web sites

_____ 4. Transmission control protocol/Internet protocol (TCP/IP)

_____ 5. Business-to-consumer e-commerce

_____ 6. World Wide Web (WWW)

_____ 7. Internet service provider (ISP)

_____ 8. Extranet

_____ 9. Hypertext

_____ 10. Host computer

_____ 11. Business-to-business e-commerce

_____ 12. Electronic commerce (e-commerce)

Column B

a. Electronic commerce that involves transactions between businesses and the end user of the goods or services; also call e-tailing.

b. A communications technology that allows different computer platforms to communicate with each other to transfer data; used by all of the commercial and public networks that make up the Internet.

c. Electronic commerce that involves transactions between companies.

d. A commercial service that connects companies and individuals to the Internet.

e. A subsystem of the Internet that consists of an information retrieval system composed of Web sites.

f. A worldwide computer network that includes both commercial and public networks and offers various capabilities including e-mail, file transfer, online chat sessions, and newsgroups.

g. A file or series of files within a Web page that link users to documents at the same or other Web sites.

h. The central computer for a Web site that stores services and data used by other computers on the network.

i. Locations on the World Wide Web consisting of a home page and, possibly, other pages with documents and files.

j. Software that allows users to access the World Wide Web with a graphical point and click interface.

k. The process of selling a product or service via the Internet; also called electronic business-to-business.

l. A private computer network that uses Internet technology and a browser interface but is accessible only to authorized outsiders with a valid user name and password.

CRITICAL THINKING EXERCISES

1. P.O.V. (Point of View)

Directions: In this exercise you will be asked to provide your personal opinion regarding some of the topics discussed in the chapter. At the completion of this exercise, your instructor may wish to poll the entire class regarding their responses.

a. The usefulness of the Internet has been overrated. It takes a long time to get connected to web sites, and security is so faulty that people are not willing to provide vendors with personal information, such as credit card and social security numbers. The improvement of the Internet as a medium for commercial and retail transactions in the future will be severely limited by these factors.

Agree _____   Disagree _____

Explain:

_____

_____

_____

_____

b. With the development of the Internet and E-commerce, consumers will have a greater number of sites from which to choose in order to purchase goods and services. Increased choice will lead to greater competition and lower prices. This will, in turn require the introduction of greater efficiencies on the part of firms that participate in E-commerce on the Internet in order for them to remain competitive. Profit will be squeezed more and more as prices are reduced. Business firms will eventually find that conducting business over the Internet is unprofitable.

Agree _____   Disagree _____

Explain:

_____

_____

_____

_____

2. Using the Internet

Directions: Internet advertising is growing and provides an opportunity for companies to get their message seen at various web sites. Go to **http://www.admedia.org**.

   a. Click on JIAD and select an article of interest to you related to Internet advertising and summarize its content.
   b. Click on Legal Beat and write a summary of the major issues being discussed.
   c. Select from Big Move, Research Front, or Innovations and review an article of interest to you.
   d. If you have any comments or opinions regarding this site, send them to the editor. What response did you receive?

3. Writing Skills

Directions: Write a short report on the main reasons for dissatisfaction with Internet shopping and how it might be changed to relieve these dissatisfactions.

NOTES ON CHAPTER 18

Chapter 19

Using Financial Information and Accounting

OUTLINE

MULTIPLE CHOICE

Directions: Place the letter of the response that best completes the questions that follow in the blank space at the left.

>lg 1   **Why are financial reports and accounting information important, and who uses them?**

_____   1. The process of collecting, recording, classifying, summarizing, reporting, and analyzing financial activities is known as:
    a. financial analysis   **c.** accounting
    b. statistics   **d.** auditing

_____   2. Balance sheets, income statements, and other special reports are known as:
    a. weekly business summaries   **c** audit reports
    b. data summaries   **d.** financial statements

_____   3. Managerial accounting:
    a. provides internal financial reports that are used inside the organization to evaluate and make decisions about current and future operations
    b. provides external reports that are used inside the organization to evaluate and make decisions about current and future operations
    c. is the process of collecting, recording, classifying, summarizing, reporting, and analyzing financial activities
    d. is the name by which the generally accepted accounting principles (GAAP) are known

_____   4. Financial accounting:
    a. provides internal financial reports that are used inside the organization to evaluate and make decisions about current and future operations
    b. provides external reports that are used outside the organization to evaluate and make decisions about current and future operations
    c. is the process of collecting, recording, classifying, summarizing, reporting, and analyzing financial activities
    d. is the name by which the generally accepted accounting principles (GAAP) are known

_____   5. The organization that is responsible for establishing financial accounting standards in the United States is known as the:
    a. Managerial Accounting Standards Board (MASB)
    b. Financial Statements Standards Board (FSSB)
    c. Generally Accepted Accounting Principles Association (GAAPA)
    d. Financial Accounting Standards Board (FASB)

_____   6. The following is the primary statement that appears in a firm's annual report:
    a. statement of cash flows
    b. income statement
    c. balance sheet
    d. all of these are primary financial statements

>lg 2   **What are the differences between public and private accountants?**

_____   7. Independent accountants who serve organizations on a fee basis are called:
    a. private accountants   **c.** consultants
    b. public accountants   **d.** financial analysts

_____ 8. Accountants employed to serve one particular organization are known as:
   a. private accountants
   b. public accountants
   c. consultants
   d. financial analysts

_____ 9. Auditing is:
   a. not required of a certified management accountant in order to earn a certified public accountant's certificate
   b. not required of a certified public accountant in order to earn a certified management accountant's certificate
   c. the process of reviewing records used to prepare financial statements
   d. can only be carried out by a Big Five accounting firm

>lg 3   **What are the six steps in the accounting cycle?**

_____ 10. Assets are:
   a. tangible and intangible things of value owned by a firm
   b. what a firm owes to its creditors
   c. the total amount of the owners' investment in a firm minus any liabilities
   d. only transactions that result in income

_____ 11. Liabilities are:
   a. things of value owned by a firm
   b. what a firm owes to its creditors
   c. the total amount of the owners' investment in a firm minus any liabilities
   d. only transactions that result in income

_____ 12. Owners' equity is:
   a. things of value owned by a firm
   b. what a firm owes to its creditors
   c. the total amount of the owners' investment in a firm minus any liabilities
   d. only transactions that result in income

_____ 13. A journal is:
   a. a listing of financial transactions in chronological order
   b. the document that shows increases and decreases in specific accounts
   c. commonly known as a trial balance
   d. the only document that is not included in the accounting cycle

_____ 14. The document used to show increases and decreases in specific assets, liabilities, and owner's equity accounts is known as a:
   a. journal
   b. trial balance
   c. cash flow summary
   d. ledger

>lg 4   **In what terms does the balance sheet describe the financial condition of an organization?**

_____ 15. The speed with which an asset can be converted into cash is called:
   a. current
   b. liquidity
   c. solvency
   d. depreciation

_____ 16. The allocation of an asset's original cost to the years in which it is expected to produce revenues is called:
   a. goodwill
   b. solvency
   c. liquidity
   d. depreciation

>lg 5   **How does the income statement report a firm's profitability?**

_____ 17. The income statement:
a. is a report of the total dollar amount of a company's sales
b. generally is used to determine the amount left after deducting sales discounts and returns and allowances from gross sales
c. can be substituted for the balance sheet when reporting income
d. summarizes the firm's revenues and expenses and shows its total profit or loss over a period of time

_____ 18. Revenues can be distinguished from sales in that:
a. sales discounts can result when price reductions are allowed
b. sales do not include income from such sources as interest, dividends, and rents
c. sales returns and allowances are included in net sales
d. none of these answers are correct

_____ 19. Once all expenses are subtracted from revenue the income statement will show:
a. net income or net loss   c. gross expense
b. gross income or gross loss   d. net revenue

>lg 6   **Why is the statement of cash flows an important source of information?**

_____ 20. The statement of cash flows:
a. summarizes the firm's revenues and expenses and shows total profit or loss over a period of time
b. is used to assess the sources and uses of money during a certain period
c. shows the amount of money left over from profitable operations since the firm's beginning
d. lists the assets that can or will be turned into cash within the next 12 months

_____ 21. Cash flows from operating activities are those related to:
a. debt and equity financing
b. the purchase and sale of fixed assets
c. the production of the firm's goods and services
d. depreciation of liabilities

_____ 22. Cash flows from investment activities are those related to:
a. debt and equity financing
b. the purchase and sale of fixed assets
c. the production of the firm's goods or services
d. depreciation of liabilities

_____ 23. Cash flows from financing activities are those related to:
a. debt and equity financing
b. the purchase and sale of fixed assets
c. the production of the firm's goods or services
d. depreciation of liabilities

>lg 7   **How can ratio analysis be used to identify a firm's financial strengths and weaknesses?**

_____ 24. The ratio of total current assets to total current liabilities is:
a. the acid test (quick) ratio   c. current ratio
b. net working capital   d. the P/E ratio

_____ **25.** The ratio of net profit to the number of shares of common stock outstanding is:
  a. the earnings per share
  b. gross profit margin
  c. net profit margin
  d. none of these answers are correct

_____ **26.** The debt to equity ratio measures the ratio of:
  a. net profit to the number of shares outstanding
  b. the speed with which inventory moves through the firm to the number of sales
  c. net profit to total owners' equity
  d. the amount of debt financing (borrowing) to the amount of equity financing (owners' funds)

>lg 8

What major trends are affecting the accounting industry today?

_____ **27.** Accountants now take an active role:
  a. advising their clients on systems and procedures
  b. delving into operating information to discover what is behind the numbers
  c. examining risks and weaknesses in a company and developing financial controls
  d. all of these answers are correct

_____ **28.** Internally generated intellectual assets include:
  a. plant and equipment
  b. supplies
  c. brands, trademarks, and employee talent
  d. raw materials

TRUE/FALSE

Directions: Place a T or an F in the space provided at the left of each question to indicate whether it is True or False.

>lg 1

Why are financial reports and accounting information important, and who uses them?

_____ **1.** The process of collecting, recording, classifying, summarizing, reporting, and analyzing financial activities that leads to the creation of financial reports is known as bookkeeping.

_____ **2.** Balance sheets, income statements, and other special reports, such as sales and expense breakdowns by product lines, are known as financial statements.

_____ **3.** Managerial accounting provides financial information that managers inside the organization can use to evaluate and make decisions about current and future operations.

_____ **4.** Accountants in the United States follow **generally accepted accounting principles (GAAP)** that are established by the **Federal Reserve Board (FRB)**.

>lg 2

What are the differences between public and private accountants?

_____ **5.** Public accountants are generally employed to serve one particular organization.

_____ **6.** Public accountants perform audits by reviewing the records used to prepare a firm's financial statements and by issuing an auditor's opinion.

_____ **7.** An examination for managerial accountants, similar to that for certified public accountants, is required for those who wish to become certified managerial accountants.

>lg 3   **What are the six steps in the accounting cycle?**

_____   **8.** Accounting and bookkeeping are synonymous. Both involve recording a firm's financial transactions and are routine, clerical processes.

_____   **9.** The accounting equation is: *Liabilities = Assets + Owners' Equity.*

_____   **10.** Assets, things of value owned by a firm, may be both tangible and intangible.

_____   **11.** Debts, also known as liabilities, are roughly equal to the value of all assets minus owners' equity.

_____   **12.** The record of a firm's transactions is kept through a system known as single entry bookkeeping.

_____   **13.** The accounting cycle refers to the process of generating financial statements that starts with a business transaction and ends with the preparation of a report.

_____   **14.** Typically, a computerized accounting package contains six basic modules that handle general ledger, sales order, accounts receivable, purchase order, accounts payable, and inventory control functions.

>lg 4   **In what terms does the balance sheet describe the financial condition of an organization?**

_____   **15.** Liquidity refers to speed with which an asset can be converted into cash.

_____   **16.** The balance sheet lists assets in the order of reverse liquidity; from least liquid to most liquid.

_____   **17.** The balance sheet summarizes a firm's financial position over a specified period of time.

_____   **18.** Current assets are those that can be converted into cash within 12 months, while fixed assets are long-term assets that are used by a firm for more than one year.

_____   **19.** Long-term assets with no physical existence are known as intangible assets.

_____   **20.** Current liabilities include the current portion of long-term debt.

_____   **21.** Owners' equity includes the owners' total investment in the business plus the value of all liabilities (both current and long-term).

>lg 5   **How does the income statement report a firm's profitability?**

_____   **22.** The income statement summarizes the firm's revenues and expenses and shows its total profit or loss over a period of time.

_____   **23.** Revenues are equal to the dollar amount of sales.

_____   **24.** Net sales are equal to gross sales minus sales discounts and returns and allowances.

_____   **25.** In a service firm, since there is no cost of goods sold, net sales are equal to gross profit.

_____   **26.** Operating expenses are the expenses of running a business that are directly related to producing or buying its products.

_____   **27.** Net income or net loss is calculated by subtracting all expenses from revenues.

>lg 6   **Why is the statement of cash flows an important source of information?**

_____   **28.** The statement of cash flows gives financial managers and analysts a way to identify cash flow problems and assess the firm's financial viability.

_____ **29.** Cash flows from investment activities are those related to debt and equity financing.

_____ **30.** Cash flows from financing activities are those related to the purchase and sale of fixed assets.

_____ **31.** Cash flows from operating activities are those related to the production of the firm's goods and services.

>lg 7 **How can ratio analysis be used to identify a firm's financial strengths and weaknesses?**

_____ **32.** The current ratio is the ratio of total current assets to total current liabilities.

_____ **33.** The acid test (quick ratio) is identical to the current ratio except that it includes inventory.

_____ **34.** Net working capital is equal to current assets minus current liabilities.

_____ **35.** The ratio of net profit to total owners' equity is called the net profit margin.

_____ **36.** The debt-to-equity ratio measures the relationship between the amount of debt financing and the amount of equity financing done by a firm.

>lg 8 **What major trends are affecting the accounting industry today?**

_____ **37.** Accountants have maintained their initial role as analysts of financial data, but have been limited in their ability to serve as consultants regarding other business matters such as information technology.

_____ **38.** The GAAP has not developed rules for estimation or reporting the value of investments in intangible, intellectual, assets.

ENHANCE YOUR VOCABULARY

Compiling	Gathering material into a single book or record; composing from materials gathered from several sources
Eye-opener	Something startling or shocking; enlightening
Fictitious	Non-existent, imaginary; unreal; purposefully deceptive; false
Generates	To bring into existence; produce
Hodgepodge	A haphazard mixture; jumble
Implemented	Put into practice; accomplished
Integrated	Made into a whole; unified
Keenly	Showing a quick and ardent responsiveness: enthusiastic; extremely sensitive in perception
Modules	A self-contained assembly used as a component of a larger system
Reconfigure	To set up (again) for operation especially in a particular way

Directions: Select the definition in Column B that best defines the word in Column A.

	Column A		Column B
_____	**1.** Modules	**a.**	Something startling or shocking
_____	**2.** Compiling	**b.**	Showing a quick response; enthusiastic; perceptive
_____	**3.** Implemented	**c.**	Gathering into a single book or record; to compose
_____	**4.** Keenly	**d.**	To set up (again) for operation

_____	5. Generates	e.	A self-contained assembly used as a component of a larger system
_____	6. Eye-opener	f.	Imaginary; unreal; false
_____	7. Reconfigure	g.	To bring into existence; produce
_____	8. Fictitious	h.	Make into a whole; unified
_____	9. Hodgepodge	i.	Put into practice; accomplished
_____	10. Integrated	j.	A haphazard mixture; jumble

REVIEW YOUR KEY TERMS

Directions: Select the definition in Column B that best defines the word in Column A.

Column A

_____ 1. Accounting

_____ 2. Annual report

_____ 3. Liquidity

_____ 4. Certified management Accountant (CMA)

_____ 5. Long-term liabilities

_____ 6. Generally accepted accounting principles (GAAP)

_____ 7. Balance sheet

_____ 8. Income statement

_____ 9. Managerial accounting

_____ 10. Certified public accountant

_____ 11. Statement of cash flows

Column B

a. An accountant who has completed a professional certification program including obtaining a bachelor's degree, passing a test prepared by the American Institute of Certified Public Accountants, and meeting state requirements. Only he/she can issue an auditor's opinion on financial statements.

b. A yearly document that describes a firm's financial status and usually discusses the firm's activities during the past year as well as its prospects for the future.

c. Short-term claims that are due within a year of the date of the balance sheet.

d. Things of value owned by a firm.

e. A method of accounting in which each transaction is recorded as two entries so that two accounts or records are changed.

f. What a firm owes to its creditors; also called debts.

g. A managerial accountant who has completed a professional certification program including passing an examination and meeting state requirements.

h. The process of collecting, recording, classifying, summarizing, reporting, and analyzing financial activities; results in reports that describe the financial condition of an organization.

i. The process of reviewing the records used to prepare financial statements and issuing a formal auditor's opinion indicating whether the statements have been prepared in accordance with accepted accounting rules.

j. Independent accountants who serve organizations and individuals on a fee basis; offer a wide range of services including preparation of financial statements and tax returns, independent auditing, and management consulting.

k. The amounts left over from profitable operations since the firm's beginning; equal to total profits minus all dividends paid to stockholders.

_____ **12.** Financial accounting

l. The total expense of buying or producing a firm's goods or services. For manufacturers, it includes all costs directly related to production; for wholesalers and retailers, it is the cost of goods bought for resale; for all sellers, it includes the expenses of preparing the goods for sale.

_____ **13.** Net income

m. The calculation and interpretation of financial ratios taken from the balance sheet, income statement, and statement of cash flows in order to assess a firm's performance and condition.

_____ **14.** Gross profit

n. The amount obtained by subtracting all of a firm's expenses from its revenues, when the expenses are more than the revenues; the final figure on an income statement.

_____ **15.** Operating expenses

o. The expenses of running a business that are not directly related to producing or buying its product; consist mainly of selling expenses and general and administrative expenses.

_____ **16.** Public accountants

p. Accounting that provides financial information that managers inside the organization can use to evaluate and make decisions about current and future operations.

_____ **17.** Depreciation

q. The amount obtained by subtracting all of a firm's expenses from its revenues, when the revenues are more than the expenses; the final figure on an income statement.

_____ **18.** Cost of goods sold

r. Accounting that focuses on preparing the financial reports used by outsiders such as lenders, suppliers, investors, and government agencies to assess the financial strength of a business.

_____ **19.** Private accountants

s. A financial statement that provides a summary of the money flowing into and out of a firm; used to assess the sources and uses of cash during a certain period, typically one year.

_____ **20.** Assets

t. The private organization that is responsible for establishing financial accounting standards in the United States.

_____ **21.** Auditing

u. The financial accounting standards followed by accountants in the United States in preparing financial statements.

_____ **22.** Retained earnings

v. A financial statement that summarizes a firm's financial position at a specific point in time; reports the company's assets, liabilities, and owners' equity.

_____ **23.** Fixed assets

w. The speed with which an asset can be converted to cash.

_____ **24.** Current liabilities

x. Accountants who are employed by one particular organization and work only for it.

_____ **25.** Financial Accounting Standards Board (FASB)

y. The total dollar amount of a company's sales.

_____ **26.** Liabilities

z. A financial statement that summarizes a firm's revenues and expenses and shows its total profit or loss over a period of time.

_____ **27.** Double-entry bookkeeping

aa. Claims that come due more than one year after the date of the balance sheet.

_____ **28.** Revenues

bb. The amount a company earns after paying to produce or buy its products but before deducting operating expenses; the difference between net sales and cost of goods sold.

_____ 29. Ratio analysis

_____ 30. Owners' equity

_____ 31. Current assets

_____ 32. Intangible assets

_____ 33. Net loss

_____ 34. Gross sales

_____ 35. Expenses

_____ 36. Net sales

_____ 37. Liquidity ratios

_____ 38. Earnings per share (ESP)

_____ 39. Inventory turnover ratio

_____ 40. Debt-to-equity ratio

_____ 41. Profitability ratios

_____ 42. Current ratio

_____ 43. Debt ratios

_____ 44. Activity ratios

_____ 45. Net profit margin

_____ 46. Net working capital

_____ 47. Acid-test (quick) ratio

cc. The dollar amount of a firm's sales plus any other income it received from sources such as interest, dividends, and rents.

dd. Long-term assets with no physical existence such as patents, copyrights, trademarks, and goodwill.

ee. Long-term assets used by a firm for more than a year, such as land, buildings, and machinery.

ff. The allocation of an asset's original cost to the year in which it is expected to produce revenues.

gg. The amount left after deducting sales discounts and returns and allowances from gross sales.

hh. Assets that can or will be converted to cash within the next 12 months.

ii. The total amount of the owners' investment in the firm minus any liabilities; also called net worth.

jj. The ratio of net profit to the number of shares of common stock outstanding; measures the number of dollars earned by each share of stock.

kk. Ratios that measure how well a firm is using its resources to generate profit and how efficiently it is being managed; for example, net profit margin, return on equity, and earnings per share.

ll. Ratios that measure a firm's ability to pay its short-term debts as they come due; for example, the current ratio, the acid-test (quick) ratio, and net working capital.

mm. The amount obtained by subtracting total current liabilities from total current assets; used to measure a firm's liquidity.

nn. The ratio of net profit to total owners' equity; measures the return that owners receive on their investment in the firm.

oo. The ratio of cost of goods sold to average inventory; measures the speed with which inventory moves through a firm and is turned into sales.

pp. Ratios that measure the degree and effect of a firm's use of borrowed funds (debt) to finance its operations; for example, the debt-to-equity ratio.

qq. The ratio of total current assets to total current liabilities; used to measure a firm's liquidity.

rr. The ratio of current assets excluding inventory to total current liabilities; used to measure a firm's liquidity.

ss. Ratios that measure how well a firm uses its assets; for example, inventory turnover.

tt. The ratio of total liabilities to owners' equity; measures the relationship between the amount of debt financing and the amount of equity financing.

uu. The ratio of net profit to net sales; also called return on sales. It measures the percentage of each sales dollar remaining after all expenses have been deducted.

_____ **48.** Return on equity (ROE)   **vv.** The costs of generating revenues.

CRITICAL THINKING ACTIVITIES

1. P.O.V. (Point of View)

Directions: In this exercise you will be asked to provide your personal opinion regarding some of the topics discussed in the chapter. At the completion of this exercise, your instructor may wish to poll the entire class regarding their responses.

   a. Accountants are no more than glorified bookkeepers. They merely take the documents that are created by others and certify that they are accurate. In order to reduce costs, during this era of increased competition in most industries, it would be advisable to allow the bookkeepers, that is those who actually work on the books, to certify that they are accurate and have been prepared properly.

   Agree _____   Disagree _____

   Explain:

   _____

   _____

   _____

   _____

   b. Accounting and accounting procedures are often complex and of little value to business people. Instinct can often be used by businessmen to make decisions, rather than having to spend large sums of money on accountants who create numerous irrelevant financial reports. In addition, the government and accounting professionals have conspired to create complex rules, regulations, and financial requirements that are often difficult for them to understand and explain to others.

   Agree _____   Disagree _____

   Explain:

   _____

   _____

   _____

   _____

2. Using the Internet

Directions: The role that accountants, both public and private, play in all aspects of the successful operation of a business has grown greatly over the years. You might want to consider accounting as a career. In order to get a better picture of what accountants do, click on **http://www.AICPA.org** and surf the site and its numerous links.

   a. Click on Ask Andy and summarize his response to the question being posed.
   b. Click on The Profession and then click on Ethics (quizzes) and answer the questions posed based upon your sense of the proper ethical response that is required. Compare your answers with the answers provided. How do your responses differ from those provided? In what ways are they the same?

3. Writing Skills

Directions: The nature of accounting has been evolving. Describe the roles that accountants now sometimes assume. Use a total of at least 3 terms from Enhance Your Vocabulary and Review Your Key Terms.

Chapter 20

Understanding Money and Financial Institutions

OUTLINE

MULTIPLE CHOICE

Directions: Place the letter of the response that best completes the questions that follow in the blank at the left.

>lg 1

What is money, what are its characteristics and functions, and what are the three parts of the U.S. money supply?

1. Anything that is acceptable as payment for goods and services is called:
   a. barter
   b. exchange
   c. money
   d. none of these answers are correct

2. A characteristic that money must possess in order for it to be a suitable means of exchange is:
   a. divisibility
   b. durability
   c. scarcity
   d. all of these answers are correct

3. When money serves as a common form of payment it functions as a:
   a. standard of value
   b. medium of exchange
   c. store of value
   d. scarce asset

4. When money is used to price items it functions as a:
   a. standard of value
   b. medium of exchange
   c. store of value
   d. scarce asset

5. When someone keeps money for future use in the form of other assets it is being used as a:
   a. standard of value
   b. medium of exchange
   c. store of value
   d. scarce asset

6. Deposits at a bank or other financial institution that pay interest but cannot be withdrawn on demand are known as:
   a. time deposits
   b. demand deposits
   c. currency
   d. credit cards

>lg 2

What are the basic functions of the Federal Reserve System, and what tools does it use to manage the money supply?

7. The central bank of the United States is the:
   a. First National Bank of the United States
   b. First National City Bank
   c. Bankers Trust Company
   d. Federal Reserve System

8. The major activity of the Federal Reserve is:
   a. carrying out monetary policy
   b. setting rules on credit
   c. distributing currency and making check clearing easier
   d. all of these answers are correct

9. The purchase or sale of U.S. Government bonds by the Federal Reserve is known as:
   a. setting reserve requirements
   b. open market operations
   c. changing the discount rate
   d. selective credit control

10. The interest rate that the Federal Reserve charges its member banks for borrowing is known as the:
    a. discount rate
    b. reserve requirement
    c. prime rate
    d. consumer rate

11. Margin requirements:
    a. determine the amount of money that banks must keep on reserve
    b. are the rate of interest charged to banks by the Federal Reserve
    c. specify the minimum amount of cash an investor must put up to buy securities
    d. are the funds that banks must keep on reserve to be held against deposits

_____ 12. The advantage gained from the time it takes a check to clear and the amount of time it takes to be withdrawn from the check writer's account is called:
a. reserve   c. float
b. margin   d. spread

>lg 3

What are the key financial institutions, and what role do they play in the process of financial intermediation?

_____ 13. When financial institutions act as go-betweens, between the suppliers and demanders of funds, they are involved in the process of:
a. creating margin
b. playing the float
c. open market operations
d. financial intermediation

_____ 14. A commercial bank is an institution that:
a. is a depository institution that is formed specifically to encourage household savings and to make home mortgage loans
b. accepts deposits, makes business and consumer loans, invests in government and corporate securities, and provides other financial services
c. operates like a savings and loan association or a savings bank
d. is a not-for-profit, member owned financial cooperative

_____ 15. A company that makes short-term loans for which the borrower puts up tangible assets as security is known as a:
a. finance company   c. insurance company
b. pension fund   d. depository financial institution

>lg 4

How does the Federal Deposit Insurance Corporation protect depositors' funds?

_____ 16. The organization that was created to insure the deposits of commercial banks is the:
a. Federal Reserve Bank
b. Federal Home Loan Insurance Corporation
c. Savings Association Insurance Fund
d. Federal Deposit Insurance Corporation

_____ 17. The Banking Act of 1933 gave the Federal Reserve System the power to:
a. set reserve requirements
b. ban interest on demand deposits
c. regulate interest rates on time deposits
d. all of these answers are correct

_____ 18. The limit of FDIC insurance on deposits at commercial banks and savings institutions is:
a. $100,000 per account
b. $150,000 per account
c. $200,000 per account
d. allowed to vary depending on the account

_____ 19. When a bank has serious financial problems, the FDIC can:
a. lend money to the bank
b. replace its management
c. cover all deposits, including those over $100,000
d. all of these answers are correct

>lg 5

What role do U.S. banks play in the international marketplace?

_____ 20. American banks were able to expand into foreign markets because they:
a. were larger
b. provided better service and had access to more funding
c. dealt only in United States currency
d. could serve United States citizens overseas

_____ 21. One difficulty related to the operation and profitability of American banks in foreign markets is that:
a. foreign banks are subject to fewer regulations
b. American owned banks must purchase a domestic bank in order to operate in the foreign market
c. American owned banks are not subject to restrictions imposed by foreign governments
d. American banks are not permitted to open foreign branches

_____ 22. An important role played by U.S. banks in global business is the area of:
a. global cash management
b. providing advanced information systems for customer use
c. supplying technological expertise
d. all of these answers are correct

>lg 6

What trends are reshaping the banking industry?

_____ 23. The use of the Internet technology to expand bank services is called:
a. email banking   c. online banking
b. ebanking   d. Interbanking

_____ 24. The trend in the U.S. banking system that has resulted in numerous bank mergers is called:
a. online banking   c. integration of banking services
b. consolidation   d. insurance and brokerage

_____ 25. The repeal of the Glass Steagal Act of 1933 and the enactment of the Financial Services Modernization Act would lead to:
a. online banking
b. a greater number of banks
c. a greater number of brokerage and insurance firms
d. the integration of bank, brokerage, and insurance services

---

TRUE/FALSE

Directions: Place a T or an F in the space provided at the left of each question to indicate whether it is True or False.

>lg 1

What is money, and what are its characteristics and functions, and what are the three parts of the U.S. money supply?

_____ 1. Banks will always maintain their ability to survive because they have been able to maintain growth in the area of commercial business.

_____ 2. Paper currency and coins are considered to be the only forms of money.

_____ 3. The federal government, through control of the money supply, can promote economic growth and stability.

_____ 4. Governments control the scarcity of money by limiting the quantity of money that is produced.

_____ 5. Scarcity, durability, portability, and divisibility are the key characteristics that money must possess in order for it to be suitable for use as a medium of exchange.

_____ 6. In order for money to function as a standard of value it must be able to retain its value over time.

_____ 7. In order for money to function as a store of value it must be able to allow for the pricing of goods and services in standard units.

_____ 8. Demand deposits are not considered part of the U.S. money supply until they are withdrawn from a bank and converted into currency.

_____ 9. Even though a credit card can be used to make a purchase, it is not considered money because it is not replacing money but rather simply allowing for deferred payment.

>lg 2

What are the basic functions of the Federal Reserve, and what tools does it use to manage the money supply?

_____ 10. In 1913 the Congress created the First Bank of the United States in order to correct the weaknesses of the U.S. financial system.

_____ 11. The Federal Reserve System, the central bank of the United States, consists of 12 district banks, each located in a major U.S. city.

_____ 12. The Fed carries out monetary policy, sets rules on credit, distributes currency, and facilitates check clearing.

_____ 13. The most important function of the Fed is to carry out the distribution of currency throughout the United States.

_____ 14. Open market operations, carried out by the Fed, are designed to cause changes in time deposit account balances held by banks for customers.

_____ 15. In order to require member banks to hold cash balances in their vaults or at a district bank, the Federal Reserve imposes a reserve requirement ranging from 3 to 10 percent on different types of deposits.

_____ 16. By controlling the discount rate, the Federal Reserve is setting credit terms on some loans made by member banks and other lending institutions.

_____ 17. Selective credit controls include the power of the Fed to specify margin requirements—the minimum amount of cash an investor must put up to buy securities.

>lg 3

What are the key financial institutions, and what role do they play in the process of financial intermediation?

_____ 18. Both national and state banks are required to obtain a charter from the appropriate authority in order to conduct banking business.

_____ 19. Savings bank depositors typically have something in common—an employer, union, professional group, or religious affiliation.

_____ 20. Insurance companies, pension funds, credit unions, finance companies, and brokerage firms are categorized as nondepository financial institutions.

>lg 4

How does the Federal Deposit Insurance Corporation protect depositors' funds?

_____ 21. During the Great Depression that followed the stock market collapse of 1929, the FDIC protected many bank depositors from losses that could have resulted when the banking system collapsed.

_____ 22. After the formation of the FDIC, the FSLIC was formed in 1934 to insure deposits at saving and loan associations.

_____ 23. The FSLIC was forced to take responsibility for administering the fund that insures deposits at thrift institutions when the FDIC went bankrupt in the 1980s.

_____ 24. The Bank Insurance Fund is administered by the FDIC and provides deposit insurance to thrift institutions.

_____ 25. Among the actions that can be taken by the FDIC to assist a bank with serious financial problems is to require the bank to use new management practices or to replace its management.

>lg 5

What role do U.S. banks play in the international marketplace?

_____ 26. An advantage that foreign banks have over U.S. owned banks in foreign markets is that the foreign banks provide better service and have access to more sources of funding.

_____ 27. U.S. banks are subject to fewer regulations than foreign banks, making it easier for them to undercut the foreign banks on the pricing of loans and services to multinational corporations and governments.

_____ 28. An important service offered by U.S. banks to foreign governments and businesses is the management of cash flows and the improvement of payment efficiency along with reducing their exposure to operational risks.

>lg 6

What trends are reshaping the banking industry?

_____ 29. An area that offers profit potential for banks is online bill presentment and payment.

_____ 30. The number of depository institutions has increased over the past 25 years due to the increase in the size of the market for banks and bank services.

_____ 31. Although there has been a decline in depository institutions overall, there has been a resurgence in the creation of small banks because many people still prefer the personal service offered by community banks.

ENHANCE YOUR VOCABULARY

Affiliates	To accept as an associate; to associate with; an associate or a subordinate
Amass	To collect for oneself: accumulate; gather; assemble
Armored	A protective, defensive covering for the body; a quality or circumstance that affords protection
Courier	A messenger especially one on urgent or official business; a tourists' guide
Lubricant	Something that lessens or prevents friction or difficulty
Perpetrate	To bring about or carry out (as a crime or deception)
Proclaims	To declare publicly, proudly

Quasi-public	Essentially public although under private ownership or control
Speculative	Theoretical rather than demonstrable; to engage in risky business ventures that offer the chance of large profits
Unscrupulous	Unprincipled; lacking moral principles

Directions: Select the definition in Column B that best defines the word in Column A.

Column A	Column B
_____ 1. Courier	a. To accept as an associate
_____ 2. Speculative	b. Unprincipled; lacking moral principles
_____ 3. Amass	c. To bring about or carry out (as a crime)
_____ 4. Quasi-public	d. Theoretical rather than demonstrable
_____ 5. Affiliates	e. To collect; accumulate
_____ 6. Armored	f. Essentially public although under private control
_____ 7. Lubricant	g. A protective, defensive covering for the body
_____ 8. Unscrupulous	h. A messenger or tourists' guide
_____ 9. Proclaims	i. Something that lessens or prevents friction
_____ 10. Perpetuate	j. To declare publicly, proudly

REVIEW YOUR KEY TERMS

Directions: Select the definition in Column B that best defines the word in Column A.

Column A	Column B
_____ 1. Money	a. The power of the Federal Reserve to influence the terms of consumer credit and margin requirements. Consumer credit rules can be used to restrict or stimulate consumer credit purchases; margin requirements can be used to accelerate or slow securities trading.
_____ 2. Reserve requirement	b. Deposits at a bank or other financial institution that pay interest but cannot be withdrawn on demand, for example, savings accounts, money market deposit accounts, and certificates of deposit; one of the three parts of the U.S. money supply (along with currency and demand deposits).
_____ 3. Discount rate	c. Money kept in checking accounts that can be withdrawn by depositors on demand; one of the three parts of the U.S. money supply (along with currency and time deposits).
_____ 4. Financial intermediation	d. The requirement that banks that are members of the Federal Reserve System must hold some of their deposits in cash in their vaults or in an account at a district bank. By changing the reserve requirement, the Federal Reserve can slow down or stimulate the economy.
_____ 5. Federal Deposit Insurance Corporation (FDIC)	e. Not-for-profit, member-owned financial cooperatives.
_____ 6. Selective credit controls	f. Anything that is acceptable as payment for goods and services; must be scarce, durable, portable, and divisible, and must also be able to function as a medium of exchange, a standard of value, and a store of value.

_____ **7.** Open market
operations

    g. The interest rate that the Federal Reserve charges its member banks. By changing the discount rate, the Federal Reserve can slow down or stimulate the economy.

_____ **8.** Time deposits

    h. The purchase or sale of U.S. government bonds by the Federal Reserve to stimulate or slow down the economy; one of the Fed's tools for carrying out monetary policy.

_____ **9.** Pension funds

    i. The process in which financial institutions act as intermediaries between the suppliers and demanders of funds. The institutions accept savers' deposits and invest them in financial products such as loans.

_____ **10.** Commercial banks

    j. An independent, quasi-public corporation backed by the full faith and credit of the U.S. government that insures deposits in commercial banks and thrift institutions up to a ceiling of $100,000 per account.

_____ **11.** Credit unions

    k. Profit-oriented financial institutions that accept deposits, make business and consumer loans, invest in government and corporate securities, and provide other financial services.

_____ **12.** Bank charter

    l. Large pools of money set aside by corporations, unions, and governments for later use in paying retirement benefits to their employees or members.

_____ **13.** Thrift institutions

    m. An operating license issued to a bank by the federal government or a state government; required for a commercial bank to do business.

_____ **14.** Demand deposits

    n. Depository institutions formed specifically to encourage household saving and to make home mortgage loans; include savings and loan associations and savings banks.

CRITICAL THINKING ACTIVITIES

1. P.O.V. (Point of View)

Directions: In this exercise you will be asked to provide your personal opinion regarding some of the topics discussed in the chapter. At the completion of this exercise, your instructor may wish to poll the entire class regarding their responses.

    a. The paper money supply of the United States and that of other nations is neither scarce nor durable. It is extremely easy to earn money and it can be found everywhere in the world. Paper currency, which is easily destroyed and counterfeited, must be constantly changed to avoid such problems.

    Agree _____   Disagree _____

    Explain:

    _____

    _____

    _____

    _____

    b. The value that is assigned by individuals to a particular currency, such as the Dollar, the British Pound Sterling, or the Russian Ruble, is determined by the quantity of precious metals into which the currency can be converted. The primary reason that currencies such as these retain their value is that central banks are willing to convert them into gold or silver, on demand, when asked to do so by other governments.

Agree _____   Disagree _____

Explain:

_____

_____

_____

_____

2. Using the Internet

Directions: The safety of bank deposits is of paramount importance in order to assure the smooth operation of a financial system. In the United States, bank account safety has only been available since the Great Depression of the 1930's and is provided by the Federal Deposit Insurance Corporation. Click on **http://www.FDIC.gov**.

   a. Click on Is My Bank Insured? Enter the name of your bank or a bank in your community. Is the bank insured?
   b. Click on Which Investments Are Not Insured? Click on Facts About Bank Investments. Which deposits are FDIC insured? Which deposits are not FDIC insured?
   c. Click on Are My Deposits Insured? Scroll down the page and click on Certificates of Deposit: Tips for Investors and summarize the advice that is provided.

3. Writing Skills

Directions: As a bank vice-president, you've been asked to give a lecture to the Economics Society of your local college. The dean of the college would like you to discuss the following question: "If America is basically a free-market economy, why do we have a Federal Reserve System?" Outline and write the lecture.

NOTES ON CHAPTER 20

Chapter 21

Financial Management

OUTLINE

I. The Role of Finance
    A. The Financial Manager's Responsibilities and Activities
    B. The Goal of the Financial Manager

II. Financial Planning
    A. Forecasts
    B. Budgets

III. How Organizations Use Funds
    A. Short-term Expenses
        1. Cash Management: Assuring Liquidity
        2. Managing Accounts Receivable
        3. Inventory
    B. Long-term Expenditures

IV. Obtaining Short-term Financing
    A. Unsecured Short-term Loans
        1. Trade Credit: Accounts Payable
        2. Bank Loans
        3. Commercial Paper
    B. Secured Short-term loans

V. Raising Long-term Financing
    A. Debt versus Equity Financing
    B. Debt Financing
    C. Equity Financing
        1. Selling New Issues of Common Stock
        2. Dividends and Retained Earnings
        3. Preferred Stock
        4. Venture Capital

VI. Finance Goes Global

VII. Risk Management

VIII. Applying This Chapter's Topics

MULTIPLE CHOICE

Directions: Place the letter of the response that best completes the questions that follow in the blank space at the left.

>lg 1

What roles do finance and the financial manager play in the firm's overall strategy?

_____   1. The art and science of managing a firm's money so it can meet its goals is known as:
        a. financing   **c.** cash flow assessment
        b. financial management   **d.** operations management

_____   2. The chief source of funding for a business should be through:
        a. debt management   **c.** revenue
        b. cash outflows   **d.** the sale of equities

_____   3. The activity known as financial planning involves:
        a. obtaining funding for the firm's operations and investments and seeking the best balance between debt and equity
        b. studying the summary of cash flows submitted by the firm's accounting department
        c. investing the firm's funds in projects and securities that provide high returns in relation to the risks
        d. preparing the financial plan, which projects revenues, expenditures, and financing needs over a given period

_____   4. The activity known as financing involves:
        a. obtaining funding for the firm's operations and investments and seeking the best balance between debt and equity
        b. studying the summary of cash flows submitted by the firm's accounting department
        c. investing the firm's funds in projects and securities that provide high returns in relation to the risks
        d. preparing the financial plan, which projects revenues, expenditures, and financing needs over a given period

_____   5. When financial managers strive for a balance between the opportunity for profit and the potential for loss, they are concerned with:
        a. risk   **c.** the risk-return-tradeoff
        b. return   **d.** none of these answers are correct

>lg 2

How does a firm develop its financial plans, including forecasts and budgets?

_____   6. To prepare a financial plan, the financial manager of a firm must consider the:
        a. existing and proposed products
        b. resources available to produce the products
        c. financing needed to support production and sales
        d. all of these answers are correct

_____   7. Short-term forecasts or operating plans:
        a. project revenues, costs of goods, and operating expenses over a one year period
        b. cover from 2 to 10 years and take a broad view of the firm's financial activities
        c. control future financial activities
        d. forecast outlays for fixed assets

_____   8. Budgets:
        a. project revenues, costs of goods, and operating expenses over a one year period
        b. cover from 2 to 10 years and take a broad view of the firm's financial activities
        c. control future financial activities
        d. forecast outlays for fixed assets

_____ 9. Long-term forecasts or strategic plans:
a. project revenues, costs of goods, and operating expenses over a one-year period
b. cover from 2 to 10 years and take a broad view of the firm's financial activities
c. control future financial activities
d. forecast outlays for fixed assets

_____ 10. Capital budgets:
a. project revenues, costs of goods, and operating expenses over a one year period
b. cover from 2 to 10 years and take a broad view of the firm's financial activities
c. control future financial activities
d. forecast outlays for fixed assets

>lg 3   What types of short-term and long-term expenditures does a firm make?

_____ 11. Cash management involves:
a. sales for which the firm has not been paid
b. collection policies
c. making sure that enough cash is on hand to pay bills as they come due and to meet unexpected expenses
d. outlays for all business activities

_____ 12. Sales for which the firm has not been paid are known as:
a. accounts payable   c. collections
b. credit terms   d. accounts receivable

_____ 13. Capital expenditures are:
a. investments in long-lived assets, such as land, buildings, machinery, and equipment
b. payment for operating expenses that can't be paid out of current revenue
c. the analysis of long-term projects and their selection based upon offering the greatest return while maximizing the firm's value
d. the use of funds to purchase inventory

_____ 14. Capital budgeting is:
a. investments in long-lived assets, such as land, buildings, machinery, and equipment
b. payment for operating expenses that can't be paid out of current revenue
c. the analysis of long-term projects and their selection based upon offering the greatest return while maximizing the firm's value
d. the use of funds to purchase inventory

>lg 4   What are the main sources and costs of unsecured and secured short-term financing?

_____ 15. An unsecured loan is given on the basis of:
a. specific assets that are pledged as collateral
b. a security deposit left with the lending institution
c. a firm's credit rating and the lender's previous experience with the firm
d. none of these answers are correct

_____ 16. A secured loan is given on the basis of:
a. specific assets that are pledged as collateral
b. a security deposit left with the lending institution
c. a firm's credit rating and the lender's previous experience with the firm
d. none of these answers are correct

_____ **17.** A trade credit:
- **a.** is an agreement between a bank and a business that states the maximum amount of unsecured short-term borrowing that is allowed over a given period, typically one year
- **b.** occurs when a seller extends credit to the buyer between the time the buyer receives the goods or services and when it pays for them
- **c.** is basically a guaranteed line of credit
- **d.** is unsecured short-term debt offered by large financially secure corporations

_____ **18.** A line of credit:
- **a.** is an agreement between a bank and a business that states the maximum amount of unsecured short-term borrowing that is allowed over a given period, typically one year
- **b.** occurs when a seller extends credit to the buyer between the time the buyer receives the goods or services and when it pays for them
- **c.** is basically a reserved line of credit
- **d.** is unsecured short-term debt offered by large financially secure corporations

_____ **19.** Commercial paper is:
- **a.** an agreement between a bank and a business that states the maximum amount of unsecured short-term borrowing that is allowed over a given period, typically one year
- **b.** created when a seller extends credit to the buyer between the time the buyer receives the goods or services and when it pays for them
- **c.** basically a guaranteed line of credit
- **d.** unsecured short-term debt offered by large financially secure corporations

_____ **20.** When a firm sells its accounts receivable outright to a firm which then collects them, it is using a form of short-term financing called:
- **a.** a line of credit
- **b.** factoring
- **c.** a revolving line of credit
- **d.** trade credit

>lg 5   How do the two primary sources of long-term financing compare?

_____ **21.** A basic rule of finance is to:
- **a.** not be concerned with the length of the debt as long as the company has the funds to pay for it
- **b.** finance short-term expenses with long-term financing
- **c.** finance long-term expenses with revolving short-term financing
- **d.** match the length of financing to the period over which benefits are expected to be received from the expenses

_____ **22.** The major drawback of debt financing is:
- **a.** the loss of ownership that takes place with it
- **b.** market risk
- **c.** financial risk
- **d.** liquidity

_____ **23.** A drawback of equity financing is:
- **a.** shareholders get voting rights and a voice in management
- **b.** it is more costly than debt financing
- **c.** dividends to stockholders are not tax-deductible
- **d.** all of these answers are correct

>lg 6 **What are the major types, features, and costs of long-term debt?**

_____ 24. Bonds are:
   a. long-term debt obligations
   b. a business loan with a maturity of more than one year
   c. securities that represent ownership in a corporation
   d. a long-term loan using real estate as collateral

_____ 25. A term loan is:
   a. a long-term debt obligation
   b. a business loan with a maturity of more than one year
   c. a security that represents ownership in a corporation
   d. a long-term loan using real estate as collateral

_____ 26. A mortgage loan is:
   a. a long-term equity obligation
   b. a business loan with a maturity of more than one year
   c. a security that represents ownership in a corporation
   d. a long-term loan using real estate as collateral

>lg 7 **When and how do firms issue equity, and what are the costs?**

_____ 27. Common stock is a:
   a. long-term debt obligation
   b. business loan with a maturity of more than one year
   c. security that represents ownership in a corporation
   d. long-term loan using real estate as collateral

_____ 28. Dividends are:
   a. profit that is to be reinvested in the firm
   b. a form of equity or ownership in the firm
   c. a form of venture capital
   d. payment to stockholders in the form of cash or stock from the corporation's profits

_____ 29. Preferred stock is:
   a. a long-term debt obligation made by the corporation
   b. an investment for which the dividend amount is set at the time the stock is issued
   c. a dividend that is paid by the corporation in the form of stock
   d. an investment in a new business made by individuals in return for part of its debt

_____ 30. Venture capital is:
   a. a long-term debt obligation made by the corporation
   b. paid a predetermined dividend amount which must be paid before common stockholders
   c. a dividend that is paid by the corporation in the form of stock
   d. an investment in a new business made by individuals in return for part of the ownership

>lg 8 **What trends are affecting the field of financial management?**

_____ 31. The common currency that will replace the currencies of the 11 European Union nations by 2002, is known as the:
   a. Euro   c. Deutschmark
   b. Shilling   d. Pound Sterling

_____ **32.** Operational risk is the risk of loss due to:
    a. default on a financial transaction or a reduction in a security's market value due to a decline in the credit quality of the debt issuer
    b. unexpected losses arising from deficiencies in a firm's management information, support, control systems, and procedures
    c. adverse movements in the level or volatility of market prices of securities, commodities, and currencies
    d. changes in the price of the firm's common and preferred stock

_____ **33.** Credit risk is the risk of loss due to:
    a. default on a financial transaction or a reduction in a security's market value due to a decline in the credit quality of the debt issuer
    b. unexpected losses arising from deficiencies in a firm's management information, support, control systems, and procedures
    c. adverse movements in the level or volatility of market prices of securities, commodities, and currencies
    d. changes in the price of the firm's common and preferred stock

_____ **34.** Market risk is a risk of loss due to:
    a. default on a financial transaction or a reduction in a security's market value due to a decline in the credit quality of the debt issuer
    b. unexpected losses arising from deficiencies in a firm's management information, support, control systems, and procedures
    c. adverse movements in the level or volatility of market prices of securities, commodities, and currencies
    d. a change in the management hierarchy of a corporation

TRUE/FALSE

Directions: Place a T or an F in the space provided at the left of each question to indicate whether it is True or False.

>lg 1

What roles do finance and the financial manager play in the firm's overall strategy?

_____ **1.** Financial management is the art and science of managing a firm's money so it can meet its goals.

_____ **2.** When accountants create financial statements, especially those that focus on cash flows, they are acting as financial managers.

_____ **3.** Financial planning, investment, and financing are all functions performed by financial managers.

_____ **4.** Both maximizing value and maximizing profits are the primary goals of financial managers.

_____ **5.** The risk-return trade-off states that, *the lower the risk, the greater the return* that must be achieved from an investment.

>lg 2

How does a firm develop its financial plans, including forecasts and budgets?

_____ **6.** The purpose of a company's financial plan is to guide the firm toward its business goals and the maximization of value. This will enable the firm to estimate the amount and timing of its investments and financing needs.

_____ 7. Operating plans typically cover 2 to 10 years and take a broader view of the firm's financial activities.

_____ 8. Strategic plans project revenues, costs of goods, and operating expenses over a one-year period.

_____ 9. Capital budgets forecast outlays for fixed assets, usually cover a period of several years, and ensure that the firm will have enough funds to buy the equipment and buildings it needs.

_____ 10. Operating budgets combine sales forecasts with estimates of production costs and operating expenses in order to forecast profits.

>lg 3   What types of short-term and long-term expenditures does a firm make?

_____ 11. Operating expenses are typically long-term in nature because they must be paid to support production and selling activities that take place over and over again.

_____ 12. Cash management assures the liquidity of the firm, making sure that enough cash is on hand to pay bills as they come due and to meet unexpected expenses.

_____ 13. Cash held in checking accounts is considered a marketable security because it provides liquidity for the firm.

_____ 14. Treasury bills, certificates of deposit, and commercial paper are popular marketable securities that businesses buy to earn income on surplus cash.

_____ 15. Accounts receivable represent sales for which the firm has yet to be paid.

_____ 16. A benefit of liberal credit and collection policies is increased sales and decreased accounts receivable.

_____ 17. The cost of inventory is included in capital expenditures because it not only includes the purchase price of the item, but also ordering, handling, storage, interest, and insurance costs.

_____ 18. The financial manager analyzes long-term projects and selects those that offer the best returns while maximizing the firm's value through a process called capital budgeting.

>lg 4   What are the main sources and costs of unsecured and secured short-term financing?

_____ 19. A loan granted on the basis of a firm's credit and the lender's previous experience with the firm is called an unsecured loan.

_____ 20. A trade credit granted when a seller extends credit to a buyer is entered on the books of the seller as an account payable.

_____ 21. A revolving credit agreement is a form of commercial paper that is issued by a bank or other thrift institution to a corporation.

_____ 22. Collateral is not required by a lending institution when a secured loan is granted.

_____ 23. Factoring allows a firm to turn its accounts receivable into cash without worrying about collections.

>lg 5   How do the two primary sources of long-term financing compare?

_____ 24. A major advantage of debt financing is financial risk—the deductibility of interest expense for income tax purposes.

_____ 25. A benefit of equity financing for the corporation is that it gives common stockholders voting rights and a voice in management.

_____ **26.** Dividends that are paid to stockholders are not tax deductible expenses.

>lg 6   **What are the major types, features, and costs of long-term debt?**

_____ **27.** A term loan is a business loan with a maturity of more than one year that can be secured or unsecured.

_____ **28.** When a mortgage loan is granted, the lender gains the right to seize the property, sell it, and use the proceeds to pay off the loan if the borrower fails to make the scheduled payments.

_____ **29.** Bonds are long-term obligations of the corporation that are issued with maturities of 10 to 30 years.

>lg 7   **When and how do firms issue equity, and what are the costs?**

_____ **30.** Common stock and preferred stock are both forms of equity that represent ownership in a corporation. Unlike preferred stock, common stockholders receive a guaranteed dividend payment prior to any payment being paid to preferred shareholders.

_____ **31.** Both cash and stock dividends are payments that are made to shareholders from the corporation's profits.

_____ **32.** Companies who already have already gone public can issue and sell additional shares of stock through *IPOs*.

_____ **33.** The use of retained earnings for dividend payments is not a common practice in public utilities.

_____ **34.** In some instances, angel investors have taken the place of venture capitalists and are emerging to help start-up firms find equity capital.

>lg 8   **What trends are affecting the field of financial management?**

_____ **35.** Managing foreign currency exposure and developing strategies to protect against increased foreign currency risk are now major activities for many financial managers.

_____ **36.** A common currency, the Escudo, will replace the currencies of the 11 European Union member nations by 2002.

_____ **37.** Risk management involves the evaluation of credit risks, market risks, and operational risks.

ENHANCE YOUR VOCABULARY

Complementary	Serving to fill out or complete; mutually supplying each other's lack
Default	To fail to fulfill a contract, agreement, or duty
Deficiency	Inadequacy; shortage
Fabricated	Invent, create; to make up for the purpose of deception
Lifeblood	Blood regarded as the seat of vitality; a vital or life-giving force
Profiled	To draw or write a profile of; a biographical essay
Residual	Remaining as a residue; remainder; what is left after something is removed
Turbulent	Causing unrest, violence, or disturbance; characterized by agitation or tumult

Underwriter   One that underwrites; guarantor; one that underwrites a policy of insurance

Volatility   Readily vaporizable at a relatively low temperature; lively; tending to erupt into violent action; explosive

Directions: Select the definition in Column B that best defines the word in Column A.

Column A	Column B
_____ 1. Underwriter	**a.** To fail to fulfill a contract, agreement or duty
_____ 2. Profiled	**b.** Readily vaporizable at a relatively low temperature; explosive
_____ 3. Complementary	**c.** Remaining as a residue; a payment made to a performer for a rerun of a television how
_____ 4. Volatility	**d.** Serving to fill out or complete
_____ 5. Default	**e.** Guarantor
_____ 6. Turbulent	**f.** Inadequacy; shortage
_____ 7. Lifeblood	**g.** Causing unrest, violence, or disturbance
_____ 8. Deficiency	**h.** A biographical essay
_____ 9. Fabricated	**i.** A vital or life-giving force
_____ 10. Residual	**j.** Invent, create; to make up for the purpose of deception

REVIEW YOUR KEY TERMS

Directions: Select the definition in Column B that best defines the word in Column A.

Column A	Column B
_____ 1. Financial management	**a.** Projections of a firm's activities and the funding for those activities over a period that is longer than a year, typically 2 to 10 years; also called strategic plans.
_____ 2. Accounts receivable	**b.** Budgets that combine sales forecasts with estimates of production costs and operating expenses in order to forecast a firm's profits.
_____ 3. Budgets	**c.** A basic principle in finance that holds that the higher the risk associated with an investment, the greater the return that is required.
_____ 4. Revolving credit agreement	**d.** Short-term loans for which the borrower does not have to pledge specific assets as security. Instead, the loans are given on the basis of the firm's credit and the lender's previous experience with the firm; include trade credit, bank loans, and commercial paper.
_____ 5. Trade credit	**e.** A form of short-term financing in which a firm sells its accounts receivable to a factor, a financial institution that buys accounts receivable at a discount.
_____ 6. Capital budgets	**f.** The process of making sure that a firm has enough cash on hand to pay bills as they come due and to meet unexpected expenses.
_____ 7. Risk	**g.** Budgets that forecast a firm's cash inflows and outflows and help the firm plan for cash surpluses and shortages.
_____ 8. Unsecured loans	**h.** Investments in long-lived assets such as land, buildings, machinery, and equipment that are expected to produce benefits over a period longer than a year.

_____ 9. Financial risk

_____ 10. Cash management

_____ 11. Capital expenditures

_____ 12. Line of credit

_____ 13. Capital budgeting

_____ 14. Risk-return trade-off

_____ 15. Risk management

_____ 16. Stock dividends

_____ 17. Cash flows

_____ 18. Factoring

_____ 19. Long-term forecasts

_____ 20. Marketable securities

_____ 21. Cash budgets

_____ 22. Short-term forecasts

_____ 23. Preferred stock

_____ 24. Bonds

_____ 25. Return

_____ 26. Operating budgets

_____ 27. Account payable

_____ 28. Mortgage loan

i. The art and science of managing a firm's money so that it can meet its goals.

j. The inflow and outflow of cash for a firm.

k. Investments in long-lived assets such as land, buildings, machinery, and equipment that are expected to produce benefits over a period longer than a year.

l. The potential for loss or the chance that an investment will not achieve the expected level of return.

m. The chance that a firm will be unable to make scheduled interest and principal payments on its debt.

n. Formal written forecasts of revenues and expenses that set spending limits based on operational forecasts; include cash budgets, capital budgets, and operating budgets.

o. Long-term debt obligations (liabilities) of corporations and governments.

p. A security for which the dividend amount is set at the time the stock is issued. Dividends on preferred stock must be paid before the company can pay any dividends to common stockholders.

q. A business loan with a maturity of more than a year; can be secured or unsecured.

r. The process of analyzing long-term projects and selecting those that offer the best returns while maximizing the firm's value.

s. Budgets that forecast a firm's outlays for fixed assets (plant and equipment), typically for a period of several years.

t. The extension of credit by the seller to the buyer between the time the buyer receives the goods or services and the time it pays for them.

u. Short-term investments that are easily converted into cash; for example, Treasury bills, certificates of deposits, and commercial paper.

v. A guaranteed line of credit whereby a bank agrees that a certain amount of funds will be available for a business to borrow over a given period, often three to five years.

w. The process of identifying and evaluating risks and selecting and managing techniques to adapt to risk exposure.

x. Unsecured short-term debt (an IOU) offered by large, financially strong corporations.

y. Projections of revenues, costs of goods, and operating expenses over a one-year period; also called operating plans.

z. Loans for which the borrower is required to pledge specific assets as collateral, or security.

aa. Payments to stockholders in the form of more stock; may replace or supplement cash dividends.

bb. A security that represents an ownership interest in a corporation.

_____ **29.** Retained earnings   **cc.** Purchases for which a firm has not yet paid.

_____ **30.** Commercial paper   **dd.** Profits which have been reinvested in a firm.

_____ **31.** Common stock   **ee.** Payments to stockholders in the form of more stock; may replace or supplement cash dividends.

_____ **32.** Secured loans   **ff.** Sales for which a firm has not yet been paid.

_____ **33.** Term loan   **gg.** A long-term loan that uses real estate as collateral.

_____ **34.** Dividends   **hh.** The opportunity for profit.

CRITICAL THINKING ACTIVITIES

1. P.O.V. (Point of View)

Directions: In this exercise you will be asked to provide your personal opinion regarding some of the topics discussed in the chapter. At the completion of this exercise, your instructor may wish to poll the entire class regarding their responses.

    a. Financial managers are under tremendous pressure to have their firms run in the 'black' and to report increased profits from operations. The best method of financing this type of growth is for these managers to borrow in the long-term bond market where interest costs are usually lower than those in the markets for short-term financing.

    Agree _____   Disagree _____

    Explain:

    _____

    _____

    _____

    _____

    b. The single best way for a business to raise funds is for it to sell stock in the equities markets. Individuals purchase the new stock and provide the firm with funds to invest in the business. If the stock cannot be sold in the United States, foreign equity markets are always a reliable source of financing.

    Agree _____   Disagree _____

    Explain:

    _____

    _____

    _____

    _____

2. Using the Internet

Directions: IPOs are an important component of equity financing for business. Go to **http://www. IPOGuys.com** and click on Educational Info:IPO University and then click on IPO Guys Glossary.

    a. What is meant by the following terms:

- IPO
- Liquidity
- Offering Price
- Prospectus
- Underwriter
- Venture Capital Funding

   b. Discuss the importance of the use of IPO's by business in the area of financial management.

3. Writing Skills

Directions: Your firm manufacturers athletic equipment and needs to raise money. As a staff CPA, write a memo to the chief financial officer outlining five ways of obtaining the funds.

Chapter 22

Understanding Securities and Securities Markets

OUTLINE

C. Security Price Quotations
1. Stock Quotations
2. Bond Quotations
3. Mutual Fund Quotations
D. Market Averages and Indexes

VIII. Market Competition Heats Up

IX. Rise of the Individual Investor

X. Applying This Chapter's Topics
A. The Time is Now
B. Tips for Online Investing

MULTIPLE CHOICE

Directions: Place the letter of the response that best completes the questions that follow in the blank space at the left.

>lg 1

What is the function of the securities markets?

_____ 1. Investment certificates issued by corporations are known as:
a. primary markets   c. securities
b. secondary markets   d. underwriting

_____ 2. The primary market is the place where:
a. the issuers of a security are not usually involved in the transactions taking place
b. new securities are offered to the public-where they are sold just once
c. old securities are bought and sold
d. *tombstone* announcements are made regarding both new and old securities

_____ 3. Investment bankers:
a. help companies raise long-term financing
b. buy and sell securities for customers and work for brokerage houses
c. issue *tombstone* announcements about firms that are going out of business
d. none of these answers are correct

_____ 4. A person who is licensed to buy and sell securities on behalf of clients is known as a(n):
a. underwriter   c. attorney
b. investor   d. stock broker

>lg 2

How do common stock, preferred stock, and bonds differ?

_____ 5. Dividends are:
a. part of the profits of a corporation that the firm distributes to stockholders
b. a security that represents an ownership interest in a corporation
c. profits that are reinvested by a firm in more buildings, equipment, and new products to earn future profits
d. a vote for each share of stock purchased

_____ 6. Retained earnings are:
a. part of the profits of a corporation that the firm distributes to stockholders
b. a security that represents an ownership interest in a corporation
c. profits that are reinvested by a firm in more buildings, equipment, and new products to earn future profits
d. a vote for each share of stock purchased

_____ **7.** Common stock is:
  a. part of the profits of a corporation that the firm distributes to stockholders
  b. a security that represents an ownership interest in a corporation
  c. profit that is reinvested by a firm in more buildings, equipment, and new products to earn future profits
  d. a vote for each share of stock purchased

_____ **8.** A major disadvantage of stock ownership is
  a. stockholders may not get any return at all
  b. stock prices are affected by economic, industry, and company factors
  c. future prices of shares can be difficult to predict
  d. all of these answers are correct

_____ **9.** Preferred stockholders:
  a. receive their dividends after common stockholders
  b. always have _cumulative preferred_ status
  c. usually receive their dividends before common stockholders
  d. are assured of increased dividend payments over time

_____ **10.** Bonds are long term debt obligations of corporations that pay a fixed amount of money called:
  a. dividends   **c.** principal
  b. interest   **d.** par value

_____ **11.** An example of a secured bond is a:
  a. debenture   **c.** Treasury bond
  b. mortgage bond   **d.** Treasury note

_____ **12.** U.S. Treasury notes:
  a. have a maturity of 10 years or less
  b. have maturities as long as 25 years
  c. mature in less than a year
  d. never mature

> **lg 3**   **What other types of securities are available to investors?**

_____ **13.** A type of security that is available to individual investors is a(n):
  a. futures contracts   **c.** purchase of shares in a mutual funds
  b. options   **d.** all of these answers are correct

_____ **14.** A mutual fund is a(n):
  a. agreement to buy or sell specified quantities of commodities or financial futures at an agreed-on price at a future date
  b. financial service that pools its investors' funds to buy a selection of securities that meets its stated investment goals
  c. contract that entitles holders to buy specified quantities of common stocks or other financial instruments at a set price during a specified time
  d. high priced (over $100 per share) debt instrument sold in bundles of $1000 or more

_____ **15.** A futures contract is a(n):
  a. agreement to buy or sell specified quantities of commodities or financial futures at an agreed-on price at a future date
  b. financial service that pools its investors' funds to buy a selection of securities that meets its stated investment goals
  c. contract that entitles holders to buy specified quantities of common stocks or other financial instruments at a set price during a specified time
  d. high priced (over $100 per share) debt instrument sold in bundles of $1000 or more

_____ **16.** Options are:
   a. agreements to buy or sell specified quantities of commodities or financial futures at an agreed-on price at a future date
   b. financial services that pools its investors' funds to buy a selection of securities that meets its stated investment goals
   c. contracts that entitle holders to buy specified quantities of common stocks or other financial instruments at a set price during a specified time
   d. high priced (over $100 per share) debt instruments sold in bundles of $1000 or more

>lg 4

Where can investors buy and sell securities, and how are these securities markets regulated?

_____ **17.** The oldest and most prestigious U.S. stock exchange is the:
   a. AMEX   **c.** NYSE
   b. OTC   **d.** Nasdaq

_____ **18.** The term used to describe the type of securities' market conditions that prevail when stock prices are falling is:
   a. raging market   **c.** boar market
   b. bull market   **d.** bear market

_____ **19.** Corrective measures that are imposed to help avoid a crisis when stock prices fall precipitously are called:
   a. safety switches   **c.** fuses
   b. circuit breakers   **d.** safety valves

>lg 5

How do investors open up a brokerage account and make securities transactions?

_____ **20.** A market order is:
   a. a purchase of less than 100 shares
   b. an order to buy or sell a security at a specified price
   c. the sale of stock if the market price reaches or drops below a specified level
   d. an order to buy or sell a security immediately at the best price available

_____ **21.** An odd lot is:
   a. a purchase of less than 100 shares
   b. an order to buy or sell a security at a specified price
   c. the sale of stock if the market price reaches or drops below a specified level
   d. an order to buy or sell a security immediately at the best price available

_____ **22.** A stop-loss order is:
   a. a purchase of less than 100 shares
   b. an order to buy or sell a security at a specified price
   c. the sale of stock if the market price reaches or drops below a specified level
   d. an order to buy or sell a security immediately at the best price available

>lg 6

Which sources of investment information are the most helpful to investors?

_____ **23.** The best known weekday publication for economic and financial information is:
   a. *Barrons*   **c.** *The Wall Street Journal*
   b. *Worth*   **d.** *Kiplinger's Personal Finance*

_____ **24.** Among the best known subscription financial advisory services is:
   a. Moody's   **c.** Morningstar
   b. Standard and Poor's   **d.** All of these answers are correct

>lg 7   **What can investors learn from stock, bond, and mutual fund quotations?**

_____ 25. Stock prices listed on the NYSE, Nasdaq, and AMEX are all quoted in:
     a. tenths of a dollar   **c.** quarters of a dollar
     b. sixteenths of a dollar   **d.** thirds of a dollar

_____ 26. The price/earnings ratio of a stock is calculated by:
     a. adding the price of a stock to its earnings per share
     b. dividing the price of a stock by its earnings per share
     c. subtracting the earnings per share of a stock from its price
     d. multiplying the price of a stock by its price per share

_____ 27. When a bond sells below its initial face value it is said to be selling at a:
     a. discount   **c.** principal
     b. maturity value   **d.** premium

_____ 28. When a bond sells above its initial face value it is said to be selling at a:
     a. discount   **c.** principal
     b. maturity value   **d.** premium

_____ 29. Mutual fund shares are quoted in dollars and cents. The price listed for a mutual fund is its:
     a. net asset value   **c.** premium
     b. maturity value   **d.** discount

_____ 30. Many market analysts prefer the S&P 500 stock index to the DJIA because:
     a. it includes the value of mutual fund shares
     b. bond prices are factored into the index
     c. of the broader base of companies included in the index
     d. the DJIA includes the prices of too many companies for it to be meaningful

>lg 8   **What are the current trends in the securities markets?**

_____ 31. Electronic stock exchanges that have emerged in recent years are known as:
     a. Nasdaqs   **c.** AMEXs
     b. ECNs   **d.** All of these answers are correct

_____ 32. Direct transactions, without the use of brokers, security exchanges, or the Nasdaq take place in what is called the:
     a. first market   **c.** tertiary market
     b. secondary market   **d.** fourth market

TRUE/FALSE

Directions: Place a T or an F in the space provided at the left of each question to indicate whether it is True or False.

>lg 1   **What is the function of the securities markets?**

_____ 1. Institutional investors are individuals who invest only in larger real estate holdings and insurance companies.

_____ 2. The primary market exists to provide for the sale of new securities to the public.

_____ 3. The secondary market is the place where securities that don't sell in the primary market are listed in order to seek buyers.

_____ 4. Underwriters are investment bankers who acquire securities for an agreed-upon price and then resell them to the public to make a profit.

_____ 5. Stockbrokers are account executives who publish *tombstones* in local papers depicting the failure of securities to sell in the primary and secondary markets and seek to sell these securities to the public.

>lg 2

How do common stock, preferred stock, and bonds differ as investments?

_____ 6. Common stock is a security that represents ownership in a corporation and has priority when dividends are distributed at the end of the year.

_____ 7. Common stockholders get one vote for each share of stock that they own and can vote on such issues as the election of the board of directors, mergers, and the selection of auditors.

_____ 8. A per-share profit of $100 on a stock that was purchased for $50 represents a 200% rate of return.

_____ 9. Most preferred stock is *cumulative preferred*, meaning that its owners will receive all unpaid dividends before any dividends can be paid to common stockholders.

_____ 10. Principal represents the fixed amount of money that a bondholder is paid on a regular schedule, typically every six months.

_____ 11. Debentures are bonds that are secured by property.

_____ 12. Convertible bonds generally carry a lower interest rate than nonconvertible bonds because they can be converted into a specified number of shares of common stock.

_____ 13. Municipal bonds can be issued in the form of general obligation bonds that are backed by the full faith and credit of the issuing government.

_____ 14. Although municipal bonds offer a low rate of interest, owners still must pay federal, state, and local taxes on them.

_____ 15. A major weakness of U.S. Treasury bills, notes, and bonds is that they are not backed by the full faith and credit of the U.S. government.

>lg 3

What other types of securities are available to investors?

_____ 16. A mutual fund is a financial service that pools its investors' funds to buy a selection of securities that meet its stated investment goals.

_____ 17. Options contracts are agreements to buy or sell specified quantities of commodities or financial futures at an agreed-upon price at a future date.

_____ 18. Futures contracts do not pay dividends or interest—their return depends solely on favorable price changes.

>lg 4

Where can investors buy and sell securities, and how are these securities markets regulated?

_____ 19. In order to make transactions in the over-the-counter market, an individual must own a "seat" in order to make the trade.

_____ 20. The AMEX is the oldest and most prestigious stock exchange in the U.S.

_____ 21. The Nasdaq system is the first electronic-based stock market, and is the fastest growing part of the stock market.

_____ 22. As opposed to having a number of dealers handle a transaction, the Nasdaq has one specialist "make a market" in a security.

_____ 23. Bull markets are associated with stock market optimism, while bear markets are associated with stock market pessimism.

_____ 24. Insider trading was encouraged by the passage of the Insider Trading and Fraud Act of 1988.

_____ 25. Circuit breakers stop trading for a short cooling-off period to limit the amount the market can drop in one day.

>lg 5 **How do investors open a brokerage account and make securities transactions?**

_____ 26. A market order is an order to buy or sell a security at a specified price.

_____ 27. A stop-loss order requires that a stock be sold if the market price reaches or drops below a specified level.

_____ 28. Stocks sold in lots of less than 100 shares are said to be sold in odd lots.

>lg 6 **Which sources of investment information are the most helpful to investors?**

_____ 29. Barron's is the best-known daily publication that provides the most complete coverage of business and financial news.

_____ 30. Standards for accuracy and integrity are lax with regard to information provided to investors over the Internet.

>lg 7 **What can investors learn from stock, bond, and mutual fund quotations?**

_____ 31. Prices for NYSE, Nasdaq, and AMEX stocks are all listed using decimal pricing.

_____ 32. A firm that has earned $1.50 per share and sells for $15 has a price/earnings ratio of 10 to 1.

_____ 33. A bond that sells for a price above 100 is said to be sold at a discount.

_____ 34. The net asset value of a mutual fund is the price at which each share of the mutual fund can be bought or sold.

_____ 35. Market indexes, such as the DJIA, measure the current price behavior of groups of securities relative to a base value set at an earlier point in time.

_____ 36. The S&P 500 is a narrower index than the DJIA and includes the prices of only 30 stocks.

>lg 8 **What are the current trends in the securities markets?**

_____ 37. The Nasdaq has successfully challenged the position of the NYSE as the undisputed leader among stock exchanges.

_____ 38. The SEC has permitted ECNs to register as exchanges and trade stock while bypassing the NYSE entirely.

ENHANCE YOUR VOCABULARY

Appreciates	To go up in or raise in value or price
Emerging	Rising up or coming forth from; to come into existence
Forge	To advance with an abrupt increase of speed; counterfeit

Integrity	Rigid adherence to a code or standard of values
Laggard	One that lags or lingers, straggler
No-frills	Marked by the absence of extra or special features; basic
Proliferation	To cause to grow or increase rapidly
Restraint	Constraint; loss of freedom; the act of restraining
Soaring	The act of gliding while maintaining altitude; to rise, glide or fly high in the air
Virtual	Existing in effect though not in actual fact or form

Directions: Select the definition in Column B that best defines the word in Column A.

	Column A		Column B
_____	**1.** Proliferation	**a.**	To rise, glide or fly high in the air
_____	**2.** No-frills	**b.**	Existing in effect though not in actual fact or form
_____	**3.** Laggard	**c.**	To go up or raise in value or price
_____	**4.** Integrity	**d.**	To cause to grow or increase rapidly
_____	**5.** Virtual	**e.**	One that lags or lingers
_____	**6.** Emerging	**f.**	Rigid adherence to a code of ethics
_____	**7.** Appreciates	**g.**	To advance with an abrupt increase in speed
_____	**8.** Forge	**h.**	Constraint; loss of freedom
_____	**9.** Restraint	**i.**	Basic
_____	**10.** Soaring	**j.**	To come into existence

REVIEW YOUR KEY TERMS

Directions: Select the definition in Column B that best defines the word in Column A.

	Column A		Column B
_____	**1.** Securities	**a.**	Bonds issued by states, cities, counties, and other state and local government agencies.
_____	**2.** Investment bankers	**b.**	Corporate bonds that are secured by property, such as real estate, equipment, or buildings.
_____	**3.** Secured bonds	**c.**	Investment certificates issued by corporations or governments that represent either equity or debt.
_____	**4.** Futures contracts	**d.**	Letter grades assigned to bond issues to indicate their quality, or level of risk; assigned by rating agencies such as Moody's and Standard & Poor's.
_____	**5.** Municipal bonds	**e.**	The process of buying securities from corporations and governments and reselling them to the public; the main activity of investment bankers.
_____	**6.** Institutional investors	**f.**	Unsecured bonds that are backed only by the reputation of the issuer and its promise to pay the principal and interest when due.
_____	**7.** Net asset value	**g.**	The first electronic-based stock market and the largest over-the-counter market.
_____	**8.** Bond ratings	**h.**	An investment company that pools investors' funds to buy a selection of securities.

_____ 9. Primary market

_____ 10. Debentures

_____ 11. Secondary market

_____ 12. Mortgage bonds

_____ 13. Mutual fund

_____ 14. Organized stock exchanges

_____ 15. Stockbroker

_____ 16. Underwriting

_____ 17. Standard & Poor's 500 stock index

_____ 18. Options

_____ 19. Interest

_____ 20. Convertible bonds

_____ 21. High-yield (junk) bonds

_____ 22. Market averages

_____ 23. Circuit breakers

_____ 24. National Association of Securities Dealers Automated Quotation (Nasdaq) system

_____ 25. Over-the-counter (OTC) market

i. Corporate bonds that are issued with an option that allows the bondholder to convert them into common stock.

j. The securities market where previously issued securities are traded among investors; includes the organized stock exchanges, the over-the-counter-market, and the commodities exchanges.

k. A fixed amount of money paid by the issuer of a bond to the bondholder on a regular schedule, typically every six months; also called the coupon rate.

l. Firms that act as underwriters, buying securities from corporations and governments and reselling them to the public.

m. Contracts that entitle the holder to buy or sell specified quantities of common stocks or other financial instruments at a set price during a specified time.

n. An important market index that includes 400 industrial stocks, 20 transportation stocks, 40 public utility stocks, and 40 financial stocks; includes Nasdaq and American Stock Exchange companies as well as those on the New York Stock Exchange.

o. Measures that under certain circumstances stop trading in the securities markets for a short cooling-off period to limit the amount the market can drop in one day.

p. The most widely used market average; measures the stock prices of 30 large, well-known corporations that trade on the New York Stock Exchange.

q. Summaries of the price behavior of securities based on the arithmetic average price of a group of securities at a given point in time; used to track market conditions.

r. A sophisticated telecommunications network that links dealers throughout the United States and enables them to trade securities.

s. Investment professionals who are paid to manage other people's money.

t. The amount borrowed by the issuer of a bond; also called par value.

u. A person who is licensed to buy and sell securities on behalf of clients.

v. Agreements to buy or sell specified quantities of commodities or financial futures at an agreed-on price at a future date.

w. Measures of the current price behavior of groups of securities relative to a base value set at an earlier point in time; used to track market conditions.

x. Markets in which securities prices are rising.

y. Organizations on whose premises securities are resold using an auction-style trading system.

_____ **26.** Price/earnings (P/E) ratio

z. The securities market where new securities are sold to the public.

_____ **27.** Principal

aa. Corporate bonds for which specific assets have been pledged as collateral.

_____ **28.** Bull markets

bb. The use of information that is not available to the general public to make profits on securities transactions.

_____ **29.** Insider trading

cc. The current market price of a stock divided by its earnings per share.

_____ **30.** Dow Jones Industrial Average (DJIA)

dd. High-risk, high-return bonds.

_____ **31.** Market indexes

ee. The price at which each share of a mutual fund can be bought or sold.

_____ **32.** Bear markets

ff. Markets in which securities prices are falling.

CRITICAL THINKING ACTIVITIES

1. P.O.V. – (Point of View)

Directions: In this exercise you will be asked to provide your personal opinion regarding some of the topics discussed in the chapter. At the completion of this exercise, your instructor may wish to poll the entire class regarding their responses.

   a. Preferred stock is the best form of investment for those who wish to achieve great gains in stock prices. Because most preferred stock is cumulative, its owners are guaranteed dividends in addition to increases in the value of the stock.

   Agree _____   Disagree _____

   Explain:

_____

_____

_____

_____

   b. Large investment companies that invest large sums of money in stocks and bonds, such as brokerage houses and mutual funds, should be provided with important corporate information related to investment in securities so that large increases or decreases in stock prices can be minimized and market stability can be maintained.

   Agree _____   Disagree _____

   Explain:

_____

_____

_____

_____

2. Using the Internet

Directions: Go to **http://www.motleyfool.com** click on Investing Basics and then click on Fool School.

- **a.** Summarize the key points made regarding getting started with investing.
- **b.** Identify the major investing pitfalls that are described.
- **c.** Continue to browse through the additional steps that are included at this site and discuss the investing concepts that are presented in terms of whether they would be used by you when investing.

3. Writing Skills

Directions: You are a sales person for mutual funds. As a way of stimulating business, you have invited potential buyers to a dinner at which you will be speaking. Explain what a mutual fund is and describe the advantages and disadvantages of owning mutual funds or owning individual stocks and/or bonds. Present all points of view, but try to create a favorable atmosphere for your products.

NOTES ON CHAPTER 22

Chapter 23

Managing Your Personal Finances

OUTLINE

MULTIPLE CHOICE

Directions: Place the letter of the response that best completes the questions that follow in the blank space at the left.

>lg 1

What is the financial planning process and how does it facilitate successful financial planning?

_____ 1. The first step in the financial management process is to:
   a. analyze the information   c. develop a plan
   b. establish financial goals   d. implement a financial plan

_____ 2. Reviewing the performance of the savings/investment vehicles used in a financial plan is known as:
   a. gathering information   c. implementing of the plan
   b. developing of a plan   d. monitoring the plan

_____ 3. The development phase of a financial plan involves:
   a. a review of the performance of the various savings/investment vehicles chosen
   b. putting the plan into action
   c. considering the various alternatives and deciding on the best plan
   d. data analysis and revision of goals if necessary

>lg 2

How can cash flow planning and management of liquid assets help you meet your financial goals?

_____ 4. Cash management is defined as:
   a. a plan for managing income and expenses, including contributions to savings and investments
   b. the day-to-day handling of one's liquid assets
   c. cash and other assets that can be converted into cash both quickly and at little or no cost
   d. a snapshot of your financial situation on a given day

_____ 5. Liquid assets include:
   a. a plan for managing income and expenses, including contributions to savings and investments
   b. the day-to-day handling of one's liquid assets
   c. cash and other assets that can be converted into cash both quickly and at little or no cost
   d. a snapshot of your financial situation on a given day

_____ 6. A cash flow plan is:
   a. a plan for managing income and expenses, including contributions to savings and investments
   b. the day-to-day handling of one's liquid assets
   c. cash and other assets that can be converted into cash both quickly and at little or no cost
   d. a snapshot of your financial situation on a given day

_____ 7. The net worth statement is:
   a. a plan for managing income and expenses, including contributions to savings and investments
   b. the day-to-day handling of one's liquid assets
   c. cash and other assets that can be converted into cash both quickly and at little or no cost
   d. a snapshot of your financial situation on a given day

_____ 8. A written order, drawn on a depository institution by a depositor, ordering the depository institution to pay on demand a specific amount of money to the person or firm on the check is a(n):
   a. check   **c.** ATM
   b. EFT   **d.** POS

_____ 9. The minimum deposit required to open a Money Market Mutual Fund account is:
   a. $5-$50   **c.** $500-$2500
   b. $100 and higher   **d.** $500-$2000

>lg 3   **What are the advantages and disadvantages of using consumer credit?**

_____ 10. Open-end credit:
   a. is a period of time after making a purchase when you do not pay interest if you pay your total balance on time
   b. includes any type of credit where you apply for the credit and then, if approved, are allowed to use it over and over again
   c. is the maximum amount you can have outstanding at any one time
   d. is a type of credit card that does not require full payment upon billing

_____ 11. A line of credit:
   a. is a period of time after making a purchase when you do not pay interest if you pay your total balance on time
   b. includes any type of credit where you apply for the credit and then, if approved, are allowed to use it over and over again
   c. is the maximum amount you can have outstanding at any one time
   d. is a type of credit card that does not require full payment upon billing

_____ 12. A grace period:
   a. is a period of time after making a purchase when you do not pay interest if you pay your total balance on time
   b. includes any type of credit where you apply for the credit and then, if approved, are allowed to use it over and over again
   c. is the maximum amount you can have outstanding at any one time
   d. is a type of credit that does not require full payment upon billing

_____ 13. A prepayment penalty:
   a. allows the lender to take back the collateral if you do not repay the loan according to the terms of the agreement
   b. will repay a loan if you die before the loan is paid
   c. is an additional fee owed if you decide to repay a loan early
   d. all of these answers are correct

_____ 14. Credit life insurance:
   a. allows the lender to take back the collateral if you do not repay the loan according to the terms of the agreement
   b. will repay a loan if you die before the loan is paid
   c. is an additional fee owed if you decide to repay a loan early
   d. all of these answers are correct

_____ 15. Security requirements:
   a. allow the lender to take back the collateral if you do not repay the loan according to the terms of the agreement
   b. will repay a loan if you die before the loan is paid
   c. represent an additional fee owed if you decide to repay a loan early
   d. all of these answers are correct

>lg 4

What are the major types of taxes paid by individuals?

_____ **16.** A type of tax that is paid directly by individuals is:
   a. sales
   b. property
   c. income
   d. all of these answers are correct

_____ **17.** The largest single tax expenditure for an individual is:
   a. income tax
   b. sales tax
   c. property tax
   d. Social Security tax

_____ **18.** The federal income tax is a progressive tax, which means that as taxable income:
   a. rises, taxes are paid at a flat tax rate
   b. falls, tax rates rise
   c. rises, numerous tax exemptions are allowed
   d. rises, tax rates rise

_____ **19.** The standard deduction, for a single person, from federal income tax is equal to:
   a. $100
   b. $1,500
   c. $2,750
   d. $4,400

>lg 5

What is the most important principle in deciding what types of insurance to purchase?

_____ **20.** Property insurance:
   a. covers financial losses from injuries to others and damage or destruction of others' property when the insured is considered the cause
   b. protects the insured from financial losses caused by automobile-related injuries to others and damage to their property
   c. covers financial losses from damage to or destruction of the insured's assets as a result of specified perils, such as fire or theft
   d. covers damage to or loss of the policyholder's vehicle due to perils such as fire, floods, theft, and vandalism

_____ **21.** Automobile liability insurance:
   a. covers financial losses from injuries to others and damage or destruction of others' property when the insured is considered the cause
   b. protects the insured from financial losses caused by automobile-related injuries to others and damage to their property
   c. covers financial losses from damage to or destruction of the insured's assets as a result of specified perils, such as fire or theft
   d. covers damage to or loss of the policyholder's vehicle due to perils such as fire, floods, theft, and vandalism

_____ **22.** Liability insurance:
   a. covers financial losses from injuries to others and damage or destruction of others' property when the insured is considered the cause
   b. protects the insured from financial losses caused by automobile-related injuries to others and damage to their property
   c. covers financial losses from damage to or destruction of the insured's assets as a result of specified perils, such as fire or theft
   d. covers damage to or loss of the policyholder's vehicle due to perils such as fire, floods, theft, and vandalism

_____ 23. Indemnity health plans:
   a. are primarily designed to provide COBRA coverage
   b. are also known as major medical insurance
   c. pay only for services that are provided by doctors or hospitals that are part of the plan
   d. reimburse the insured for medical costs covered by the insurance policy

_____ 24. HMOs:
   a. except in the case of an emergency, will not pay for care that is given by non-HMO providers
   b. provide health care services for a fixed periodic payment
   c. have gatekeeper physicians, known as PCPs, manage patient care
   d. all of these answers are correct

>lg 6   What personal characteristics are important when making investment decisions?

_____ 25. According to the Investment Risk Pyramid, the investment with the highest risk of loss of principal and with the highest potential for gain through appreciation is:
   a. high grade municipal bonds, personal residence equity, and fixed annuities
   b. growth stocks, growth mutual funds, and income mutual funds
   c. futures, derivatives, commodities, and naked puts/calls
   d. FDIC-insured accounts, MMMF, U.S. EE savings bonds, cash value life insurance, and Treasury bills/notes/bonds

_____ 26. According to the Investment Risk Pyramid, the investment with the lowest risk of loss of principal but which has the lowest potential for gain through appreciation is:
   a. high grade municipal bonds, personal residence equity, and fixed annuities
   b. growth stocks, growth mutual funds, and income mutual funds
   c. futures, derivatives, commodities, and naked puts/calls
   d. FDIC-insured accounts, MMMF, U.S. EE savings bonds, cash value life insurance, and Treasury bills/notes/bonds

_____ 27. A DRIP is:
   a. identical to a money market mutual fund
   b. an automatic transfer of money from your checking account to a mutual fund or stock so that a given amount is regularly invested
   c. a collection of investments
   d. none of these answers are correct

_____ 28. A portfolio is:
   a. identical to a money market mutual fund
   b. an automatic transfer of money from your checking account to a mutual fund or stock so that a given amount is regularly invested
   c. a collection of investments
   d. none of these answers are correct

>lg 7   What are the emerging trends in personal financial planning?

_____ 29. An employee benefit plan that allows them to pick from a selection of benefits that meet their needs is known as a:
   a. self-directed retirement account
   b. dividend reinvestment plan
   c. universal life plan
   d. cafeteria-style benefit plan

___ **30.** A plan that requires employees to decide how their money should be invested for retirement is called a:
   a. self-directed retirement account
   b. dividend reinvestment plan
   c. universal life plan
   d. cafeteria-style benefit plan

TRUE/FALSE

Directions: Place a T or an F in the space provided at the left of each question to indicate whether it is True or False.

>lg 1

What is the financial planning process and how does it facilitate successful financial management?

___ **1.** Financial planning is a process that starts with having a sum of money to invest.

___ **2.** Establishing financial goals is involved with analyzing financial data that has been gathered, including both objective and subjective information.

___ **3.** Reviewing the performance of the savings/investment vehicles used in a financial plan is part of the last step in financial planning - monitoring the plan.

>lg 2

How can cash flow planning and management of liquid assets help you meet your financial goals?

___ **4.** Cash management is the use of cash and other assets over an extended period of time.

___ **5.** Liquid assets include cash and other assets that can be converted into cash quickly and at little or no cost.

___ **6.** The cash flow plan, also known as a budget, is an important tool for cash management and includes a plan for managing income and expenses, including contributions to savings and investments needed to accomplish one's financial goals.

___ **7.** The net worth statement is a snapshot of your financial situation over a period of time.

___ **8.** The cash flow statement is a snapshot of your financial situation on a given day.

___ **9.** A check is a written order, drawn on a depository institution by a depositor, ordering the depository institution to pay on demand a specific amount of money to the person or firm named on the check.

>lg 3

What are the advantages and disadvantages of using consumer credit?

___ **10.** A line of credit is a type of credit that allows the borrower to exceed a set credit limit when necessary.

___ **11.** Credit cards that do not require full payment upon billing are called grace period debt instruments.

___ **12.** Open-end credit includes any type of credit where you apply to receive the credit, and then, if approved, are allowed to use it over and over again.

___ **13.** When a specific amount of money is borrowed, the amount of money that you must repay based upon the rate of interest is called the principal.

_____ 14. Loans may require that a prepayment penalty is owed if the borrower seeks to repay the loan before maturity.

>lg 4 What are the major types of taxes paid by individuals?

_____ 15. The federal income tax is based upon a progressive system, which requires those with higher taxable income to pay a higher percentage of their income as tax.

_____ 16. The greater the number of withholding allowances claimed by an individual, the more an employer will withhold from income.

_____ 17. Increasing the number of personal exemptions increases the amount of income on which someone pays taxes.

>lg 5 What is the most important principle in deciding what types of insurance to purchase?

_____ 18. Property insurance covers financial losses from damage to or destruction of the insured's asset as a result of specified perils, such as fire of theft.

_____ 19. Liability insurance covers financial losses from injuries caused by others to the insured, including damage or destruction of the insured's property.

_____ 20. Comprehensive automobile insurance protects the insured from financial losses caused by automobile-related injuries to others and damage to their property.

_____ 21. An indemnity health insurance plan reimburses the insured for medical costs covered by the insurance policy.

_____ 22. Under major medical insurance, the insured pays a deductible and then pays a portion called coinsurance, typically 15 to 25 percent, of covered expenses.

_____ 23. Whole life insurance covers the insured's life for a fixed amount and a specific period, typically five to twenty-five years.

_____ 24. Universal life insurance covers the insured's life, as long as premiums are paid, and has a cash value that earns interest over the life of the policy.

>lg 6 What personal characteristics are important when making investment decisions?

_____ 25. Every investor should start with this question: "What do I want to achieve with my investment program?"

_____ 26. Covered puts/calls, collectibles, speculative common stock, and junk bonds are reasonable investments for a young conservative investor.

_____ 27. Automatic transfers from a checking account to purchase a mutual fund or shares of stock on a regular basis can be achieved through the use of a DRIP.

>lg 7 What are the emerging trends in personal financial planning?

_____ 28. An important trend in personal finance is for employers to take greater responsibility for employee investment choices.

_____ 29. In a typical cafeteria-style benefit plan, employees pick from a menu of benefits provided by the employer, with the employee free to choose the benefits that best fit their needs.

_____ 30. Guaranteed investment contracts (GICs) are insurance company products that look very much like mutual funds.

ENHANCE YOUR VOCABULARY

Chimes in	To break into, as a conversation; interrupt; to join in harmoniously
Facilitate	To make easier or help bring about; assist
Forgo	To give up; relinquish
Fraudulent	Characterized by deliberate deception
Impulsively	Tending to act on impulse rather than thought; produced by impulse; uncalculated actions
Incrementally	Something added in small installments; a series of regular contributions
Knack	A specific talent or skill; a clever way of doing something
Longevity	A long duration of individual life; length of life; durability
Monitoring	Checking, watching, or keeping track of, often by an electronic device
Self-restraint	Self-control; restraint of one's emotions, desires, or inclinations

Directions: Select the definition in Column B that best defines the word in Column A.

Column A	Column B
_____ 1. Impulsively	a. A clever way of doing something
_____ 2. Self-restraint	b. Interrupt; to break into, as a conversation
_____ 3. Knack	c. Length of life
_____ 4. Chimes in	d. To make easier; assist
_____ 5. Facilitate	e. Uncalculated actions; produced by impulse
_____ 6. Longevity	f. Self-control
_____ 7. Monitoring	g. Characterized by deliberate deception
_____ 8. Incrementally	h. To give up; relinquish
_____ 9. Forgo	i. Checking; watching, or keeping track of
_____ 10. Fraudulent	j. Something added in small installments

REVIEW YOUR KEY TERMS

Directions: Select the definition in Column B that best defines the word in Column A.

Column A	Column B
_____ 1. Financial planning	a. An income tax that is structured so that the higher a person's income, the higher the percentage of income owed in taxes.
_____ 2. Line of credit	b. Any type of credit where the borrower applies for the credit and then, if approved, is allowed to use it over and over again; for example, credit cards.
_____ 3. Credit life insurance	c. The process of managing one's personal finances to achieve financial goals; involves establishing financial goals, gathering information, analyzing the information, developing a plan, implementing the plan, and monitoring the plan.
_____ 4. Revolving credit cards	d. The period after a purchase is made on a credit card during which interest is not owed if the entire balance is paid on time.

_____ 5. Filing status

_____ 6. Standard deduction

_____ 7. Automobile physical damage insurance

_____ 8. Universal life insurance

_____ 9. Cash management

_____ 10. Diversification

_____ 11. Liquid assets

_____ 12. Open-end credit

_____ 13. Replacement cost average

_____ 14. Withholding allowances

_____ 15. Comprehensive (other than-collision) coverage

_____ 16. COBRA

_____ 17. Whole life (straight life, cash value, continuous pay) insurance

_____ 18. Indemnity (fee-for-service) plans

e. Homeowner's and renter's insurance that pays enough to replace lost and damaged personal property.

f. Amounts that are deducted from the income tax that would otherwise be withheld by a taxpayer's employer; vary according to the number of dependents and other criteria. The more allowances, the less tax withheld.

g. The status of a taxpayer as a single, married, or some other status on the income tax return.

h. A program in which dividends paid by a stock are automatically reinvested in that stock along with any additional contributions submitted by the stockholder.

i. A cash management tool that provides a plan for managing income and expenses, including contributions to savings and investments needed accomplish financial goals.

j. Deductions that reduce the amount of income on which income tax is paid. Each taxpayer is entitled to one exemption, but the exemption can be used only once, so a taxpayer who is claimed as a dependent by someone else cannot also claim the exemption.

k. Provisions that allow a lender to take back the collateral if a loan is not repaid according to the terms of the agreement.

l. An amount that most taxpayers can automatically deduct from their gross income in computing their income tax; not permitted if the taxpayer itemizes deductions.

m. Automobile insurance that covers damage to or loss of the policy-holder's vehicle due to perils such as fire, flood, theft, and vandalism; part of automobile physical damage insurance.

n. Insurance that covers damage to or loss of the policy-holder's vehicle from collision, theft, fire, or other perils; includes collision coverage and comprehensive (other-than-collision) coverage.

o. The day-to-day handling of one's liquid assets.

p. Network of health care providers who enter into a contract to provide services at discounted prices; combines features of major medical insurance plans with features of health maintenance organizations.

q. The total amount borrowed through a loan.

r. An investment strategy that involves investing in different asset classes, such as cash equivalents, stocks, bonds, and real estate, and combining securities with different patterns and amounts of return.

_____ **19.** Personal exemption

_____ **20.** Automobile liability insurance

_____ **21.** Cash value

_____ **22.** Managed care plans

_____ **23.** Earned income

_____ **24.** Actual cash value

_____ **25.** Unearned income

_____ **26.** Coinsurance (participation)

_____ **27.** Cash flow plan

_____ **28.** Grace period

_____ **29.** Progressive tax

_____ **30.** Net worth statement

_____ **31.** Principal

_____ **32.** Term life insurance

_____ **33.** Health maintenance organizations

_____ **34.** Preferred provider organization (PPOs)

_____ **35.** Prepayment penalties

_____ **36.** Waiting period (elimination period)

_____ **37.** Security requirements

s. A federal regulation that allows most former employees and their families to continue group health insurance coverage at their own expense for up to 18 months after leaving an employer.

t. Life insurance that covers the insured's life for a fixed amount and a specific period and has no cash value; provides the maximum amount of insurance for the lowest premium.

u. Health insurance plans that reimburse the insured for medical costs covered by the insurance policy. The policy holder selects the health car providers.

v. Life insurance that covers the insured's entire life, as long as the premiums are paid; has a cash value that increases over the life of the policy.

w. Insurance that protects the insured from financial losses caused by automobile-related injuries to others and damage to their property.

x. Income that is not earned through employment such as interest, dividends, and other investment income.

y. The market value of personal property; the amount paid by standard homeowner's and renter's insurance policies.

z. Income that is earned from employment such as wages, tips, and self-employment income.

aa. A summary of a person's financial situation on a given day; provides information about both assets and liabilities.

bb. Insurance that will repay a loan if the borrower dies while the loan is still outstanding.

cc. Cash and other assets that can be converted to cash quickly at little or no cost, such as checking accounts.

dd. For credit cards, the maximum amount a person can have outstanding on a card at any one time.

ee. Health insurance plans that generally pay only for services provided by doctors and hospitals that are part of the plan.

ff. A percentage of covered expenses that the holder of a major medical insurance policy must pay.

gg. The dollar amount paid to the owner of a life insurance policy if the policy is cancelled before the death of the insured.

hh. In disability income insurance the period between the onset of the disability and the time when insurance payments begin.

ii. In disability income insurance, the length of time the insurance payments will continue.

jj. A combination of term life insurance and a tax-deferred savings plan. Part of the premium is invested in securities, so the cash value earns interest at current market rates.

kk. The process of committing money to various instruments in order to obtain future financial returns.

_____ **38.** Guaranteed investment contracts (GICs)

ll. Managed care organizations that provide comprehensive health care services for a fixed periodic payment.

_____ **39.** Duration of benefits

mm. Insurance company products that are similar to bank certificates of deposit.

_____ **40.** Investing

nn. Additional fees that may be owed if a loan is repaid early.

_____ **41.** Emergency fund

oo. A collection of investments.

_____ **42.** Dividend reinvestment contracts (DRIP)

pp. Liquid assets that are available to meet emergencies.

_____ **43.** Portfolio

qq. Credit cards that do not require full payment upon billing.

CRITICAL THINKING ACTIVITIES

1. P.O.V. (Point of View)

Directions: In this exercise you will be asked to provide your personal opinion regarding some of the topics discussed in the chapter. At the completion of this exercise, your instructor may wish to poll the entire class regarding their responses.

a. As workers begin to live longer and longer, it is the responsibility of the Federal Government to provide increased benefits for those workers when they retire. For example, social security and Medicare payments to retirees should reflect real purchasing needs rather than a small dollar amount on which it is impossible for retirees to live. Workers cannot be expected to plan for the future when current living costs are so high.

Agree _____   Disagree _____

Explain:

_____
_____
_____
_____

b. Life insurance salespeople are the best source of information for individuals seeking retirement. They sell various types of insurance that are promoted as 'allowing you to save for your future.' These policies can be counted upon to provide you with needed coverage when you retire.

Agree _____   Disagree _____

Explain:

_____
_____
_____
_____

2. Using the Internet

Directions: Go to **http://www.creditguide.com**.

   a. Click on Debt Warning Signs and complete the quiz on Debt Detection. Could you or anyone you know answer Yes to any of the questions? What advice would you give someone who answered Yes to one or more of the questions?

   b. Set up a personal budget that reflects your income and expenses. Make sure that it is a realistic budget that you actually can live with.

   c. What role do you feel financial planning will play in assuring your future business and personal success?

3. Writing Skills

Directions: You are running as mayor of a small town. You would like to replace property taxes with a local progressive income tax. Prepare a speech to present your position at a local town hall meeting.

Answer Key

Solutions to Chapter 1

Multiple Choice
1. D 2. C 3. A 4. B 5. C 6. D 7. C 8. D
9. A 10. B 11. D 12. B. 13. C 14. D 15. C
16. D 17. B 18. D 19. B 20. A 21. C 22. D
23. C 24. A 25. B 26. C 27. D

True/False
1. F 2. T 3. F 4. F 5. T 6. F 7. F 8. F 9. T
10. T 11. T 12. F 13. T 14. F 15. F 16. T
17. T 18. F 19. F 20. F 21. T 22. F 23. F
24. T 25. F 26. F 27. T 28. T 29. F 30. T
31. F

Enhance Your Vocabulary
1. D 2. G 3. B 4. J 5. H 6. I 7. F 8. C
9. A 10. E

Review Your Key Terms
1. C 2. E 3. M 4. Q 5. W 6. G 7. S 8. GG
9. HH 10. EE 11. F 12. P 13. T 14. D 15. I
16. K 17. J 18. N 19. BB 20. AA 21. Y
22. DD 23. R 24. U 25. CC 26. FF 27. B.
28. V 29. H 30. O 31. Z 32. L 33. X 34. A

Solutions to Chapter 2

Multiple Choice
1. C 2. A 3. B 4. A 5. D 6. C 7. B 8. D
9. C 10. A 11. D 12. D 13. A 14. C 15. B
16. A 17. A 18. C 19. A 20. D 21. B 22. C
23. D 24. B 25. D 26. C 27. A 28. D

True/False
1. F 2. T 3. F 4. T 5. F 6. T 7. T 8. F
9. F 10. T 11. F 12. F 13. T 14. T 15. F
16. F 17. T 18. T 19. F 20. F 21. T 22. T
23. F 24. T 25. F 26. T 27. F 28. T 29. F
30. T 31. F 32. T 33. T 34. F 35. T

Enhance Your Vocabulary
1. C 2. G 3. E 4. H 5. I 6. J 7. F 8. B
9. D 10. A

Review Your Key Terms
1. PP 2. V 3. X 4. PP 5. MM 6. NN 7. OO
8. QQ 9. Y 10. A 11. D 12. U 13. B
14. CC 15. G 16. N 17. F 18. O 19. H
20. EE 21. L 22. P 23. T 24. J 25. K

26. W 27. I 28. M 29. GG 30. C 31. Q
32. KK 33. S 34. AA 35. JJ 36. BB 37. LL
38. DD 39. Z 40. II 41. HH 42. FF 43. R.

Solutions to Chapter 3

Multiple Choice
1. C 2. D 3. A 4. B 5. D 6. C 7. A 8. D
9. B 10. D 11. C 12. C 13. D 14. C 15. C
16. A 17. B 18. D 19. A 20. B 21. C 22. C
23. B 24. A 25. D 26. A 27. C 28. D 29. D
30. B 31. B

True/False
1. T 2. F 3. F 4. T 5. F 6. F 7. F 8. T
9. T 10. T 11. F 12. F 13. T 14. F 15. T
16. T 17. F 18. T 19. F 20. T 21. F 22. F
23. T 24. F 25. F 26. T 27. F 28. T 29. T
30. F 31. F 32. T 33. F 34. F 35. F 36. T

Enhance Your Vocabulary
1. I 2. H 3. D 4. A 5. G 6. B 7. J 8. C
9. E 10 F

Review Your Key Terms
1. KK 2. E 3. P 4. N 5. H 6. DD 7. S 8. L
9. CC 10. X 11. O 12. GG 13. F 14. AA
15. A 16. W 17. BB 18. D 19. T 20. II
21. B 22. G 23. C 24. M 25. FF 26. U
27. EE 28. Q 29. J 30. K 31. Z 32. HH
33. V 34. JJ 35. I 36. R

Solutions to Chapter 4

Multiple Choice
1. B 2. C 3. D 4. A 5. C 6. A 7. B 8. D
9. B 10. C 11. D 12. A 13. D 14. B 15. B
16. D 17. C 18. C 19. A 20. D 21. C 22. B
23. A 24. C 25. D

True/False
1. F 2. T 3. F 4. T 5. T 6. F 7. F 8. T
9. F 10. T 11. T 12. F 13. F 14. T 15. F
16. T 17. F 18. T 19. F 20. F 21. F 22. T
23. T 24. T 25. T 26. F 27. T

Enhance Your Vocabulary
1. H 2. F 3. A 4. E 5. I 6. C 7. J 8. D
9. B 10. G

Review Your Key Terms

1. CC 2. G 3. EE 4. E 5. C 6. Y 7. R 8. V
9. B 10. N 11. AA 12. A 13. BB 14. Z
15. M 16. H 17. D 18. DD 19. J 20. L
21. Q 22. U 23. F 24. K 25. S 26. W 27. P
28. O 29. I 30. T 31. X

Solutions to Chapter 5

Multiple Choice

1. A 2. D 3. B 4. D 5. A 6. C 7. C 8. D
9. B 10. A 11. D 12. B 13. D 14. A 15. A
16. C 17. C 18. C 19. B 20. D 21. D 22. A
23. A 24. C 25. B 26. C 27. C 28. D 29. C
30. C

True/False

1. F 2. F 3. T 4. T 5. F 6. T 7. T 8. F
9. T 10. T 11. F 12. F . 13. T 14. F 15. T
16. T 17. F 18. F 19. F 20. T 21. T 22. F
23. T 24. F 25. F 26. T 27. T 28. F 29. F
30. F 31. T 32. T 33. F 34. F 35. T

Enhance Your Vocabulary

1. G 2. E 3. A 4. D 5. C 6. F 7. H 8. B
9. J 10. I

Review Your Key Terms

1. N 2. I 3. M 4. O 5. A 6. K 7. F 8. T
9. B 10. E 11. V 12. Q 13. D 14. C 15. R
16. L 17. P 18. G 19. W 20. H 21. J 22. S
23. U

Solutions to Chapter 6

Answer Key:

1. D 2. C 3. B 4. C 5. B 6. D 7. D 8. A
9. C 10. D 11. B 12. D 13. C 14. A 15. A
16. C 17. D 18. B 19. C 20. A 21. B 22. D
23. C 24. A 25. B 26. B 27. A 28. C 29. C
30. D 31. D

True/False:

1. T 2. F 3. F 4. T 5. F 6. T 7. F 8. T
9. T 10. F 11. F 12. T 13. F 14. F 15. T
16. T 17. F 18. T 19. F 20. F 21. T 22. F
23. T 24. F 25. F 26. T 27. F 28. F 29. T
30. T 31. F 32. F 33. T 34. F 35. T

Enhance Your Vocabulary

1. F 2. J 3. D 4. E 5. A 6. H 7. B 8. C
9. G 10. I

Review Your Key Terms

1. C 2. G 3. J 4. B 5. C 6. H 7. D 8. A
9. E 10. I

Solutions to Chapter 7

Multiple Choice

1. C 2. B 3. B 4. A 5. C 6. B 7. D 8. C
9. D 10. A 11. B 12. C 13. D 14. D 15. C
16. B 17. A 18. A 19. D 20. C 21. D 22. B
23. C 24. A 25. A 26. D 27. A 28. C 29. D
30. B

True/False

1. F 2. T 3. F 4. T 5. F 6. T 7. F 8. F
9. T 10. T 11. F 12. T 13. T 14. F 15. T
16. T 17. F 18. T 19. F 20. F 21. F 22. T
23. T 24. T 25. F 26. T 27. T 28. F 29. F
30. T 31. T 32. F

Enhance Your Vocabulary

1. F 2. D 3. C 4. E 5. I 6. B 7. A 8. J
9. G 10. H

Review Your Key Terms

1. F 2. M 3. Z 4. A 5. X 6. L 7. H 8. G
9. O 10. R 11. U 12. KK 13. V 14. P 15. C
16. Q 17. BB 18. GG 19. J 20. II 21. HH
22. FF 23. I 24. D 25. AA 26. DD 27. Y
28. B 29. EE 30. N; 31. W 32. CC 33. T
34. S 35. JJ 36. K 37. E

Solutions to Chapter 8

Multiple Choice

1. C 2. C 3. D 4. B 5. B 6. B 7. A 8. D
9. C 10. B 11. D 12. A 13. D 14. C 15. D
16. A 17. A 18. D 19. C 20. B 21. B 22. D
23. D 24. A 25. D 26. D 27. C 28. C

True/False

1. T 2. F 3. F 4. T 5. F 6. F 7. T 8. T
9. F 10. F 11. F 12. T 13. F 14. T 15. T
16. F 17. T 18. F 19. T 20. F 21. T 22. T
23. T 24. F 25. F 26. T 27. F 28. F 29. T
30. T 31. F 32. T 33. F

Enhance Your Vocabulary

1. I 2. E 3. H 4. C 5. F 6. G 7. A 8. J
9. D 10. B

Review Your Key Terms

1. D 2. K 3. E 4. F 5. J 6. M 7. Y 8. O
9. B 10. C 11. S 12. G 13. R 14. Q 15. H
16. L 17. U 18. N 19. I 20. T 21. A 22. P
23. Z 24. W 25. V 26. X 27. BB 28. CC
29. AA

Solutions to Chapter 9

Multiple Choice
1. B 2. C 3. D 4. A 5. B 6. C 7. D 8. C
9. A 10. B 11. D 12. C 13. A 14. B 15. B
16. C 17. D 18. D 19. C 20. A 21. D 22. B
23. A 24. C 25. C 26. A 27. D 28. B 29. D
30. C

True/False
1. F 2. T 3. F 4. T 5. F 6. F 7. F 8. F
9. T 10. F 11. T 12. F 13. T 14. F 15. F
16. F 17. T 18. F 19. T 20. F 21. T 22. T
23. F 24. T 25. T 26. F 27. F 28. T 29. F
30. T 31. F 32. T 33. F 34. T 35. F 36. F

Enhance Your Vocabulary
1. B 2. E 3. A 4. J 5. I 6. G 7. F 8. C
9. H 10. D

Review Your Key Terms
1. Q 2. Z 3. A. 4. P 5. X 6. BB 7. AA
8. D 9. W 10. O 11. T 12. K 13. L 14. V
15. H 16. F 17. CC 18. FF 19. N 20. U
21. Y 22. EE 23. GG 24. R 25. S 26. DD
27. G 28. B 29. C 30. M 31. J 32. E 33. I

Solutions to Chapter 10

Multiple Choice
1. D 2. B. 3. A 4. C 5. C 6. B 7. C 8. D
9. A 10. D 11. D 12. C 13. A 14. B 15. C
16. D 17. A 18. D 19. C 20. B 21. B 22. D
23. A 24. B 25. C 26. A 27. C 28. B 29. D

True/False
1. F 2. T 3. T 4. F 5. T 6. F 7. T 8. F
9. F 10. T 11. F 12. T 13. F 14. T 15. F
16. T 17. T 18. T 19. F 20. T 21. F 22. F
23. F 24. T 25. T 26. F 27. F 28. T 29. T
30. F 31. F 32. F 33. T 34. T 35. T

Enhance Your Vocabulary
1. D 2. E 3. H 4. F 5. I 6. G 7. B 8. C
9. J 10. F

Review Your Key Terms
1. H 2. J 3. K 4. N 5. M 6. C 7. Q 8. A
9. O 10. B 11. L 12. F 13. I 14. D 15. G
16. U 17. T 18. E 19. R 20. P 21. S

Solutions to Chapter 11

Multiple Choice
1. D 2. C 3. B 4. A 5. D 6. C 7. B 8. A
9. D 10. C 11. B 12. B 13. D 14. B 15. C
16. C 17. A 18. B 19. D 20. A 21. D 22. C
23. B 24. B 25. A 26. A 27. D 28. C

True/False
1. F 2. F 3. T 4. F 5. T 6. T 7. F 8. T
9. F 10. T 11. F 12. T 13. T 14. F 15. T
16. T 17. F 18. F 19. F 20. F 21. T 22. T
23. F 24. T 25. T 26. F 27. T 28. F 29. T
30. F

Enhance Your Vocabulary
1. C 2. F 3. G 4. J 5. A 6. H 7. E 8. D
9. B 10. I

Review Your Terms
1. B 2. N 3. G 4. Q 5. T 6. S 7. I 8. C
9. E 10. A 11. L 12. BB 13. II 14. P 15. Y
16. O 17. D 18. X 19. U 20. V 21. J 22. H
23. R 24. F 25. AA; 26. M 27. K 28. W
29. KK 30. JJ 31. HH 32. DD 33. CC 34. GG
35. Z 36. EE 37. FF 38. NN 39. LL 40. OO
41. PP 42. MM

Solutions to Chapter 12

Multiple Choice
1. C 2. D 3. B 4. A 5. A 6. C 7. D 8. A
9. B 10. C 11. D 12. D 13. D 14. A 15. C
16. D 17. C 18. B 19. B 20. C 21. A 22. A
23. C 24. B 25. D 26. B 27. C 28. D 29. A
30. C

True/False
1. F 2. T 3. T 4. F 5. F 6. T 7. F 8. T
9. T 10. F 11. F 12. T 13. T 14. F 15. T
16. T 17. F 18. T 19. F 20. T 21. F 22. T
23. F 24. F 25. T 26. F 27. T 28. T 29. F
30. T 31. T 32. F

Enhance Your Vocabulary
1. I 2. G 3. D 4. A 5. B 6. C 7. H 8. J
9. F 10. E

Review Your Key Terms
1. C 2. JJ 3. G 4. H 5. A 6. N 7. KK 8. D
9. K 10. U 11. M 12. W 13. R 14. T 15. DD
16. Q 17. E 18. AA 19. Y 20. BB 21. V
22. L 23. FF 24. B 25. CC 26. S 27. J
28. EE 29. Z 30. P 31. I 32. HH 33. X
34. II 35. O 36. GG 37. F 38. NN 39. QQ
40. PP 41. LL 42. MM 43. RR 44. OO

Solutions to Chapter 13

Multiple Choice
1. B 2. A 3. C 4. C 5. D 6. B 7. C 8. A
9. D 10. C 11. B 12. D 13. A 14. B 15. C
16. D 17. C 18. D 19. D 20. B 21. A 22. C
23. D 24. B 25. D 26. A 27. B 28. A 29. C
30. D

True/False
1. F 2. F 3. F 4. T 5. T 6. F 7. T 8. T
9. F 10. T 11. T 12. F 13. F 14. F 15. T
16. F 17. T 18. T 19. F 20. T 21. T 22. F
23. F 24. T 25. F 26. T 27. T 28. T 29. T
30. F 31. T

Enhance Your Vocabulary
1. C 2. F 3. D 4. I 5. E 6. A 7. J 8. H
9. G 10. B

Review Your Key Terms
1. F 2. CC 3. J 4. U 5. H 6. Z 7. I 8. G
9. L 10. B 11. D 12. FF 13. E 14. R 15. K
16. Q 17. A 18. O 19. T 20. AA 21. V 22. S
23. N 24. DD 25. C 26. Y 27. W 28. X
29. P 30. EE 31. GG 32. M 33. LL 34. BB
35. JJ 36. HH

Solutions to Chapter 14

Multiple Choice
1. D 2. C 3. B 4. C 5. A 6. D 7. A 8. C
9. B 10. D 11. A 12. B 13. C 14. B 15. D
16. D 17. D 18. A 19. D 20. C 21. B 22. A
23. C 24. D 25. D 26. B 27. A 28. C 29. C
30. B 31. A 32. D 33. C

True/False
1. F 2. T 3. F 4. T 5. T 6. F 7. F 8. T
9. T 10. F 11. T 12. F 13. F 14. T 15. F
16. F 17. T 18. F 19. T 20. T 21. F 22. T
23. F 24. T 25. T 26. F 27. T 28. F 29. T
30. F 31. T 32. F 33. T 34. F 35. T 36. F
37. F 38. T

Enhance Your Vocabulary
1. B 2. G 3. D 4. J 5. H 6. I 7. A 8. E
9. F 10. C

Review Your Key Terms
1. E 2. C 3. Y 4. V 5. J 6. P 7. K 8. D
9. B 10. F 11. Q 12. G 13. I 14. H 15. T
16. N 17. O 18. M 19. X 20. W 21. FF
22. L 23. S 24. A 25. R 26. AA 27. Z 28. U
29. LL 30. MM 31. CC 32. NN 33. DD
34. BB 35. PP 36. HH 37. EE 38. GG
39. KK 40. QQ 41. JJ 42. II 43. OO

Solutions to Chapter 15

Multiple Choice
1. C 2. A 3. D 4. D 5. B 6. C 7. B 8. A
9. C 10. A 11. B 12. C 13. D 14. C 15. B
16. A 17. C 18. D 19. B 20. A 21. A 22. D
23. C 24. C 25. B 26. D

True/False
1. F 2. T 3. F 4. F 5. F 6. T 7. F 8. T
9. T 10. F 11. T 12. T 13. T 14. F 15. F
16. T 17. F 18. T 19. T 20. F 21. T 22. T
23. F 24. F 25. T 26. F 27. T 28. T 29. T
30. F

Enhance Your Vocabulary
1. C 2. F 3. H 4. G 5. J 6. I 7. A 8. B
9. D 10. E

Review Your Key Terms
1. H 2. W 3. T 4. B 5. K 6. J 7. I 8. A
9. N 10. F 11. Z 12. O 13. DD 14. S 15. V
16. C 17. U 18. Y 19. X 20. L 21. CC
22. AA 23. BB 24. EE 25. G 26. Q 27. M
28. E 29. P 30. D 31. R

Solutions to Chapter 16

Multiple Choice
1. D 2. B 3. C 4. A 5. D 6. B 7. A 8. D
9. C 10. C 11. D 12. B 13. A 14. C 15. B
16. D 17. A 18. D 19. C 20. A 21. D 22. B
23. B 24. D 25. C 26. B 27. A 28. D 29. C
30. C

True/False
1. F 2. T 3. T 4. F 5. T 6. F 7. T 8. F 9. F
10. T 11. F 12. T 13. T 14. F 15. F 16. T
17. T 18. F 19. T 20. F 21. T 22. F 23. F
24. T 25. F 26. T 27. F 28. T 29. F 30. F
31. T 32. T 33. F 34. T 35. F 36. T

Enhance Your Vocabulary
1. F 2. E 3. D 4. B 5. C 6. A 7. H 8. J
9. G 10. I

Review Your Key Terms
1. F 2. G 3. I 4. O 5. R 6. B 7. C 8. D
9. H 10. U 11. M 12. X 13. AA 14. T 15. L
16. S 17. K 18. P 19. J 20. Q 21. A 22. W
23. BB 24. V 25. E 26. Y 27. EE 28. Z
29. N 30. CC 31. DD

Solutions to Chapter 17

Multiple Choice
1. D 2. C 3. B 4. A 5. A 6. C 7. D 8. B
9. D 10. C 11. A 12. B 13. D 14. C 15. B
16. A 17. C 18. B 19. D 20. C 21. B 22. C
23. D 24. D 25. A 26. B

True/False
1. T 2. F 3. F 4. T 5. F 6. F 7. T 8. F
9. T 10. T 11. T 12. T 13. T 14. F 15. T
16. T 17. T 18. F 19. F 20. T 21. F 22. F

23. T 24. T 25. T 26. F 27. F 28. T 29. F
30. T 31. F 32. F 33. F 34. T

Enhance Your Vocabulary
1. H 2. A 3. J 4. E 5. D 6. G 7. C 8. I
9. B 10. F

Review Your Key Terms
1. F 2. Q 3. A 4. CC 5. R 6. DD 7. M 8. I
9. II 10. L 11. KK 12. B 13. GG 14. C
15. B 16. O 17. D 18. N 19. HH 20. U
21. X 22. AA 23. S 24. LL 25. J 26. GG
27. BB 28. V 29. T 30. EE 31. W 32. Y
33. JJ 34. FF 35. P 36. Z 37. H 38. K

Solutions to Chapter 18

Multiple Choice
1. D 2. A 3. B 4. B 5. C 6. D 7. C 8. A
9. C 10. B 11. D 12. C 13. D 14. B 15. A
16. D 17. C 18. D 19. A 20. C 21. D 22. A
23. B 24. C 25. D

True/False
1. T 2. F 3. T 4. F 5. F 6. T 7. F 8. F
9. T 10. T 11. F 12. F 13. T 14. T 15. F
16. T 17. T 18. F 19. F 20. T 21. F 22. T
23. F 24. T 25. T 26. T 27. F 28. T 29. T
30. F 31. F 32. T 33. T 34. F 35. T

Enhance Your Vocabulary
1. B 2. H 3. E 4. F 5. G 6. A 7. J 8. C
9. D 10. I

Review Your Key Terms
1. F 2. J 3. I 4. B 5. A 6. E 7. D 8. L
9. G 10. H 11. C 12. K

Solutions to Chapter 19

Multiple Choice
1. C 2. D 3. A 4. B 5. D 6. D 7. B 8. A
9. C 10. A 11. B 12. C 13. A 14. D 15. B
16. D 17. D 18. B 19. A 20. B 21. C 22. B
23. A 24. C 25. A 26. D 27. D 28. C

True/False
1. F 2. T 3. T 4. F 5. F 6. T 7. T 8. F
9. F 10. T 11. T 12. F 13. T 14. T 15. T
16. F 17. F 18. T 19. T 20. T 21. F 22. T
23. F 24. T 25. T 26. F 27. T 28. T 29. F
30. F 31. T 32. T 33. F 34. T 35. F 36. T
37. F 38. T

Enhance Your Vocabulary
1. E 2. C 3. I 4. B 5. G 6. A 7. D 8. F
9. J 10. H

Review Your Key Terms
1. H 2. B 3. W 4. G 5. AA 6. U 7. V 8. Z
9. P 10. A 11. S 12. R 13. Q 14. BB 15. O
16. J 17. FF 18. L 19. X 20. D 21. I 22. K
23. EE 24. C 25. T 26. F 27. E 28. CC 29. M
30. II 31. HH 32. DD 33. N 34. Y 35. VV
36. GG 37. LL 38. JJ 39. OO 40. TT 41. KK
42. QQ 43. PP 44. SS 45. UU 46. MM
47. RR 48. NN

Solutions to Chapter 20

Multiple Choice
1. C 2. D 3. B 4. A 5. C 6. A 7. D 8. D
9. B 10. A 11. C 12. C 13. D 14. B 15. A
16. D 17. D 18. A 19. D 20. B 21. A 22. D
23. C 24. B 25. D

True/False
1. F 2. F 3. T 4. T 5. T 6. F 7. F 8. F
9. T 10. F 11. T 12. T 13. F 14. F 15. T
16. F 17. T 18. T 19. F 20. F 21. F 22. T
23. F 24. F 25. T 26. F 27. F 28. T 29. T
30. F 31. T

Enhance Your Vocabulary
1. H 2. D 3. E 4. F 5. A 6. G 7. I 8. B
9. J 10. C

Review Your Key Terms
1. F 2. D 3. G 4. I 5. J 6. A 7. H 8. B
9. L 10. K 11. E 12. M 13. N 14. C

Solutions to Chapter 21

Multiple Choice
1. B 2. C 3. D 4. A 5. C 6. D 7. A 8. C
9. B 10. D 11. C 12. D 13. A 14. C 15. C
16. A 17. B 18. A 19. D 20. B 21. D 22. C
23. D 24. A 25. B 26. D 27. C 28. D 29. B
30. D 31. A 32. B 33. A 34. C

True/False
1. T 2. F 3. T 4. F 5. F 6. T 7. F 8. F
9. T 10. T 11. F 12. T 13. F 14. T 15. T
16. F 17. F 18. T 19. T 20. F 21. F 22. F
23. T 24. F 25. F 26. T 27. T 28. T 29. T
30. F 31. T 32. F 33. F 34. T 35. T 36. F
37. T

Enhance Your Vocabulary
1. E 2. H 3. D 4. B 5. A 6. G 7. I 8. F
9. J 10. C

Review Your Key Terms
1. I 2. FF 3. N 4. V 5. T 6. S 7. L 8. D
9. M 10. F 11. K 12. E 13. R 14. C 15. W
16. AA 17. J 18. E 19. A 20. U 21. G 22. Y
23. P 24. O 25. HH 26. B 27. CC 28. GG
29. DD 30. X 31. BB 32. Z 33. Q 34. EE

Solutions to Chapter 22

Multiple Choice
1. C 2. B 3. A 4. D 5. A 6. C 7. B 8. D
9. C 10. B 11. B 12. A 13. D 14. B 15. A
16. C 17. C 18. D 19. B 20. D 21. A 22. C
23. C 24. D 25. B 26. B 27. A 28. D 29. A
30. C 31. B 32. D

True/False
1. F 2. T 3. F 4. T 5. F 6. F 7. T 8. T
9. T 10. F 11. F 12. T 13. T 14. F 15. F
16. T 17. F 18. T 19. F 20. F 21. T 22. F
23. T 24. F 25. T 26. F 27. T 28. T 29. F
30. T 31. F 32. T 33. F 34. T 35. T 36. F
37. T 38. T

Enhance Your Vocabulary
1. D 2. I 3. E 4. F 5. B 6. J 7. C 8. G
9. H 10. A

Review Your Key Terms
1. C 2. L 3. AA 4. V 5. A 6. S 7. EE 8. D
9. Z 10. F 11. J 12. B 13. H 14. Y 15. U
16. E 17. N 18. M 19. K 20. I 21. DD 22. Q
23. O 24. G 25. R 26. CC 27. T 28. X
29. BB 30. P 31. W 32. FF

Solutions to Chapter 23

Multiple Choice
1. B 2. D 3. C 4. B 5. C 6. A 7. D 8. A
9. D 10. B 11. C 12. A 13. C 14. B 15. A
16. C 17. A 18. D 19. D 20. C 21. B 22. A
23. D 24. D 25. C 26. D 27. B 28. C 29. D
30. A

True/False
1. F 2. F 3. T 4. F 5. T 6. T 7. F 8. F
9. T 10. F 11. F 12. T 13. F 14. T 15. T
16. F 17. F 18. T 19. F 20. F 21. T 22. T
23. F 24. T 25. T 26. F 27. T 28. F 29. T
30. F

Enhance Your Vocabulary
1. E 2. F 3. A 4. B 5. D 6. C 7. I 8. J 9. H
10. G

Review Your Key Terms
1. C 2. DD 3. BB 4. QQ 5. G 6. L 7. N
8. JJ 9. O 10. R 11. CC 12. B 13. E 14. F
15. M 16. S 17. V 18. U 19. J 20. W
21. GG 22. EE 23. Z 24. Y 25. X 26. FF
27. I 28. D 29. A 30. AA 31. Q 32. T
33. LL 34. P 35. NN 36. HH 37. K 38. MM
39. II 40. KK 41. PP 42. H 43. OO